WHAT

GOD

HATH

JOINED

Also by Terrance A. Sweeney

A CHURCH DIVIDED

WHAT GOD HATH JOINED

TERRANCE A. SWEENEY
PAMELA SHOOP SWEENEY

BALLANTINE BOOKS • NEW YORK

Library of Congress Cataloging-in-Publication Data
Sweeney, Pamela Shoop.
What God hath joined / Pamela Shoop and Terrance A. Sweeney.—
1st ed.
p.   cm.
ISBN 0-345-38203-X
I. Sweeney, Terrance A. 2. Sweeney, Pamela Shoop.
3. Ex-priests, Catholic—United States—Biography.
4. Actors—United States—Biography.
5. Celibacy—Catholic Church—Controversial literature.
I. Sweeney, Terrance A. II. Title.
BX4668.3.S88S88 1993
282'.092'—dc20
[B]   92-54488
CIP

Manufactured in the United States of America
First Edition: May 1993
10 9 8 7 6 5 4 3 2 1

B
Sweeney

In memory of
Pat, Shoopy, Dan
and Devon.

"FROM THE BEGINNING OF CREATION
GOD MADE THEM MALE AND FEMALE.

THIS IS WHY A MAN MUST LEAVE FATHER AND MOTHER,
AND CLING TO HIS WIFE, AND THE TWO BECOME ONE BODY.
THEY ARE NO LONGER TWO, THEREFORE, BUT ONE BODY.

SO, THEN, WHAT GOD HATH JOINED,
MAN MUST NOT DIVIDE."

JESUS

INTRODUCTION

The rule of mandatory celibacy for Roman Catholic priests has caused pain, suffering, and suicide for over sixteen hundred years. It is one of the most divisive and crippling problems threatening the survival of the priesthood today.

Since 1955 over one-third of the worldwide total of priests have married. Since 1965 over 110,000 priests have resigned, including 20,000 in the United States alone. By the year 2000 there will be more married priests in the United States than celibate parish priests. Surveys conducted over the past twenty-five years indicate that the majority of Catholic laity and priests, and even a substantial number of bishops, feel that the Gospel and the Church would be better served by a priesthood that includes both celibacy and marriage. A May 1992 Gallup poll revealed that seventy-five percent of American Catholics would approve of a married priesthood. Even so, the Vatican refuses to consider changing the policy.

The Roman Catholic Church maintains that priestly celibacy is a great virtue because it is modeled on Jesus' own life, a celibate life dedicated entirely to inspiring faith in God, and love of both God and neighbor. Certainly the many priests throughout history who have lived in this manner have proven that celibacy can be a profound witness.

But the Church goes far afield of the teachings and example of Jesus when it makes celibacy a legal requirement for the priesthood. Jesus did not require his apostles to be celibate. In fact, most of them were married. There is nothing in the Bible to suggest that Jesus married, nor is there anything to suggest that Jesus made a vow not to marry. Yet the Church, citing the life of Jesus, makes celibacy a prerequisite for the priesthood and warns priests that falling in love would be a betrayal of their vocation.

Many priests who have fallen in love have known the sting of ostracism, guilt, and slander. A priest in love faces a dilemma: He must give up either the woman he loves or his priesthood. Some, unable to reject either one, are forced to live a double standard—loving in secret, then donning the vestments of the celibate priest to face the Sunday congregation.

Behind each tortured priest there lies the hidden tragedy: that of a woman alone . . . in the silence . . . in the shadows. A woman in love with a priest must face the desperate confusion of heart and reason at war within her soul as she waits in lonely isolation in the back of the church, unrecognized and unacknowledged. In love with a man who has promised to be celibate, her future rests in his decision; for it is his vow, not hers, that comes between them. Whether he chooses marriage or celibacy is between him, his conscience, and God. The woman's choice is whether or not to sit and wait as the man she loves battles his way to the light of his own personal truth. She can turn and walk away from her love, assuring herself that it is the noble and right thing to do. But if the love is truly from God, no such assurances will ever fill the void left in her soul.

The greatest tragedy in all of this is that it need not be. It should not be. Peter, the first pope, was married. More than forty popes were married. For over a thousand years there was a married priesthood. For all of its great contributions, the Church today is one of the few worldwide institutions that has twentieth-century laws built on fourth-century opinions. And sadly those fourth-century opinions, conceived in error and formulated into laws mandating celibacy, continue to undermine the very heart of the priesthood.

The Church teaches that everyone is free to choose a state in life; yet, it forbids women to choose priesthood and it won't allow men to become priests without first promising never to marry. The Church teaches that marriage is sacred and inviolable; yet, from the fourth century to this very day laws of the Church have forbidden priests, under threat of punishment and expulsion, to make love to their wives or to have children.

Requiring celibacy by law and under threat of sanctions demeans the virtue of celibacy freely and lovingly chosen. It affronts the dignity of marriage and preempts the inalienable, God-given right to marry.

We have known the pain of loving with a divided heart, of struggling to discern whether priestly intimacy and love are a sin or a blessing. We know what it costs to move from fears that love is wrong to a consciousness that love, of all life's graces, is the most sacred.

Our personal story reflects the hardships endured by countless thousands of couples since the celibacy canons were first imposed so long ago.

We hope that sharing our story will help to ease the pain of all those priests who still feel that falling in love is a sin and all those women who have never been able to walk down the aisle to marry the men they love.

Perhaps our painful journey, and the deep joy we now feel for saying yes to love, will make their way easier.

WHAT
GOD
HATH
JOINED

I

TERRY

Even through her bridal veil her eyes glistened with tears. As the violinists began playing the hauntingly beautiful theme from "Homecoming," Pamela clasped her stepfather's arm tightly and stepped forward into the church. The wedding guests looked back toward my bride with an audible sigh of wonder. Tiny white flowers nestled in her red-blond curls. The diamond solitaire necklace she had borrowed from her mother rested reassuringly over her heart. Her bridal bouquet of white hibiscus and white roses cascaded from her hand. Her floor-length bridal gown was Austrian lace over white satin, and with each movement bursts of light danced off the hundreds of pearls hand-sewn into the lace. She glided forward surrounded by an aura of loveliness and grace.

How often had I stood at the altar as a priest and watched other brides come to meet their beloved. Now I was the groom, and this radiantly beautiful woman was smiling at me, walking toward me. My eyes whispered back to her: *Love is more than a dream, more than the heart's passionate aching for union—love is a person, and your name is Pamela.*

As the music carried her closer, the tears streaming from her eyes reminded me that love is not all joy and ecstasy, and that love, of

---

all powers on earth, demands sacrifice. For two years and ten months Pamela had born the burden of my divided heart. She knew the torment of loving a priest. She had felt the pain of unfulfilled love and had still refused to run away.

Even as we stood in this church that was not ours, before three courageous Episcopal priests who welcomed us when all of my Roman Catholic priest friends had turned us away, I still felt the anguish of love divided. In my soul I heard the cries of those priests and their wives whose marriages had been crushed by the Church. I felt deep sorrow that the Roman Catholic Church was still, after seventeen centuries, enforcing laws that destroyed love—laws that were, at this very moment, claiming the power to invalidate our marriage.

As Pamela looked into my eyes, she knew that our love would ban me from the priesthood that was so much a part of my soul. As I looked into hers, I knew that no man should be deprived of the enduring love of holy matrimony.

The music floated off to a romantic silence as Pamela and Bill came to rest in front of the sanctuary. For a brief moment an expectant stillness permeated the church. Without words, I looked into Pamela's heart and whispered the reassuring biblical truth that was warming my entire being:

> *Love, no floods can quench,*
> *No torrents drown . . .*

2

PAMELA

Where do you go when to-morrow arrives and yester-day's dreams are still way out of reach?

Across from my bed, the firelight cast a shimmering glow over the darkened room. I leaned back against the pillows, mesmerized by the beauty of the flames and the shadows they cast dancing over the walls and the eighteen-foot ceiling of my New York City apartment. The tinsel from my Christmas tree caught the firelight, scattering it into shafts of color. Over in the corner my suitcase sat propped open against the wall.

When I was a little girl growing up in Los Angeles, I had dreamed of Broadway lights, musty theaters, of the backstage door and opening-night jitters. But Broadway had been as far away as the end of the rainbow and as impossible to reach. It had existed only as a daydream haunting me from a picture postcard taped to my mirror. When I had finally taken the step to move to New York six months ago, it had seemed that, at last, I was taking a step closer to my dream. But as I sat in the firelight, I wondered whether it was already too late.

Beginning my professional career at age nineteen at the Drury Lane Theatre in Chicago, I had acquired a vast amount of theatrical experience in productions all over the country. Logically, the next step should have been to pursue my childhood dream and move to New York. Instead, life in Hollywood had led me into the world of television.

All throughout my twenties, television had provided for me a lucrative and rewarding training ground. I had come to relish the intimacy of the smaller screen and the world of movie studios. Getting up at four o'clock in the morning had proved to be not so bad, and I had grown to love breakfast burritos in the makeup trailer, costume fittings in the wardrobe department, and the nervous energy behind the cameras of a darkened soundstage. But it wasn't just the actor's life I loved; it was acting itself. I loved creating a personality from head to toe. I loved jumping into someone else's skin, even just for a short time, and being transported into a world of different color, sound, and texture. I loved the range of emotions that accompanied each new character. Acting was my profession, and going to work was a pleasure.

However, as time passed, I had begun to find myself greatly unchallenged by the material that was presented to me. As a television actress I had become quite successful, but I was finding it virtually impossible to break from that particular mold into areas of more creative and dramatic substance. The opportunity to audition for quality roles seemed to elude me. Even with the volume of work I had done, I was finding it increasingly difficult to move up the ladder and into films. It's common stuff for actresses, but it bred in me a desperation so acute that it began to undermine my self-confidence, even in my personal life. It became difficult to separate woman from actress. Eventually the actress has to jump out of the character and back into her own skin and, looking into the mirror, face who she really is. Eventually she has to ask herself, *Where do I go from here?*

From time to time throughout my life, even at the most successful points in my career, a restlessness would come over me. I would become filled with a longing for unknown sights and sounds, for new faces, new adventures. But more than that, I felt restless with who I had become. At times like these, the urgency to challenge myself seemed impossible within the confines of my complacent routine. At times like these, I would pack a suitcase and head for the airport. Paris had beckoned to me like this once. For three months I had explored a new language, a new culture, back streets, museums, and outdoor cafés. But, most importantly, in wandering these streets alone, I had explored the deepest parts of myself.

This time, however, my unrest had come from somewhere far deeper in my soul. It had seemed to be connected to the deepest longings of my heart and to my talent itself. I had begun to feel a yearning to return to my dreams of the past. I'd started to realize that I had been complacent far too long and that my life would continue on as it had unless I had the courage to take a step in a new direction. But what was the step I was to take? More and more I had grown to believe that if I just had the courage to step out of the familiarity of my present, my future would fall into place. So, in the summer of 1984, I fled to New York.

The embers in the fireplace faded into nothingness as I pondered what the last six months had taught me. And I wondered why it was that still I felt no peace in my soul.

The suitcase was unbelievably heavy as I lugged it down the steep steps from my apartment to the curb. There was a winter chill in the air, though the first snow had not yet fallen on the city. I hoped that I wouldn't miss it while I was away over the Christmas holidays. Having grown up in California, I eagerly anticipated a bout with cold weather. A block away, the leaves had fallen from the trees in Central Park, leaving them to wait patiently until the park would become a snowy fairyland. That's what winter should be, I thought, snow and wind, hot chocolate and ice-skating.

My taxi tooted its horn as my suitcase landed with a thud at the bottom of the steps. I dragged it out into the center of the street and, with a final glance at my apartment, hopped into the backseat of the taxi. This holiday would be a good one. Though I hated to leave New York, I'd missed my family, and returning home for a few days might help to give me a little bit of perspective. As we began to weave in and out of traffic, the anticipation of Christmas crept into my heart. I sat back in the taxi and decided to count my blessings.

I had grown up in the happiest of family surroundings. My mother had been an actress. Under contract to Warner Bros. Studios, who had changed her name from Jacqueline Wells to Julie Bishop, she had appeared in such films as *Action in the North Atlantic* opposite Humphrey Bogart, *Sands of Iwo Jima* and *The High and the Mighty* opposite John Wayne, and *Northern Pursuit* opposite Errol Flynn. She did eighty-two films in all, as well as the television series "My Hero." Her career had been very successful, as had her marriage to my father, Major General Clarence A. Shoop, which had begun with a romantic honeymoon during the war at Hyde Park as guests of President and Mrs. Roosevelt. My mother's life had always seemed idyllic to me, and I often marveled at her ability to move so gracefully from career to family life. Our house was frequently filled with visiting dignitaries and guests of all kinds. Often Howard Hughes, who had been a close friend of my father, would visit. Our summers had usually been spent abroad, my brother, Steve, and I traveling with our parents wherever my dad had business. We were as close as a family could be, and as I look back on it now, I realize that I was a very, very lucky girl.

After my father passed away, my mother married Dr. William Bergin, a general surgeon practicing in Los Angeles. When he retired, they moved up north to the little town of Mendocino on the California coast. Together they shared a tranquil life in this peaceful haven. Bill had been a pilot during the war and had flown with the Chinese American Combat Wing. This unit was composed of American Air Force pilots who volunteered to lead the Chinese in combat missions with the hope that the Chinese would eventually be able to take over their own squadrons. Bill encouraged my mother to learn to fly, and eventually she, too, got her pilot's license. She loved to take us whale watching in their plane; and often we'd swoop down close enough to see the barnacles on the whales' backs as they swam close to the surface.

In the years since my father's death my brother, Steve, had managed to incorporate both the worlds of aviation and medicine into the man he had become. A pilot and a surgeon, he seemed to embody the best of both my father and of Bill. I not only loved him as a brother, but also had great respect for him as an individual. At times his abilities made me feel that, both professionally and personally, there was still a great deal more I needed to contribute to life.

Christmas was perfect. My parents' house is nestled in the trees overlooking an enormous meadow leading to the cliffs and sea beyond. Waves crested high over the top of the bluff, then crashed wildly on the rocks below. Across the headlands deer loped gently in search of shelter. The setting is both wild and serene. It is a very special place.

Steve had rented a plane to fly up for Christmas and had brought my dog, Devon, along with him. She is a beautiful black Labrador and my very best friend in the world. I'd had her since she was four months old, and until now we'd been inseparable. She had remained in L.A. with a friend of mine while I was in New York finding a place to live and getting my life in order. It was wonderful to have her with me again, and I couldn't wait to introduce her to Central Park. My plan was to take her back to New York with me when I went. Together we all took long walks over the headlands. It was a happy family Christmas.

I had planned to spend a couple of days in Los Angeles visiting friends before heading back east, but decided to spend a few extra days alone with my parents first. Steve had to get back to his patients at the hospital and took Devon back to L.A. with him. Helping Mom take down the Christmas tree and put away all the decorations gave us a good chance to visit, and I was beginning to feel the serenity of Mendocino lulling me into its peaceful way of life. My mother's love always comforts me.

However, as the day approached when I would have to leave, I grew more and more restless. I began to feel that familiar uneasiness return.

I awoke to a pouring rain and thick fog on the morning I was to say good-bye. Unable to fly in this awful weather, Bill and I drove the three hours to San Francisco over winding California roads. There I would catch a commercial flight to Los Angeles. As we drove, we talked at great length. Bill is a gentle, caring person, and he was terribly worried about me. He longed for me to marry and to have a child, and had often expressed his concerns in this regard. He seemed to feel that by not committing myself to marriage, I was not taking responsibility for my life. How often he had said, "Pam, I think you're just afraid of growing up." I tried, once again, to explain.

Marriage, to me, represented a unique and precious union, a bond of heart and spirit. It was not a commitment made for social or economic reasons or simply for companionship. Though I could appreciate those reasons for marriage for some people, I knew that they would be wrong for me. I had been in love before; yet, deep inside, I knew that the love I would feel for the man I would someday call my husband would be on a far deeper spiritual and emotional level than any love I had so far experienced. I believe that there are many people we can love in our lives and that there are varying degrees accompanying each of these loves. But caring enough to spend time with someone is not the same to me as saying, "Take my hand, I want to walk through life with you." That was a commitment I would make only once. And it would be forever.

I looked at Bill in the driver's seat. I loved him so much, and it saddened me that I could not explain myself to him in a way that he could understand. But how could he understand when there was so much I couldn't understand myself? Even this trip to L.A. didn't make much sense. I had no real need to return there. I could have taken my dog back to New York from Mendocino, but I chose not to.

Looking back on it now, it seems as if my future, my destiny were leading me on a course I was bound to follow.

Cradled in the hills above Los Angeles, about an hour out of the city, is the tiny town of Lake Hughes. If you wind for a few miles over the crest of the mountains overlooking the serenity of the

Antelope Valley, eventually you will come to a peaceful mailbox standing alone on the side of the road. Bear right and head down the dusty, graveled driveway and you will come to an immense oak tree—the tunnel tree, we used to call it as kids. Many a race on horseback was won or lost as we sped beneath its branches with screams of laughter and the pounding of horses' hooves. Off to the right stands a grand old Victorian farmhouse. As I looked, the Christmas lights twinkled back at me over the snowy field. Ginger's family and mine had co-owned this ranch many years before. When, finally, we sold our half to her father, her family turned it into a quarter-horse racing operation and chose to live there full-time, keeping their home in Beverly Hills as well. My best friend welcomed me with hot dogs and soup, then a long hike through the frosty forest. When the snow began to fall at last, we retreated to the house, poured a couple of hefty glasses of wine, and threw ourselves onto the floor in front of the fire.

There are few things in life as gratifying as an old friendship . . . someone who has known you since childhood, gone through all the ups and downs and questions of growing up: the mistakes, the triumphs, the daydreams and nightmares . . . someone who perhaps knows you in ways better than you know yourself. Ginger was one of those friends. She was worried about me, that was clear. For hours I lay there, tearfully pouring out my questions, my unhappiness, my failure. For, indeed, I felt like a failure. She reminded me, however, that I had starred in five films, a soap opera for a year, and countless television shows.

"Okay, that sounds like a lot. But what am I doing now? Nothing. I don't know whether I belong in New York or L.A. I'm not even sure I'll be able to support myself in New York if I leave all my contacts behind. Besides, I'm lonely."

Ah! That was it. Girl talk inevitably gets around to men. It always does, don't ask me why. And Ginger, always the premier pragmatist, once again reminded me that I had had several proposals of marriage and that if I was so "gol-durn" lonely, I did have an option or two!

"I know, I know," said Ginger, "you're still waiting for that perfect love. Well, it may not exist, and meanwhile you could be living a very comfortable and exciting life with someone and you wouldn't be sitting here crying on my floor!"

Of course she had a point, but with every fiber of my being I knew that I had not found what I was looking for. "But, Ginger, I know I'll find it. I just know I will. Don't you remember when we were small, I always used to say that I was waiting for something, and that I would know it when I saw it? Well, I haven't seen it yet."

"How do you know you haven't already found it and just didn't recognize it? We all were looking for the White Knight, Shoop. But the rest of us have grown up to realize that he's just not out there and you have to be realistic. This is the real world, not some storybook fairy tale."

But my notion was far too elusive to put into words. Even if I could have, it probably would have sounded naive. It always seemed to me that behind a gossamer veil lay some intangible "something" for which I had my being, and that if I listened hard enough, I would be led.

I put another log on the fire and reflected on the notion of intuition. Why is the inner voice that speaks to us silently so frightening to follow? Why is it so impossibly unrealistic to depend upon what we cannot see or touch or understand? If only we could simply believe what our hearts declare, without everything having to be proven to us. Ginger brought me back to the present with a start.

"When are you going to realize that you have to make decisions and stick by them?"

I sighed. But I had made a decision. I believed that I had to wait, and flounder, if I must. If there was one thing of which I was very sure, it was that I had not yet found my heart's home.

I propped myself up on my elbow and looked at Ginger in the firelight. "If you're right and I never find what I'm looking for—do you think I could pull up my rocking chair and park it on your porch? Probably thirty years from now we'll be sitting here, rocking away, having the same kind of conversation. And all we'll have is each other."

She laughed. "Sure, Shoop."

It was a comforting thought that we might not have to be alone.

The next day was New Year's Eve, and Ginger and I awoke to a blue sky and the brightest of suns reflecting off the snowy meadow. It was clear and gorgeous as we donned our boots and plodded out into the field toward the duck pond.

The crisp air helped to wake me as we walked in the silence of the early morning. Ginger has found her God in the mountains, she says.

Over the last few years I had begun to feel a spiritual yearning, and a deep longing to feel the peace and comfort of God's presence I'd known as a child. Attending Sunday school in the Christian Science faith had given me a deep sense of Love, and I had had a very clear understanding of God in my life. I had grown up in a religion without fear, based on Divine Love. It had always given me great peace. But as the frustration in my professional life grew, so too, did my spiritual unrest, and in reaching out to find God again, I had begun searching for a different church. I had attended many different types of service, but more and more found myself drawn to the sacraments celebrated in the Catholic faith. This spiritual quest was an important process to me. I longed to feel again the innocence and trust I had felt as a child. I needed to belong. Tomorrow would be the beginning of a new year, and I hoped that I could somehow take the tranquillity of this majestic setting with me through whatever would come my way.

Because New Year's Eve was only hours away, we drove back down the hill to Ginger's parents' home in Los Angeles for Ginger to prepare for her date. Since I had sublet my Beverly Hills apartment when I moved to New York, I had no place to stay on this trip, so Ginger had offered me the guest room. I had accepted happily; however, I was feeling particularly sorry for myself as I watched her apply makeup and don the slinkiest of outfits. When the phone rang and my brother invited me to go with him and his girlfriend, Suzanne, to a party, I was greatly relieved. I dressed rapidly and actually left the house before Ginger's date arrived.

The party was small and the evening quiet. Too quiet. Good-byes have always been difficult for me. And New Year's, to me, was good-bye, an ending rather than a beginning. It always seemed to be the saddest night of the year. A few minutes before midnight I snuck outside by myself to the street in an attempt to see the moon, which was playing cat and mouse through patches of fog. For a fleeting second, the moon cast a shimmer of radiance over the darkened street. *Please, God, where do I belong?*

3

TERRY

"I'm dissolving Jesuit Media Associates, Terry. I want you to resign as president."

The Provincial's words of three weeks earlier once again echoed in my mind. Since our December 12th meeting I had tried repeatedly to find something positive in his decision that would have enabled me to say, "I can see from your perspective that some good will come of this." But the intervening weeks, and my first actions of closing out the corporation, had left me with the gnawing feeling that his decision was destroying a unique opportunity for the Jesuits and for those who hoped media would inspire as well as inform and entertain.

I finished glancing over the list of things I still had to do in order to shut down JMA. I was trying to be an obedient Jesuit, not only doing what the Provincial had asked, but doing so in accord with his own thinking, as "one who stood in the place of Christ." But no matter how hard I tried, I just couldn't make myself agree with his thinking.

I got up from my desk, walked over and turned off the floor heater. A stark memory of a burial in East Los Angeles forced its way into my thoughts. Mrs. Lopez, dirt in hand, stood over the casket of her fifteen-year-old son who had been blown away by gang members. Jorge's mother stretched her arm over his casket but wouldn't release the dirt. Her arm began to tremble. She looked at me and sobbed, "I can't do it, Father, I can't." Other mourners, feeling her grief, began to cry. Her husband came up to her and forced open her hand. As the dirt fell on Jorge's casket, she let out a soul-piercing wail.

I switched off the lights and walked out of my room. *There's violence everywhere,* I thought: *on the streets, in human hearts, even in obedience.*

The hallway was cold. Wind swept through the open windows of the adjacent laundry room. But the chill of this unheated dormitory during Christmas break seemed nothing compared to the silence of two hundred empty rooms. Where once there were four hundred university students talking, laughing, shouting, and studying, now there were only deserted hallways and locked doors.

I walked out of McKay Hall and started across the campus of Loyola Marymount University toward the Jesuit Community parking lot. A campus security car patrolled the road behind the library and communication-arts buildings. Subdued voices filtered out of the second-story recreation room of the Jesuit Community Residence. The lights of a large, elaborately decorated Christmas tree twinkled through the window.

As I got into my car and drove off campus, I realized that I was not the least bit interested in going to a big, noisy, New Year's Eve party. What I really wanted to do was go back to my room and sort through my fears about the demise of JMA, and the increasingly unsettling obedience that demanded it. Mona Moore, on JMA's advisory board, must have sensed my mood. Perhaps that's why she had asked me to go with her to this New Year's celebration—to talk things out, then relax for a few hours.

The palm trees on Santa Monica's Ocean Avenue swayed in the wind. Lights from Santa Monica Pier shimmered on the water below. Since Mona's counsel and contacts had played such an important part in JMA, I knew that JMA's dissolution must have disappointed her also. Mona and I had first met in the late 1970s. For three and a half years I had worked as a priest with Chicano street gangs in a 7.9-square-mile area known as Unincorporated East Los Angeles. This area had a population of 113,000 people.

It also had the highest rate of gang-related homicides in the United States.

The more street work I'd done with gang members, the more I'd realized it was necessary to get some kind of historical perspective on the problem. Mona had that perspective. Not only was she thoroughly familiar with Hispanic culture and history, she had spent several years living in Mexico before finally settling in Los Angeles. Many times she was involved in finding gang members work or helping them with family problems. This background, coupled with her many years as an executive both in business finance and feature-film production, had prompted me to seek out her advice many times over the years.

"Any word from the Provincial?" Mona asked as we drove down Sunset Boulevard.

"He called, said he didn't want the dissolution process to drag on."

"How are you holding up?" she asked.

"I've been better."

"I know it's hard, but try to look at the positive side. Your gang documentary won an Emmy. You have a contract with one of the best producers in the world to do a feature film on Rutilio Grande's assassination. Puttnam, Zeffirelli, and others want to work with you."

"I tried to explain it to Father Clark, but he didn't seem to care. The gang documentary wasn't just a piece of film. It helped convince the city and the county to set up a gang program. Homicides in East L.A. have been reduced by fifty percent. That means more 'homeboys' are finally agreeing to talk things out rather than shoot them out. It means fewer children will die from a bullet intended for a nearby gang member!"

"You can't expect him to feel the same way you do about this. He hasn't lived there. Besides, you don't need JMA to continue your work."

"I know. But the Jesuits have always been committed to educating. One of the best ways to do this today is through creating mass-media programs. JMA was the first serious effort in this direction. Now it's history."

"Well, if you want to be a Jesuit, I suppose that's part of it. Some decisions are made that aren't easy to accept." Mona's tone was pragmatic, yet sympathetic.

"It's more complicated than that. Ignatius was very emphatic about the importance of obedience: Jesuits are supposed to see in the voice of the superior, the voice of Christ, in all things except where sin is involved. They say that Ignatius had reached such a perfect level of obedience that if the Pope had suppressed the Society, Ignatius would have been able, within fifteen minutes of prayer, to accept his decision peacefully."

"Interesting . . ." Mona commented.

"Well, nineteen full days have passed since JMA's suppression and I still can't accept it. Not only has prayer brought me no peace, it's precisely then that I feel the most uneasy."

"Do you think the Provincial's shutting down of JMA is sinful?" Mona asked.

"I can't say it's sinful. But I can't see the voice of Christ in it either."

"You're not the first, you know. There's Teilhard de Chardin. He obeyed. . . ."

"But should he have?" I replied. "Chardin had one of the finest creative minds of the century. His thinking would have been even more refined if he had been allowed to publish his writings and benefit from the constructive criticism of his peers. What good is an 'obedience' that restricts and limits the search for truth?"

Mona answered, "Well, if a situation becomes intolerable, you have to ask yourself what other options you have. Have you made up your mind yet?"

"About final vows, you mean?"

"Yes," she replied.

"No, I haven't."

"One way or another, your doubts about obedience are going to have to be resolved," she said.

"In twenty-three years this is only the third time I've disagreed with a superior's judgment. It's not the Jesuits that worry me so much. It's Rome. Their declarations on birth control, on excluding women and marriage from the priesthood, on the faithful's owing 'assent, with sincere mind and ready will' to all Church teaching—these worry me a great deal."

"None of your books or films have dealt with any of those issues."

"I know. I've deliberately avoided them because I was afraid discussing them would get me in trouble."

"So, why now?"

"Because this pope, for all the good he's done, is polarizing the Church. Priests and nuns are leaving in droves, theologians are being silenced, and more and more women are feeling alienated from the Church."

Mona looked puzzled. "Jesuits have a reputation for being the most educated and sophisticated of religious orders. Are you saying you can't objectively explore any issue, that you can only repeat what the Church teaches?"

"To cut through the rhetoric and thousands of treatises on obedience, there are in actuality two kinds of obedience operating in the Church. One maintains that the Pope, bishops, and superiors have, on earth, the authority of Christ. This obedience means following their commands and promoting their teachings as though they came from Christ Himself."

"This, I assume, is the obedience the Vatican expects," Mona said.

"Yes. The other kind of obedience holds that both Church leaders and the Catholic community are servants of God's will, and if there is ever a conflict between what Church leaders teach and God's will, then Catholics have an obligation to challenge that teaching."

"Turn left at the signal," Mona said. "Of course, you feel it's the second."

"Yes. How could I possibly promote certain Vatican declarations that seem to go against Christ's teachings and against basic human dignity?"

"You're beginning to sound like Martin Luther," she chided.

"Even before the Reformation, the papacy of corrupt popes had given Catholics reason not to trust blindly in papal authority. During the Western Schism of 1378 to 1417, three men claimed to be pope, each one excommunicating all those who did not accept his authority. This conflict left the entire Church under the shroud of a formal declaration of eternal damnation."

" 'Absolute power corrupts absolutely,' " Mona quoted. "So, which model of obedience do the Jesuits expect?"

"Depends on whom you ask. Some say it's the first; others the second. Even Jesuit superiors are divided on this."

"If the Society is big enough to encompass both, you should be okay."

"It's more complicated than that. If I take final vows, one of them would be a vow of obedience to the Pope regarding education and missions."

Mona nodded her head, "Now I see the problem. So, what are you going to do?"

"With JMA I'll do what the Provincial has asked. As for final vows, I just don't know."

"You can't keep putting them off. How long has it been now?"

"Seven years. The more research I do, and the more people I listen to, the more difficult it is to decide. If the vows related only to the Jesuit order, I think I could accept that. But obeying this pope—well, given all that's going on, I don't know if I could live with that."

A parking valet took my VW as we arrived at the house. Mona and I got out and walked toward the front door.

She looked at me intently. "You'll have to choose."

"I know."

The party was in full swing. The living room, kitchen, den, and patio were all crowded with people. Helium balloons with streamers floated throughout the house. Music was playing, but whatever it was could be only faintly heard through the din of cocktail banter. Mona was pulled into a crowd of people she knew as a waiter asked me what I wanted to drink.

At 11:59 people began shouting out the last sixty seconds of 1984: "Thirty, twenty-nine, twenty-eight . . ." Champagne bottles were popped. A woman halfway across the room was staring at me, smiling. I wasn't wearing my Roman collar, so that eliminated one possible explanation. Another woman with a large diamond ring glittering on her wedding finger kissed the two men standing closest to her, then glanced over at me with a worn stupor in her eyes. A man with a party hat blew on his kazoo, lifted his champagne glass, and sang, "To eighty-four and all the girls I loved before, to eighty-five and keeping it alive!" The woman next to him threw a handful of streamers in his face.

"Fifteen! Fourteen! Thirteen!" the crowd's voices crescendoed. As the last seconds of 1984 were racing away, I took refuge behind the wet bar, dreading the prospect of being grabbed and kissed by a stranger. I didn't even feel like toasting champagne. What I felt was apprehension and inner coldness.

4

PAMELA

As I awoke early on New Year's Day, the sound of the Rose Parade and the smell of coffee filtered into the softly decorated suite I now occupied. Stretching slowly, my mind beginning to focus, I recognized those pale-green curtains and was instantly comforted by the familiarity of a home in which my childhood memories seem to lurk mischievously in every corner. I tiptoed into Ginger's bedroom, and there she was, propped up on an abundance of pillows, the TV close to the bed so that she wouldn't wake me, taking the most delicious bite of toast with jam and peanut butter.

I crawled under the covers beside her, pulled a stuffed animal under my chin, and focused on the Rose Parade. I felt warm and toasty as we recounted the events of the most popular "date night" of the year. Hers hadn't gone too well, it seemed, and she consoled herself with yet another chunk of toast and jam. We were giggling like school kids when Ginger's housekeeper, Lennie, knocked at the door.

"Hi, there, Bombshell," Lennie said as she placed a breakfast tray in front of me and gave me a hug. I was so happy to see her. Lennie is the best. She had been the housekeeper for Ginger's family since I was about nine years old, and she never changed. The food looked so inviting, and I felt like a queen, luxuriously having my breakfast brought to me in bed. Lennie made some wisecrack about her employer's "not-so-hot" date and then retreated. She can get away with those things.

A few hours later Ginger headed back up to the ranch. As I dressed for church, I felt peaceful and somewhat expectant. Content behind the wheel of my own car again after six months of New York City taxicabs and subways, I drove to the Church of the Good Shepherd in Beverly Hills through Sunday-quiet streets, warm and sunny for a California New Year's Day. I walked up the steps of the beautiful old Spanish-style church with the warmth of the sun on my back and an unusual and unexpected pleasure in my heart that I was coming "home." Quietly, I opened the rear door of the vestibule. I was a few minutes late and people were already seated, so I let the door close gently behind me. A voice was reciting the opening prayer. The church was crowded, so as quietly as I could, I tiptoed down the center aisle looking for a seat. *Please, God, let me find one—I hate being late!* With a sigh of relief, I spied one. Silently I slipped into it, and for the first time my eyes came to rest on the altar. It was then that I saw him. He stood in his vestments before the congregation, his gentleness reaching out across the pews. At that very moment something happened to me. A voice whispered in my heart: "There's the answer. Now, what's the question?"

I stood very still. My heart began to pound in my chest and my eyes filled with tears. The words had been as crystal clear as if someone next to me had tapped me on the shoulder and uttered them. I felt at once alert, cautious, stunned. I looked around to see if anyone else had heard. They hadn't. Eyes were intent upon the altar and this gentle soul now giving the sermon. It wasn't just that his unusually handsome face held a sweetness one doesn't often see, or that his quiet voice commanded a reassuring calm, or the earnestness with which he spoke of God's love and compassion. He obviously believed deeply in what he was saying, but there was more than that. He seemed to be speaking "with" us, the congregation, not "to" or "at" us, as so many priests do. He didn't seem compelled to teach, but rather to share—and the humility of his approach was obviously appealing, not only to me, but to everyone.

Maybe it wasn't any one of these things. Or maybe it was all of them. I watched and made myself concentrate on my breathing. I was sure it was so loud that everyone could hear. I thought back to those words. Those words. What did they mean? Where did they come from? I forced myself to breathe, to think. I had asked God for guidance—was this His answer? Think, Shoop! What had I prayed for? To know where I belonged, to find love, to have a deeper meaning to my life, to feel a sense of fulfillment in my career, to know how to proceed with my career and where, to feel a sense of purpose. I'd asked a thousand questions! Which answer was this?

Perhaps God was calling me to religious life. Maybe that was the plan.

When the Mass was ended, I took a deep breath and threaded my way up to the front of the church and the Christmas crèche at the side of the altar. I waited for the parishioners to say a little prayer and then depart. Eventually it was my turn, and I felt a real sense of peace come over me as I approached the miniature manger. The scene was so very tender: the shepherds, Mary, Joseph, Jesus . . . and the most adorable donkey. I knelt down and reached out to pat his nose. For the first time in months I felt at home, comfortable, secure, and warm. I didn't have any desire to leave. I prayed very hard. Gradually the church began to empty and only a few people remained inside, lost in their own thoughts. My knees began to ache a bit, so I sat down on the steps where I had been kneeling and leaned against a pillar. I smiled at the donkey. I sat there for about forty-five minutes or so, feeling safe and content. In the still and quiet, I longed to know where God needed me.

5

TERRY

"**B**ody of Christ."
          "Amen."
          "Body of Christ."
"Amen."

The parishioners who had just received Communion stood up from the altar rail and stepped away as the usher directed others to kneel in their places. I moved down the Communion rail to the next person as the altar boy shuffled silently backward over the beige-carpeted floor. From the choir loft the melodious voice of the soloist, Gary Bachlund, resonated throughout the congregation, somehow drawing attention not to the excellent quality of his voice, but to that inner world of intimate thought and prayer.

"Body of Christ."

"Amen."

As I walked down the length of the altar rail to begin a new row of communicants, I remembered the negative judgments I had made of these Beverly Hills parishioners five years earlier, resenting the imperiousness and eccentricities that so often accompany Rolls-Royces, expensive clothing, and jewelry. I blushed at how I had laughed at one priest's quip: "Instead of collecting money, we should ask the women to put in one earring each!" It was a kind of culture shock for me to work during the week in East Los

Angeles with parents whose sons were murdered, or with gang youth living always on the edge of survival, and then on Sundays to be with a congregation whose pastor wanted me to keep Masses well under an hour in order to avoid parking-lot gridlock. But my disquiet over the obvious inequality of living standards evanesced as I learned to look beyond the standards and trappings of life to the people living it.

I lifted another Host from the ciborium. "Body of Christ, John." As he accepted Communion in his hands, I wondered if he'd ever see his mother again. She lived in Pakistan; John was born in India. If he left the United States to visit her, he might lose his bid for U.S. citizenship, for which he had already paid thousands of dollars to an "attorney specializing in citizenship." If he made it into Pakistan, he might have his India passport confiscated, which would leave him a person without a country.

"Body of Christ, Barbara." Barbara's husband, a prominent film producer, had suffered a stroke during the middle of production. His death broke her heart.

"Body of Christ, Jane." Her husband of twenty-five years had walked into the breakfast room one morning and announced that he was moving out. That night he moved in with another woman. Jane thought of divorcing him, then decided she could never love another man. She is now waiting for him to "come home."

"Body of Christ, Jim." His seventeen-year-old daughter won third place in a horse-riding competition. The night of the competition she attended a victory party, had a violent attack of asthma, and died. Jim's faith is strong, so is Eva's, his wife, but even their deep faith cannot heal all the grief from their daughter's death.

"Body of Christ, Cathy." Cathy had escorted an East Coast executive of her company to a VIP bash. After the party he had raped her.

While giving Communion, these personal details of people's lives would stir in my heart, evoking a silent prayer—*Lord, heal her body. . . . Lord, strengthen their faith. . . . Lord, help him to love again, to really trust.* Sometimes, there would be no prayer, only feelings too deep for words. Sometimes my thoughts and feelings would fall totally silent, becoming wholly absorbed in that precise moment of Communion during which the most mundane of all human acts, transformed by love and faith, became the very action through which the human heart experiences the abiding touch of God.

It was through Communion that I realized that gang members in East L.A. and "stars" in Beverly Hills were the same. Take away the guns and the gems, take away the clothes and the cars—we're all naked; we all hunger, fear, misjudge, sin, love, die.

After Communion I walked back up to the altar and purified the chalice. Gary finished his solo as I moved over to the celebrant's chair and sat down. Those in the congregation still kneeling took this as a signal to sit. In a few seconds the entire church fell silent. When I had first started saying Mass at Good Shepherd, the lectors would leave about ten seconds for the Communion Meditation, then jump up and start the parish announcements. When I first asked them to wait for a nod from me, so that there would be longer time for silent, personal prayer, there would be signals of discomfort and anxiousness from the congregation, such as repeated coughing, rustling in the pews, or people just getting up and walking out before the final blessing. After just a few short weeks, however, the parishioners seemed to really value these few minutes of quiet time for Communion reflection, almost as though these brief minutes were the only ones in the entire week where God was number one on the agenda. Now, five years later, the original discomfort had totally given way to a peaceful and prayerful silence in which four hundred people, for at least these fleeting moments, valued nothing more than talking to God or listening to God's voice speaking in their own hearts.

As I sat there listening to that silence, it struck me that these Eucharistic moments were epiphanies, our few grace-filled moments of gazing at the Light, of hearing the truth speak within the depths of our souls, calling us ever more deeply into the heart of all Life. The dissolution of JMA, the stressful quandary regarding obedience, the insecurity I felt regarding what the future might bring—all these anxieties drifted into distant background as I felt both in the congregation and in me light, warmth, acceptance, peace.

As we stood for the final prayer and blessing, I looked out into the congregation. I could see in many faces a tranquillity, a joy.

After Mass I waited outside the church to greet the parishioners and listen to any special requests. Since I didn't want them to feel obligated to say hello, I always stood not at the entrance of the church, but at one of the side doors. The greetings would take anywhere from fifteen minutes to forty-five, most often consisting of a friendly hello and a comment or criticism of my homily. Frequently there were requests for prayers or special requests for confession, a marriage, a baptism, counseling, or a funeral. I found it difficult to say no to any personal request, but after years of constant overextension I was finally able to say no occasionally.

A good friend, Jeanne Sully, came up to me. After greeting me with a kiss, she turned and gestured to a young woman standing next to her. I remembered first seeing this woman five days earlier as I was walking out of the sacristy following the twelve-fifteen New Year's Day Mass. She and an elderly Spanish lady had been kneeling at the crèche, praying. The Spanish lady had a black-lace mantilla on her head with rosary beads in her hands, and she was looking at the statue of Mary, quietly whispering the rosary prayers in Spanish. This younger woman, with tears in her eyes, was reaching over the Communion rail and touching the face of the donkey. In all the years I had been at Good Shepherd, I had never seen anyone contemplate the manger scene with such tenderness and feeling. The expressiveness in her eyes and gesture had prompted me to wonder what exactly she was feeling.

"Terry," Jeanne said, "I want you to meet a very special person, Pamela Shoop. Pammy, this is Father Terry Sweeney." A quiet voice, somewhere inside of my brain, said, *Careful, Terry, she's attractive.* I extended my hand to her. As she shook it, she blushed heavily. "Nice to meet you." "And you," I said. As I looked into her eyes, I saw anticipation, uncertainty, restlessness.

Jeanne went on, "Pammy's parents and I have known each other for many years. Robert and I went down with them to their vacation home in Puerto Vallarta and had the most wonderful time. Pammy was raised in Christian Science, so imagine my surprise when I saw her here at Good Shepherd." Jeanne laughed good-naturedly, touching Pamela's arm to make her feel more at ease. "Anyway, she has some questions about the Catholic religion, and I told her you were the best priest to ask. I'll leave you two. Give your mom my best. Call me, Terry. Robert and I want to catch up." She hugged me good-bye and left.

Pamela blushed again. "I've never talked to a priest before. As Mrs. Sully said, I'm not Catholic, but I have some questions that are very important to me."

"What questions?" I asked.

"About God, faith, the Sacraments, other things," she answered.

"How is it that you came to this church? Do you live in this area?" I asked.

"Not now. I live in New York. I came in for the holidays. But prior to my moving to New York, I came to this church for two years, to the Sunday-evening Masses."

As soon as she said that she lived in New York, I felt a sense of relief. From the look in her eyes, I knew her questions were vital, and that they would take a long time to answer. I also felt safer having someone else answer them. "I'll be away for a few weeks, but I know some priests in New York who may be able to help you."

"Thank you, that would be nice, but actually I don't know when I'm going back there," she said. There was uncertainty and disappointment in her voice.

"Do you have a pen and a piece of paper?" I asked.

She reached into her purse, "Yes."

"A few miles from here there is a church called Saint Paul's. There is a priest there—here's his name and phone number. Give him a call, tell him I asked you to call and that you have some questions about the Catholic faith. Also, there is a book called *Christ Among Us* by Anthony Wilhelm. You can pick up a copy of the book at Saint Paul's and read it. It answers a lot of basic questions."

She thanked me again as I handed back her pen and piece of paper. Though part of me felt guilty about sending her off to another priest, a different part of me said it was the "prudent" thing to do. The prudent side reminded me that I was at this time too vulnerable emotionally. Twelve years of priestly counseling had proven too many times how difficult it is to avoid falling in love when someone shares her soul with you. Further, I had been researching and praying over the Church's laws on celibacy for the past eight years, and I had developed radical misgivings about their validity. Yes, sending this woman, Pamela Shoop, to another priest was the wise thing to do, even if it meant that I would never see her again.

6

PAMELA

Funny how things happen, isn't it? Life and Timing. I had moved across the country to breathe some life into my career, had come home for three short days, and now I suddenly found myself besieged with interviews. Of course, pilot season does that. In a matter of days, having your own television show can become a real possibility, and lifestyles can change overnight. During these few months of the year, the new shows for the fall season are cast, and life becomes utter chaos. Agents are frantic, phones never cease ringing, actors scurry about from interview to interview, changing clothes in gas stations and learning lines at stoplights. Urgent messages are left with answering services all over town as panicked secretaries try to remember which actor is where at four o'clock and can he be somewhere else by five! At red lights from Universal City in Burbank to MGM in Culver City, lone individuals in their cars can be seen speaking animatedly with themselves, gesturing at the rearview mirror, repairing lipstick, and heaving enormous sighs of desperation.

As I sat in my pew waiting for Mass to start, I wondered if I could take it one more year. I wondered if it had been the right decision to accept a couple of interviews and postpone my return to New York. I certainly needed the money. Rent and expenses back east were very high, and with the exception of residuals, I'd had no income for over six months. Then, too, I wondered if I was taking a step backward. But there is a big difference between being an episodic actress and the star of your own series. The quality of the work is basically the same, but the work schedule is much more hectic and rewarding. A steady job, I guess you could call it. Having analyzed the dire straits of my financial situation, I'd thought about it for three or four seconds and decided to stay for a few days.

The last two weeks had been very busy. Having exhausted the proper length of time at Ginger's, I'd moved to my brother's for a few days, and now was house-sitting for some friends before moving down to my girlfriend Ellen's apartment in Santa Monica. Living out of a suitcase was fun. I'd had four interviews, one of which had led me to the network reading for a new pilot called "Family Honor." If you think pilot season sounds bad, you should see a network reading. This is an audition for the heads of the network (this one was ABC) for the final five to ten actors for a role. It's hair-raising. Your agent makes your deal and sets your salary for the next five years ahead of time, and when you arrive at the audition, everyone knows this is the final moment. To get this far, you've had to beat out probably over a hundred or more actors for the same role. One by one you are ushered into a room of about twelve to fifteen people sitting in the dark. You do your scene. They say, "Thank you." You exit as quickly as possible . . . and wait. It's devastating. I'd auditioned on Friday, now it was Sunday and I was waiting, waiting, waiting. I wanted the job, and I didn't. What about New York?

But in my heart, I knew there was another reason I was still here. Two weeks had passed since the Feast of the Epiphany, but the feeling lurking in the back of my mind remained. Snatches of conversations began to race through my mind. "Terry, I'd like you to meet someone very, very special." *Terry, Terry. He doesn't look like a Terry.* I remembered the steadiness of his gaze as he looked me directly in the eyes, giving me his full attention. It was very flattering until I realized he did this with everyone. There was nothing perfunctory about this man. It was obvious that he cared deeply about each person who reached out to him. He had a kindness about him, a sense of calm and joy that seemed to draw people into his presence. "I loved your sermon. It was beautiful," I'd said. "I've always thought they should have actors do the homily to make it more interesting, but yours was really very good." I remembered the flush of horror I'd felt as those words had escaped . . . not what I meant at all . . . and the sound of his genuine laughter in response to my awkward compliment.

The music began. At last the procession started, and I was actually surprised to see Father Sweeney. I'd assumed he would still be away. As I watched him approach the altar, I couldn't help but notice how he sang with a smile on his face. It made me happy just to be still and listen. Suddenly I was very hot. I pulled off my sweater.

After Mass I nervously approached the side of the church where Father Sweeney stood to greet people after each service. I ended up last in line, and as I waited, I noted the tender hugs passing between priest and parishioner: grandmothers and children, men and women alike. To my surprise, he remembered who I was and seemed a little startled that not only had I read the book he'd suggested, but had already met with the priest at Saint Paul's.

"How did it go?" he asked.

"Well, he told me when the instruction classes were, and talked about a variety of people who attended the classes."

"And?" He clearly sensed my discomfort.

"Actually, I have a difficult time with cigar smoke—and when he started making some critical remarks about Christian Science, I felt I had to defend my religious background."

I could see the disappointment on his face. From my purse I pulled out a long list of questions I had written down.

"Oh dear," he said. "A few questions, huh?"

"I don't mean to bother you . . ."

"I just got back into town, and there's a lot of work I have to catch up on. I won't have any time to talk to you for a couple of weeks. Look, do you have time right now? Would you like to have some lunch, or something?"

I was stunned! "Yes, of course."

"I just have to go change out of my vestments. It'll only take a minute."

"Okay. I'll wait here."

I paced back and forth in the courtyard, growing more and more nervous. After all, this was the first priest I'd ever met! What was protocol? Was there protocol? I needed to comb my hair. Oh, well, I'd do it at the restaurant. At last he came through the door dressed in his black clerical shirt and collar.

"There's a little restaurant called the Magic Pan just down the street. Is that all right?"

"Sure. I love it. My car's out front." *How to make conversation?* "Did you see the Super Bowl?" *Do priests watch football?*

"Yes, I saw it on TV in San Francisco. I was up there visiting friends. The city got pretty wild that night after the victory."

I unlocked the door to my car. "You were in San Francisco? So was I. Would you like a T-shirt?" *Why did I say that! I bought that T-shirt for someone else!*

He laughed. "Well, yes, I would. Thank you very much."

I pulled it out of the paper bag in the backseat. As I handed it to him, I gritted my teeth. *I just gave a Super Bowl "Dolphin Buster" T-shirt to a Roman Catholic priest! Do they even wear T-shirts?*

The streets of Beverly Hills were very quiet on that Sunday afternoon. We parked, and as we started toward the restaurant, a silver Alfa Romeo pulled up alongside. I recognized my brother as he tried to cover up the look of shock on his face.

"What a coincidence. Father Sweeney, I'd like you to meet my brother, Steve."

(Later that evening at a family dinner, my brother would recount with glee the initial thought he'd had upon seeing his sister walking up the street. He'd thought, "What's Pam up to now? What kind of guy wears all black on a Sunday?")

Father Sweeney and I entered the restaurant, and the waitress seated us at a small table for two next to the wall.

"Did I introduce you correctly? I wasn't sure how to address you."

"Some people call me Father Sweeney, some call me Father Terry, others just Terry."

———

"What do you prefer?"

"I prefer my name to a title—but whatever makes you most comfortable."

"I think I'll try Terry. I'm not used to calling people 'Father.' So, do you have any brothers or sisters?"

"Two older brothers, and a younger brother and sister. Dudley's the oldest, then Pat. My sister's name is Therese. Dan's the youngest."

"Do you ever wish you had your own family?"

"Sure, all the time, especially on the holidays. Just four Sundays ago I became godfather to my nephew Michael, Dudley and Dori's baby. Not much more you can give to Life than life born of love."

How beautiful, I thought.

"Well, I really appreciated your suggesting that book, but I still have a lot of questions." As I pulled out my list, I thought I caught a twinkle in his eye. "My main problem is original sin."

This was to be the first of many discussions on this subject. Actually *debates* would be a better word!

I asked lots of questions, which he tried to answer between bites. Some were theoretical; some were personal. I tried to explain the disquiet I felt, and the gnawing sense that there was something for which I seemed to be searching.

"I feel so lost sometimes. The other day I was looking at the manger scene at Good Shepherd, and I really began to feel peaceful. It's beautiful, isn't it? Sometimes I just wish I could sit there all day. It makes me feel safe. You see, I just don't know where I belong."

I had felt safe as a child, nurtured and protected in the haven of a loving family. The disquiet I felt in my life at present made it all the more difficult to answer Father Sweeney's questions about my father, who had died of cancer in 1968. Though years had passed, there were still many unanswered questions and moments of darkness. I have never gotten over his death, nor the fact that I was not by his side. For the first time in years I found myself speaking about my sense of loss to this man sitting opposite me.

"The last social event my dad attended before he found out he had cancer was my debutante ball. He'd lost a lot of weight by then, but he looked so radiant in his white tie and tails and white gloves. When he presented me to the room, he had the biggest smile on his face. But then, he always had a smile on his face. Two days later we received a phone call from his doctor saying that he had to have surgery, and soon."

I explained to Terry that I had been in school in Florence, Italy, and had flown home for only a few days to attend the National Charity League Ball. With this news, I postponed my return to school for another month, but eventually I had to go back. My father underwent four operations over the next thirteen-month period. Fortunately I was able to be there for all of them, but it wasn't enough.

When I returned from Italy, I was asked to replace Bob Cummings's daughter in the play *Generation*. Our families were very close, and my mother had worked with Uncle Bob many times, so I was the logical choice. My father had even been able to attend my opening performance in Chicago. A few months later I was asked to do the show again in Phoenix, Arizona, for three weeks. Though he knew this would take me away from him at a very crucial time in his life, my father urged me to go. I remember standing by his bed, holding his hand.

"I know God won't let anything happen to you while I'm away."

"We've all been through a lot, Pamsy, but I think it's almost over now."

At the time, I assumed he meant he was starting to get well. When the phone rang in my hotel room at six o'clock in the morning a few days later, I knew in my heart that was not what he had meant at all.

My father passed away the night of the dress rehearsal. After long deliberation I realized that I had a commitment to the people in the cast, the producers, and the audience; so we opened the show the next night, and a plane flew to pick us up and fly us to L.A. for the funeral the next day. Uncle Bob was to be one of the pallbearers.

"I remember sitting in the cockpit, not wanting to talk to anybody, watching the pilot's hands on the controls, and I was thinking, 'Those aren't my father's hands.'"

We landed on the familiar airstrip at Hughes Aircraft, which brought back so many happy memories of the past. As well as being commander of the Air National Guard for California, my father had been the head of Flight Test for Howard Hughes and, subsequently, vice president of Hughes Aircraft Company until his death. All of my life I had been privileged with many takeoffs and landings on that runway with my family. With my dad at the controls, I had flown in different types of aircraft, at times in the cockpit, my dad trying in vain to teach me the basics. I had driven him out to the "plant," as he called it, during his illness not long before he died, and I had landed there for the last time on the day of his funeral.

I went on to explain about my father's military funeral, the largest at that time in the history of Forest Lawn Cemetery in Glendale. Since I wasn't home for the preparations, I didn't know exactly what was going to take place.

The casket was closed. When the chapel finally emptied after the long procession of people paying their respects, my mother asked for the casket to be opened. She knew I had not said good-bye. A member of the honor guard pulled back the American flag and opened the lid. I looked down at my dad's thin face. I had been strong up until then, but all of a sudden it became a reality. He was dead. I touched his hand; his long, beautiful fingers were cold. My mother, brother, and I kissed him and wished our silent good-byes. And then the lid was closed on my father forever.

Gathering all our strength, my mother, brother, and I held each other's hands and walked through the door of the chapel into the sunlight through the hundreds of faces, following the flag-draped coffin of my father to his grave.

As we stood at the gravesite, the minister mentioned something about dust to dust, ashes to ashes. Instinctively I started toward the coffin, but someone pulled me back and held my arm firmly. The color guard lifted the American flag and held it taut a few inches above the casket. A volley of gunshots sounded. Men in uniform saluted as the lonely echo of taps rang through the Court of Freedom. The flag was folded into a tight triangle. Three shell casings from the rifles that had just been fired were tucked inside. The flag was placed into my mother's hands . . .

"On behalf of the President of the United States and a grateful nation . . ."

And then the thunder overhead. Suddenly from out of nowhere in the crystal sky came a flyby of three C-97s in formation. Everyone looked to the sky. As the planes disappeared over the mountains, a flight of four F-102 jets soared above us in the traditional missing-man formation—one missing plane in honor of my father. I hadn't known that was going to happen. After they had passed and the deafening engine noise had subsided, the only sounds remaining were wind and tears.

When it was time to go, I wanted to touch the casket one more time, but my friend, Greg Gilford, who had sung so beautifully for us at the funeral, put his arm around me forcefully and led me away saying, "He's not there, Pam."

As the car wound its way down the hairpin curves of Forest Lawn, leaving the others behind, I leaned out the window and waved up toward the top of the hill. I felt as if I were being ripped away from everything I wanted to feel.

I told Terry how I was taken immediately from the graveside to the airport, where I was flown back to Arizona to be onstage with Uncle Bob again that night.

When we got back to Phoenix, I went directly to the theater. It was early, so I lay down on the couch which was part of the set on the stage. The theater was perfectly quiet. Soon it would be filled with laughter. How could I possibly make people laugh with such emptiness in my heart? I longed to grieve with my mother and with Steve; with my half-sister, Sally; with my Uncle Slim and my Uncle Dick. They all had each other, but I was alone.

"In the darkened theater all I could think of was, 'I wasn't there when he died.' I'll never forgive myself for that."

Father Sweeney's gentle eyes softened as he listened.

"Steve told me later how he watched from his window as the ambulance carried our father down the driveway in the dark, away from his home for the very last time. Sometimes I envy him that memory. After that, Steve lost his faith for many years. He said he couldn't understand how so many people could have prayed so hard and Daddy still died. I think that's why Steve became a doctor—to stop people from dying."

A groundswell was starting. I could feel it. I'd been choking back emotion for over an hour. I tried to stare intently at the white brick wall beside me, touching it with my fingertips. Though I felt too shy to look at him, I knew Father Sweeney was looking at me and feeling my pain.

Finally, he began to speak. "My dad died alone."

"I'm sorry."

The waitress deposited the check on the table.

"He had advanced stages of arterial sclerosis and was supposed to have his legs amputated. But he wouldn't do it. Gangrene set in."

Terry pushed the bill aside as he began to speak more animatedly. His father had been an alcoholic and left the family when Terry was only eight years old. His mother had been left with the responsibility of raising all five children on her own without any child support. This left her, understandably, with a great deal of bitterness toward her children's father. Terry had been in Mexico City when he had received word that there had been a death in the family.

"I knew instantly that it was my father. Dad had said he was thinking about moving back to L.A. to be close to the family, or at least be able to visit us. He said he wouldn't recognize Dan. He hadn't seen him for fifteen years. But he never made it. In a run-down hotel room in Portland, Oregon, he died in his sleep."

"Did Dan ever get to see him?"

"No. Not even during the wake service. He was at home going through withdrawal. He had shot up heroin. I couldn't figure out why Therese and Dudley weren't at the wake service either. When I got to Mom's house for the reception after the service, I heard this screaming coming from the back room. I went back there and found Dan on the floor, pinned down by Dudley and Therese. Dan had saliva all over his mouth. He started shouting, 'I'm not an animal! I'm not an animal! Let me go! Dad never cared about me—he never loved me. . . .' A few hours later he slit his wrists."

Terry stopped talking for a minute, and I just sat there, waiting.

Haltingly he began again. "But he made it to the funeral the next morning, his wrists covered with bandages. I had spent the night in a Laundromat because the rectory door had been locked when I'd returned at midnight. Mom and I had gotten into a really ugly argument over Dad. She said he had lied to me about insurance papers. I said, 'I've never tried to interfere in your relationship with Dad. I wish you would respect my relationship with him and not call him a liar, at least until after he's buried.' She shouted back at me, 'I loved your father more than you ever did or could!' I said, 'You have a strange way of showing it. You can't stand to be near him, and you can't even talk about him without tears or suspicion.' The last words she said to me were, 'Listen, Mister Priest, Mister Perfect, you think you know so much about love? You don't know anything about love!'

"During the funeral Mass, as I was reading that passage from I Corinthians 15 about how at the sound of the last trumpet we shall not all die, but we will all be changed 'and this mortal flesh will put on immortality and this corruptible flesh will put on incorruptibility,' I looked down and saw my father's casket. A powerful, desperate feeling surged through me: This must be true, there has to be a resurrection. Immediately a brutal feeling swept through me that it was all a lie. As I saw my father's corpse and realized that he had been snatched away from me just when I was finally learning to love him, I thought, 'What difference does it make whether there is life after death or not? He is gone!' The feeling filled me with such despair that I could no longer continue the reading from the Bible. I walked to the pew and sobbed for the entire duration of the Mass."

Father Sweeney fell silent for a long time. When he began again, it was on an even more personal, more emotional level. He told me about his crisis of faith, his rage against God. "When my father was buried, my faith went with him. Death can cause faith and love to be enemies. . . ."

So much was said—and I knew that some of it was very precious, very private. At one point he swallowed and said, "I've never told that to anyone before except one priest." Then he started to cry. Spontaneously my hand reached out to stroke his hair, but I hastily pulled it back, reminded by his collar that this vulnerable human being was also a priest. With no embarrassment whatsoever, Terry grabbed my hand and squeezed it as the tears rolled down his cheeks. Quietly he said, "It's okay. Thank you."

I looked at this man across the table from me. I no longer saw the Roman collar. I saw only a man loved by many, surrounded by friends; yet there was no one with whom he could share his own pain. I saw a man in need of love and companionship. I thought, *Here is a man who goes out every day to help people through their heartache, despair, anguish . . . a voice on the other end of the telephone in the middle of the night when your son's car has just gone off the road, or your husband left you, comforting you for hours on end until the terror subsides. Who takes care of this man? Who holds this man when he cries?* With everything inside of me I wanted to reach out and comfort him. I wanted to wipe away the years of restraint and caution, to let him know that it was all right for him to share his weakness with me, to befriend and trust me. I did none of those things. But I believe that in that moment, words were spoken in the grasping of our hands.

By now the restaurant was almost completely empty. It was already four o'clock, and neither of us had noticed. Our lunch had taken nearly three hours, and as we walked up the street, Terry remarked somewhat shyly how amazing the experience had been. A bond had been formed. To me it was a recognition in two hearts of a promise—an uncommon level of trust for a stranger . . . who wasn't really a stranger at all.

I dropped him off at his car and went home to call the airline. I knew I was going nowhere until I spoke with this man again.

That night I called my friend Ginger to share the incredible experience I'd had. Her reaction totally surprised me.

"Pam! What can you be thinking of? A priest!" Ginger exclaimed. "Didn't you ever read *The Thorn Birds?*"

"No, I didn't."

"You're kidding! They made it into my favorite miniseries of all time! Rachel Ward falls in love with this priest, Richard Chamberlain, and of course he never leaves the priesthood . . . but they're madly in love—you never saw it?!"

"Okay, so I'm media deprived."

"Pam, I'm serious. I have a feeling we're in trouble here."

"Ginger, it was just a lunch."

But Ginger had heard something in my voice, something she'd never heard before, something even I hadn't recognized as yet.

"Shoop, I'm worried. Be careful, okay?"

7

TERRY

Immediately inside the main entrance to the Jesuit Community Residence is a switchboard and a waiting room. In the waiting room is a Renaissance painting of the child Jesus standing in the Temple of Jerusalem, speaking to a group of elders whose eyes reveal amazement at His words. As I sat in that room, expecting Pamela to arrive shortly, the painting reminded me of our meeting five days earlier. I wondered, with the thousands of words people encounter each day, through print, radio, TV, conversation, why is it that so few words really amaze us? Why is it that people's cries for help are so easily and so often unheard? Was the priest at Saint Paul's too busy smoking his cigar and challenging Pamela's religion to realize she longed for a deeper experience of God, not an argument about religions? Why is it that their words together caused tension and our words together caused amazement and elation?

I was annoyed at hearing how poorly their meeting had gone, and I thought about the many people I'd known who had turned away from the Catholic faith because of one hurtful encounter with a priest. This terrible possibility and the look of disappointment in Pamela's eyes prompted me to reevaluate my earlier decision to refer her to another priest. I had tried that. It had failed, and I felt partially responsible. Here she was, asking for help once more. When I realized that I was putting my own emotional vulnerability ahead of her faith quest, I decided then and there to help, regardless of the risk. Also, though I wouldn't admit it at the time, I enjoyed seeing her.

As I gazed at the clear light in Jesus' eyes, I tried to understand more clearly why my lunch meeting with Pamela had made such a profound impression on me. The questions she had asked about good and evil, forgiveness, Confession, Eucharist, God, her work, her father's death, seemed to come from her very soul, not merely out of an intellectual curiosity. It was much more than wanting to know. She *had* to know. And her life, her peace, her happiness depended on that knowing. When she had described her attraction to the manger, there was such feeling and longing in her description that I intuited immediately that what she needed was a manger of her own, a husband, a child, the fullness that comes with knowing that this love and this life are born of God.

Even though Pamela had been too nervous to eat, and the importance of her questions seemed to make her very shy in asking them, there was such naturalness, such a pure depth of feeling in the way she talked, especially of her father, that I found myself not only listening intently to her every word, but also attending to how her words resonated in my own heart. In the midst of that conversation I learned the difference between "words" and "communication." Words alone are simply one person's expression of thoughts or feelings. Communication is the language of one mind relating to another mind, one heart relating to another heart. When Jesus spoke, people listened. Their intense reactions of love, hatred, longing, rejection could only have happened because His words, "like a two-edged sword, penetrated through bone and marrow" to the heart. They heard His words inside their own hearts—that is why their reactions were so intensely personal. When Pamela had said, with tears in her eyes, that she would never forgive herself for not being with her father when he died, her grief reached right into my own soul and unleashed the anguish I felt over my own father's death. Rarely in my life had another's words touched me so deeply.

Because of the urgency and integrity of her words, because they came from her heart, and because they so powerfully stirred up my own soul, I began at that moment to appreciate what it means to listen with the Third Ear, to listen with the Ear of the Heart. I began to realize that deep within each person is a reservoir of instincts and feelings, always ready to speak, if only we would listen. I had taken Pamela to lunch to help her. In the end it was she who had helped me.

It was as if some interior part of my life, which before had been dark or hidden, was suddenly suffused with light. Rarely had I allowed myself to be vulnerable enough to share the deepest levels of my joy and pain with another, and the few times I had shared on this level, it was only after prolonged periods of building trust. Yet with this woman, in the space of one conversation, I was acting as though she were the closest of friends. I was amazed. In the very act of sharing our questions about God and life, I found myself being pulled through my standard defenses and emotional reservations right into the heart of a friendship, without ever saying the word or intending the reality. How could I tell Pamela that her questions animated some of the deepest levels of my own faith? How could I explain to her, whose religion had no priests, that she had been a "priest" to me? How could I say to her that I could no longer look upon our conversations as those between a priest and a parishioner, or counselor to counselee? We were both learners, we were both priests, we were both human beings longing for God.

For however long she was in L.A., I felt privileged to help and to learn from this extraordinary woman. No matter how soon she might return to New York, I knew that our conversation the previous Sunday would never be forgotten. I knew, even if the word were never used between us, I would always regard her as that rare, precious, and enriching person we call "friend."

Pamela walked through the door and greeted me with a huge smile on her face.

"I have a couple of books for you, but we'll talk about them later. The dining room is down this way."

As we walked down the first-floor corridor, she said, "Well, this is a first. I've never been in a Jesuit Community before."

"There are some seventy of us living on campus. Most live here in this building; others, including me, are scattered around campus living in the student dorms as counselors."

"How many students are there?" she asked.

"About sixty-two hundred, including undergraduate, graduate, and law school."

We walked into the carpeted, well-lighted dining room. Paintings by Michael Tang hung on several walls. "We eat buffet style here."

We got our meals, and Pamela followed me to a table in front of the floor-to-ceiling glass window. She looked out toward Marina del Rey and the Santa Monica Mountains.

"What a spectacular view!"

"Yes, for several months of the year we can sit here and watch the sun set over the water. We keep on hoping to see the green flash during sunset."

"Have you ever seen it?"

"I think so, once. Would you like to pray?"

"Yes."

I said a short, informal prayer, then took out *The Church* and *On Being a Christian* by Hans Kung. "These might be of help to you, but I want to make sure they're not overwhelming. What were the last three books you read?"

"Hemingway's *A Movable Feast*, *Fruits of the Earth* by André Gide, and Nietzsche's *Beyond Good and Evil.*"

"Then you shouldn't have any difficulty with Kung's books."

"I've been wanting to read *The Thorn Birds*, but I don't have a copy," she added.

"I do. It's a great book. You can borrow my copy if you like."

"That would be great. Did you see the miniseries? My best friend, Ginger, said it's her favorite TV show of all time."

"Actually I was technical adviser on it."

She looked at me incredulously. "You're kidding! How did that happen?"

"The producer, Stan Margulies, wanted to have an adviser for Richard Chamberlain, and someone to answer all questions from the writer, cast, and crew on Church-related matters."

"Were you on set and everything?"

"Yes, except for the love scenes. They didn't seem to want my advice there."

"Oh, what I wouldn't give to be on a project like that! Unfortunately in this town it's so easy to get slotted as an actress. You do leading roles and guest shots in episodic and they think that's all you're good for."

"What are some of the shows you've done?"

"Well, let's see, I've done a miniseries, movies-of-the-week, over a hundred shows in all. I had the lead opposite Tom Selleck in the pilot for "Magnum P.I."—that was one of my favorites. Also I've been in a few movies. I had the lead with Jack Palance in *Dead on Arrival*; I was up for the lead in *Body Heat*, across from William Hurt. I got down to the final screen tests—but Kathleen Turner got it."

"That's impressive."

"Well, sort of. I've reached a point in my career where I'm considered a workhorse actress, but for episodic. No one's offering the really good feature roles. That's why I moved back to New York, to get a fresh start."

"Speaking of New York, when are you going back?"

"I've changed my plane ticket a couple of times already. I'm not sure, really."

For the next hour we talked about questions she still had from Wilhelm's book, *Christ Among Us*. She was particularly interested in knowing more about the Eucharist. Though she didn't know how the Catholic Church defined the Eucharist, she felt instinctively drawn to Communion. This was in fact why she had started attending Catholic Masses. She wanted to know more about the Church and the Sacraments. I mentioned that the Kung books would give her a historical summary of some of the many different perceptions of Jesus and the Church.

She looked down at her plate, but still hadn't eaten very much.

"Not hungry?" I asked.

"No, sorry. But the food is delicious."

I stood up and took her plate. "I'll take this away for you. Can I get you anything more, coffee? Ice cream?"

"No, thank you."

After dinner we walked over to see the Jesuit Community chapel.

"How peaceful. How beautiful." She knelt down for a long time, with her head bowed. The tabernacle light flickered against the gold plating of the tabernacle and sent silent shadows dancing against the cedar-paneled walls. I wondered what He thought of this woman praying before Him. I thanked Him for bringing her into the world.

We walked out to the hillside overlooking Hughes Aircraft. As she looked down at the landing strip, her eyes glistened. "All the times we landed on this runway . . . it's so unbelievable to be standing up here now. I used to look up at Loyola and wonder what it was like. My daddy's office was over there, in that complex. Can you see it? Oh, I wish I could just walk into his office, see him sitting there. . . ."

"Maybe he does too."

She wiped tears away from her eyes. "Thank you for showing me this. I can't tell you how much it means to me." She fell silent for a long time, as though carrying on a secret conversation with her father. Lights from the nearby university chapel cast a soft glow over her face. Finally she spoke.

"At the end of my school year in Italy, my mom and dad flew over to meet me, and then I traveled with them to the various cities where my father had business. He was in charge of the International Division for Hughes. He and Steve, who had just joined the Air National Guard, had planned to meet and fly back on their first military flight together—Daddy as the senior officer and Steve as the junior—but he never made it. By then his cancer had worn him down until he was extremely thin and he was in constant pain. But he wanted to continue working. I remember one morning he had an important meeting in Geneva. My mom and I dropped him off, then sat in the car and watched as he walked up the steps of the hotel where the meeting was to be held. He was all doubled over in pain, but when he reached the middle of the steps, he stopped, pulled back his shoulders, and straightened himself until he was standing at his full height, and then he walked into the building. My mom and I just sat there and cried. That's the kind of man he was. We flew home commercially a few days later and went directly to the hospital. They operated on him within the hour."

She looked over at me and in a broken whisper asked, "Do you think we will ever see our fathers again?"

"I hope so," I replied.

The chimes from the university chapel bell tower rang out. "About *The Thorn Birds,* I can pick it up and bring it to where you're parked, or you can come up to my dorm office—it's kind of a mess, though."

"Sure, let's go. Do you believe in reincarnation?"

"I don't, but some people I greatly respect do. Reincarnation, in some respects, is similar to Catholic teaching about purgatory. The soul undergoes a period of purgation and cleansing in preparation for seeing God. Reincarnational theory proposes successive life-forms as a way for the soul to evolve through its imperfections to finally attain enlightenment. The concepts of purgatory and reincarnation address the same dilemma: How does the human person evolve from imperfection to perfection?"

"Interesting. I hadn't thought of it that way before," Pamela said.

We started climbing the stairs in McKay Hall. The students passing by said hello. "I have a hard time accepting that the same unique soul can at one time be animal life, then later a person, and even later a different person. What do you think?"

"I think reincarnation is very possible," she replied. "This is a co-ed dorm?" she asked incredulously.

"Bottom three floors used to be for girls. Fourth floor used to be all guys. Then housing decided to alternate the fourth-floor suites—two rooms for guys, two rooms for girls, and so on. Now it's all girls. Heaven only knows what it'll be next year."

"How does it feel living up here with all girls?"

"Louder."

I unlocked the door to my dorm-room office and switched on the light. She walked in, looking the room over. In the center of the room was a coffee table, flanked by a couch and chair. Against the wall were bookcases, a filing cabinet, a typewriter, and a cart with a television and a tape recorder on it. She walked to the large windows on the far wall and looked out at the blinking lights shimmering along the coastline.

I reached over to a shelf, pulled out my copy of *The Thorn Birds*, and handed it to her.

"What are those? Are they what I think they are?" she exclaimed.

"Yes," I answered.

"For what shows?" she asked.

"One was for a documentary on East L.A. gangs, another for a Christmas special, the others for a television series I produced called *Insight.*"

She walked over and began reading their inscriptions: "Four Emmy awards! Makes me wonder what I've done with my life."

Suddenly, reminded of JMA, I felt very uncomfortable. I began removing file folders and research that had been stacked up on the far end of the couch.

"Enough about me. Tell me about yourself. And please, don't look upon this as a counseling session—you've taught me far too much already. In fact would you mind sitting over here? I know that chair is comfortable, but it makes me feel too much like I'm counseling you. I don't want to be your counselor." As I started to set the things down on the coffee table, I dropped them.

She laughed.

"Sorry," I said. "Normally I'm not this messy, or this clumsy. I've been working on too many things lately."

"What things?" she asked.

"Sixteenth-century China, obedience, celibacy, the homeless . . ."

"The homeless?"

"I'm writing and producing a documentary on homelessness. There are between two and three million homeless in the U.S., more than at any time since the Great Depression. We're starting production on it soon."

"Where?"

"New York, Washington, D.C., L.A."

I finished gathering my debris, set it on the coffee table. I was embarrassed and still blushing over my awkwardness, but I looked at her anyway. "You can sit wherever you like. It's just that so much happened last Sunday, I've had this strange feeling as if we've known each other for a long time, or that we're the closest of friends. I hope I'm not being forward in saying this—but I would really like it if you would be my friend. That is, if you want. . . ."

She smiled. "Yes, I'd like that."

She stood up, walked to the other end of the couch, and sat down. She talked about her family, her schooling, work, and her restlessness to understand what she was meant to do with her life.

I walked over to my closet, opened it and pulled out a Styrofoam-wrapped package. As I did this, helium balloons floated out.

"What are the balloons for?" she asked.

"My birthday."

"Your birthday! When was that?"

"Last Saturday."

"The day before our lunch. Why didn't you tell me?"

"Should I have?"

"Of course. Happy birthday!"

"Thanks."

"How old are you?"

"Forty."

"Forty? You don't look forty!"

I put the package down on the coffee table in front of her. "I think you should open this. Maybe one day your talent will be recognized with one of these."

She opened the package, wide-eyed, and let out a joyful scream. "It's another Emmy! How fantastic! When did you get it?"

"It arrived by mail in November. I couldn't make it back to New York for the awards in June. We were in production then."

She looked at me in sheer disbelief. "It's been sitting in your closet for two months!"

"Well—yes. I knew what it was from the size of the package and the return address. But it seemed strange somehow to open an award like that all alone."

Five hours after she had arrived for dinner, we walked back

across campus to her car. The hours had seemed like minutes.

As she got into her car, she said, "This was an absolutely incredible evening. Well, if you ever want to do this again. . . ."

I shook her hand and said good-bye.

She waved as she drove off into the night.

8

PAMELA

Ellen's apartment was in a beautiful high rise overlooking Santa Monica beach and the ocean. She had stayed with me at my apartment in New York, so I felt comfortable about parking on her couch for a while. It was fun having a roommate, especially Ellen, who was also an actress. We would read scripts at night and commiserate over the makeup mirror in the morning. She had about five interviews to my one, and I was always envious. Ellen would sit in her bedroom rehearsing her lines for the next day out loud, and I would sit cross-legged on the couch in her living room doing the same. Often screams of frustration would pierce the bedroom door.

"This is awful! I can't say this stuff! I'm going crazy, I'm a nervous wreck!"

"Ellen, just calm down. At least you've got interviews. Be positive. Wanna switch scripts?"

"I hate this, Shoop. We're too old for this torture!" Then we'd hit the peanut butter. Peter Pan peanut butter. We didn't bother with bread or crackers—all we needed was a spoon.

But today was Saturday, and Eggs Bennie at the local omelet parlor were in order. It was a glorious day, and as we walked up

Main Street, a lovely crystal geode in one of the windows caught my eye.

"Oooo—I have to buy that."

"Your suitcase is already stuffed!"

"Actually," I stammered, "I think I might give it to someone."

But I hadn't a clue when I would see Father Sweeney again. I felt elated and terrified, all at the same time. I remembered how he had looked in the parlor where he'd met me before dinner at the Jesuit Community. He had been wearing tan jeans and a blue shirt—real clothes. He had looked up and smiled, and I savored the memory of the still and quiet and warmth of that smile.

And today, in the sunlight walking back to Ellen's apartment with the crystal geode in my purse, I wondered if I would ever see him like that again. I didn't have very long to wait. At five o'clock the phone rang.

"How would you like to get a bite to eat?"

"Great!"

"I'm just up at Paulist Productions, on Pacific Coast Highway, cleaning out my desk. I'll be there in twenty minutes."

"Okay. Terrific. I'll be ready."

Twenty minutes! Is he kidding? Whirlwind Time! I jumped into the shower, washed my hair, dried my hair, put on makeup, and finished dressing just as the buzzer rang!

As I raced out of the elevator toward the car, I saw Terry standing facing the entryway with his hands behind his back waiting for me with an enormous grin on his face. There was a poise, an elegance about him, coupled with a shy vulnerability, that was tremendously appealing. We had found on our previous two meetings that there seemed to be so much to say to one another, so much to learn, and we were both eager to understand each other's world. I learned a lot about Terry that night. His background had been so completely different from mine, and it fascinated me.

As we drove to Pancho Villa's, a Mexican restaurant high atop a building in Santa Monica, he talked about his experiences in Latin America and India. He spoke with great anguish about the impoverished countries. In the hopes of enlightening Westerners, he and Father Herbert de Souza had filmed a documentary on India a few years before. I found myself amazed at the scope of his life and how far his desire to serve had led him. I was reminded of a quote by André Gide in *Fruits of the Earth*: "So far as my dreams may carry me, so far will I go."

But it was when he began to talk about his work with Chicano street gangs in East Los Angeles that I could sense his passion and frustration. I could read the desperation in his heart as he whispered, "I couldn't stop them from killing themselves."

When the waiter finally seated us at our table by the window, I realized that I had been completely oblivious of the noisy UCLA students around us.

"By the way, I have something for you."

I handed him the geode. He held it in his hands and looked at it quietly, then placed it on the window ledge.

"That's very thoughtful," was all he said.

At last we returned to Ellen's apartment, where she and Terry had a chance to meet before she and her boyfriend, John, went out. Terry was on the board of trustees of the Humanitas Prize, which is an award given to writers who help to promote human values in their scripts. John had been nominated for an episode of a show which he co-produced called "St. Elsewhere," so they had a lot to talk about. After they left, Terry flopped on the floor, determined to fix Ellen's stereo. As I watched him, I was enveloped in a wave of tenderness and peace. I realized that I had shared more of myself with this person than with anyone else in my life for a long, long time—if ever. And there was something I wanted to say, but I couldn't seem to phrase it correctly, even to myself. I became tentative and shy.

"You know, what you did at Loyola the other night, taking me out to look at the landing strip, that meant a lot to me. I really don't know how to put this, but it's as though you have filled the emptiness in my heart my father's death left behind. I don't feel so alone anymore."

Terry looked at me very hard, in the same way he had when I had handed him the geode. He didn't smile or say thank you. He just looked at me. Then finally he spoke.

"I just want to be your friend." He looked me in the eyes with a kind of desperation, though his voice was soft. "You have to be careful. Sometimes you think you're stepping into a bathtub and it can suddenly become the Atlantic Ocean."

I could feel the heat from my flushed face; my reaction was sudden and unexpected. I felt as if I were choking inside, yet I sat very still. From the depths of my being, I knew I was already in the Atlantic Ocean.

The next morning I replaced the pillows on the couch and pulled from my suitcase my comfortable old Yankee jacket and tennis shoes. It was cold on the beach, I knew, but I needed to walk and to feel the salt air about me.

There were fairly few people about that day, an occasional jogger passing by. I began to walk very fast, my heart beating to the rhythm of my steps, in an effort to force from my head the thoughts that were making me so restless. *The faster I walk, the less I will have to think! Breathe!*

I stopped as a sob broke from my throat, and suddenly quiet tears were mixing with the salty air. Slowly, then, I began again— one foot in front of the other, my hands thrust deep into my pockets. A seed . . . a tiny terror . . . was beginning to engulf me. I knew that I couldn't just wish it away. It was there. A key had unlocked the door to that secret chamber in my heart, and there was no way to deny it. I knew what it was, and for the first time I had to admit it to myself.

I had recognized from our first lunch the unusually strong bond Terry and I had both experienced, but I knew now that it could be far deeper for me than a friendship. I knew that I could love this man, and I also knew that I would be in love with a man whom I could never have. The impossibility of that situation was overwhelming to me that day as I walked for hours on a drizzly beach. I was glad no one could see my tears. I knew I had finally found what I had been searching for. I knew it with unquestionable clarity—and I also knew that this knowledge would be my only comfort. In the real world Terry could never be mine. I was sure that I would never embrace this man or feel his heart against my chest. I realized that I could never hold him. More importantly, I also realized that I would never, ever let him know how I felt.

Something strange was happening inside me, and as I walked, I tried to clarify things for myself. I knew that Terry was a priest . . . a celibate priest. He had chosen this course for his life. He was a vital part of the lives of so many people—they needed him, and that was where he was content to be. But I also recognized his instinctive reactions to me, the subtle indications of his lack of fulfillment: his need to share his own private hurts and dreams, his need to laugh, his need to cry. Surrounded by people who loved him, he was lonely. I knew that he, consciously, was unaware of these things.

At that moment in our relationship I don't think I felt the guilt for my emotions that a Catholic woman in my position might have felt. One of the basic beliefs of the Christian Science faith is that all men and women are created in the image and likeness of God. Therefore, each of us has the capability of attaining perfection. In a Christian Science service there are no priests, but simply readers who present the weekly lesson to the congregation. No one is holier than anyone else—perhaps more committed, more advanced in understanding, more dedicated, but no group is set above another. So I was unused to the notion of a priest. Of course, I understood what a priest represents, how the Catholic Church defines him, and how he perceives himself. But I didn't have any preconditioned ideas about priestly behavior. I saw Terry as someone committed to the service of God and his fellow man; but because of my background, I could also recognize his needs and desires. Had I been more educated in the Catholic religion, I might not have perceived so clearly my heart—and I think, now, that my uncomplicated view of things at that time was a blessing. I didn't rationalize away my feelings as a need for counseling, or any of the other delusions available. I recognized that what I felt for Terry was love . . . and I needed to behave accordingly.

My terror lay in the fact that my heart was on such shaky ground. Should I return to New York, for the rest of my life contenting myself with lesser passions? At least I would always know that I had found my heart's home. Surely that would be the honorable thing to do . . . to walk away. But what about those tears on his cheeks? Would I be deserting something that I could not yet, perhaps, understand?

Was it by God's law or man's law that Terry Sweeney lived alone and lonely? Was celibacy his choice, or had it been chosen for him? Was the tenderness I felt a remarkable impropriety, or a godsend for us both?

I resolved to sit back and wait. I realized that if ever there were to be the possibility of a relationship between us, everything must come from him. If I were to instigate anything at all, years down the line he might feel compromised or manipulated. If he questioned his celibacy, I could not tempt that questioning—for I would only lose. I would wait a week or two. I would not call him or try to see him. I would wait. And I would pray.

9

TERRY

The counseling session with my spiritual adviser, Father Donald Merrifield, was coming up shortly, and I wanted to ask his advice about how an "obedient" Jesuit would go about correcting errors in the Church's policy regarding the priesthood. The question was not merely hypothetical.

A 1976 Vatican Declaration had stated that women would not be ordained priests because "Christ himself was and remains a man," and Jesus "did not call any woman to become part of the Twelve." Most of the arguments advanced by the Vatican to support their conclusions crumbled before an objective biblical and historical analysis. I had known this when the Declaration had first been announced, but I did not join my voice with others objecting to it. I was afraid that doing so would be "disobedient" and that such dissent would lead to reprimand.

Compounding this exclusion of women from the priesthood were other serious problems. Priestly vocations were dwindling at an alarming rate. Since Vatican II over 100,000 priests had resigned. In the United States alone, seminary enrollment had plummeted from 48,000 in 1965 to 10,400 in 1985. A nationwide survey of resigned priests, conducted in 1970 by the National

Opinion Research Center, had shown that the two major causes of priestly resignations were conflict with authority and problems with celibacy. A 1984 study by Dean Hoge, entitled "Men's Vocations to the Priesthood and the Religious Life," had stated that the strongest obstacle for Catholic men considering a vocation to the priesthood is that they are "not allowed to marry," and if "married men could be ordained, the number of men seeking ordination would increase, as an estimate, fourfold or more."

From historical studies I had learned that many of the Reformers had vehemently objected to the priestly celibacy discipline, calling it unnatural. Also I knew that many of the apostles and some forty popes had been married and that celibacy had not become a requirement for the Roman Catholic priesthood until the Second Lateran Council in 1139. But what I had never been taught at any point in my Jesuit training was why the celibacy laws were first enacted. To answer this question, I had to begin not in the twelfth century, but in the fourth. The first extant canon regarding continence and celibacy dated from that period, and it forbade, under threat of dismissal from the clerical state, all married bishops, presbyters, and deacons to have conjugal relations with their wives or to have children. Reading this canon filled me with horror and shame. Here was the Church, which had always defended the sacredness of the marriage bond, enforcing a law that violated the very heart of marriage.

I read everything I could obtain about the celibacy canons, how the married clergy and their wives reacted to them, why various popes and bishops would enforce them, and why others would completely ignore them and themselves marry. After several years of this research a very distressing picture had begun to emerge: that even though celibacy had been in the lives of many saints a profound witness and virtue, many of the celibacy laws were used as legal instruments of punishment to break up the marriages of priests. The motives for doing this varied: Some popes thought conjugal intercourse was a defilement and that a priest should always be "pure" to celebrate the Lord's Supper; others felt priests should be totally devoted to prayer and to the Church, not to the cares of wife and children; still others wanted to ensure that donations to the local priest would not pass from priest father to priest's son, but to the Church; and still others felt that celibacy was a witness to the celibate life of Jesus.

Because many of the married clergy ignored these canons, saying that such laws violated God's law and the marriage bond, increasingly severe punishments were inflicted on married priests and their wives and children. These sanctions included fines, beatings, imprisonment, imposed fastings, women having their heads shaved, armed attacks by papal order, and the wives and the children of priests made slaves of the Church.

This distressing knowledge had made me aware of the terrible probability that the priestly celibacy discipline was unethical and unchristian.

As I walked into the Jesuit Community Residence that day, I was still too immersed in the research to know how to respond to this probability. All I knew was that there was a profound disorder in the Church and that if Jesuit obedience meant mirroring the mind of the Pope, everything I said about my doubts would be a threat, either to Rome, to the Jesuits, or to my vocation. Also I had learned, from three years of lobbying efforts (with city, county, and state officials) to set up the gang-violence-reduction program, that trying to effect institutional change was very difficult and frustrating. How much more demanding it would be to try to effect change in the largest organized religion in the world! The mere thought of it was oppressive.

Maybe Don could help me sort things out. I climbed the stairs to the second floor, walked down the hallway to room 209. Don had a Ph.D. in Physics from MIT, had been president of Loyola Marymount University for fifteen years, and was now chancellor. Though some in the Jesuit Community regarded him as aloof and cynical, I thought of him as a good friend and as a man who made light of his substantial service to the university and to the Los Angeles community. Even after his quadruple bypass, he stayed on as president of the university, knowing that the pressures could only aggravate his health. When push came to shove, Don valued the university more than his own life. Several years after the bypass, and only when a suitable replacement as president could be found, did he resign. With time I grew to trust Don both as my spiritual adviser and friend. He knew my hopes, my weaknesses, and my sins.

I knocked on his door. "Come in," he said.

Don put aside the book he was reading and greeted me with a smile. "Have a seat. Sorry to hear about JMA. Charlie's been trying for years to get the Province involved in a serious way in media. He thought JMA would work."

"So did I."

"What are you going to do now?"

"I'm shutting it down. But it hasn't been easy. It's bringing back into play my fears about obedience. The more people I talk with and the more research I do, the clearer it becomes that there are two models of obedience in the Society and in the Church. One model says obedience means conforming ourselves to Vatican teachings; the other model says obedience means communicating the truth, even if that sometimes means contesting Vatican teachings. Which do you think it is?"

Don thought for a moment, then replied, "The President can't have members of his cabinet criticizing his policy. Neither can the Pope."

"But the Church is more than a political institution. Church policy should be formulated by the entire Church, not just the Pope and his bishops. And that policy should be based on what is good, what is true. If it isn't, then our responsibility as Christians, and especially as priests, is to stand up and say so. How can the Church move forward if, in the name of obedience and authority, it suppresses valid criticism?"

"The Church has her flaws, but overall she's done fairly well over the last two thousand years," Don answered.

He was looking out the window when I replied, "The Church will stagnate if she is not open to the truth."

"Truth—what is that?" Don said with a wry grin on his face. "And whose version of the truth? The Pope's? Yours?"

His cynicism wasn't the counsel I was seeking. "For example, the truth about celibacy."

Don looked straight at me, then swiveled his chair around to stare again out the window: "I can't imagine anyone having told you it was going to be easy."

"I'm not talking about the personal struggle of trying to live it, I'm referring to the actual historical origins of the laws of celibacy. The more I read about the history of the laws, the more unbelievable it gets."

"What do you mean?" he asked.

"We were taught all about the virtues of celibacy, but nothing about the vices that brought the laws into being. Why did I have to learn about it on my own? Why weren't we told that the first celibacy laws were laws requiring total abstinence of validly married clergy? Why didn't our seminary teachers tell us that married priests and their wives who refused to follow mandatory abstinence were forced out of the priesthood, were beaten, imprisoned, and sometimes even murdered?"

Don spun around in his chair and looked uneasily at me. From the length of time it took him to answer, and the more serious tone of his reply, it seemed as though what I had just said was something he, too, had not been taught. "The Church is a human institution. Her history has never been perfect."

"I'm not talking about perfection, I'm talking about evil. It was evil to interfere with the marriage bond; it was wrong to assert that conjugal intercourse was impure and that married priests must refrain from conjugal relations. It was wrong to punish those clerical couples who refused to follow the canons mandating abstinence and celibacy."

"That was long ago," Don said. "You can't use a twentieth-century ethical mentality to evaluate laws passed centuries ago."

"Twentieth-century? It was Jesus who said, 'What God hath joined let no man divide.' It doesn't matter whether you're talking about the first century or the twentieth century, those marriages were blessed by God. And married people certainly don't want to be told that their lovemaking is a sin, which is exactly what some of the popes and papal legates enforcing celibacy laws were pushing down married clergy's throats."

"Sex has never been one of the Church's strong points, but the body of her teachings on marriage has been very positive."

The conversation was becoming very frustrating. I guess I had expected Don to share my outrage over the mired origins of the celibacy laws; instead he seemed to be brushing them aside as a remote and not overly significant action of the distant past. I could feel the color rushing to my face. "I agree, but I'm not talking about her teachings on marriage. I'm talking about the actual history of the celibacy laws, and about particular popes who broke up marriages while enforcing those laws. The first known celibacy canon dates from the fourth century, and it ordered bishops, priests, and deacons to totally abstain from their wives and not to have children; if they did so, they would be dismissed from the clerical state. There is a direct relationship—in some canons the wording is almost identical—between the current canons and those dating all the way back to the fourth century."

Don, who normally had a quick response to every statement, fell silent. I pressed my argument: "Abstinence and celibacy canons that interfere with the matrimonial bond are wrong, from every point of view you can think of—biblical, philosophical, theological, ethical. . . ."

While my voice was getting louder, his became softer. "Catholic priests today aren't married. You knew celibacy was a requirement going in. No one forced you to become a priest."

"That's right, no one forced me to become a priest. But Church law wouldn't allow me to become one without first promising never to marry. Jesus didn't force his disciples to be celibate, why does the Church? Sure, in our seminary training we were told all about the great virtue of celibacy, how it makes us more available to people and to preaching the Gospel, more Christ-like. But why were we never told of the error-ridden and bloody historical foundations of the celibacy laws?"

"Even if celibacy were made optional, that would not affect you. You're a Jesuit."

"Yes, but one who wants the freedom to tell the truth about the real origins of mandated celibacy. I want to tell people that it's just not right to mandate celibacy by law. It was wrong when it was first imposed, it is wrong now."

"That is your opinion," Don said.

"I'm not alone. Every survey over the last twenty years shows that the majority of priests and laity think celibacy should be made optional. And that's without even knowing the actual violent origins of the celibacy laws."

"This pope won't change the celibacy laws," Don said definitively.

"I keep hearing that: 'This pope won't change, maybe the next pope, or the one after that.' Meanwhile centuries go by. What am I supposed to do, keep my mouth shut? Pretend I don't know what I know? Pretend that I don't know that one third of the worldwide total of priests ordained since 1965 have married? And that canon law automatically suspends them and cuts them off from their ministry? Don, the priesthood is dying!"

Don swiveled his chair to the right, then to the left, then back to face me. His answer was calm, matter-of-fact—and for those reasons all the more disturbing: "Under this pope, no matter what you say or do, the celibacy laws will not change—and your efforts will only get you into trouble."

I left Don's room and went out the backdoor to the lawn behind the Residence. Branches in the tall palm trees swayed with gusts of wind sweeping up from Marina del Rey. I needed to feel the ocean breeze against my face, to see something peaceful and simple, such as sailboats gliding over the water. I needed to calm down. I looked out toward the water, but it was no use. My attention was all inward, on the multiyear dilemma now manifesting itself yet again. The Provincial was telling me to obey and not to presume to know more than the Vatican; other very prominent Jesuits had told me that obedience was to God and that if there were a conflict between God's revelation and papal teaching, we were obligated to try to correct the Pope; Don was telling me that taking issue with the Pope on the current priesthood policy would only end in trouble.

Extensive travel through some of the poorest countries in the world had burned into my heart the conviction that "with knowledge comes responsibility." What I was learning about authority and the priesthood was obligating me to some form of action. But I also knew from previous pastoral and political experience that the world is a very imperfect place and that one person can only do so much. Reforming the priesthood policy would be a massive undertaking, and I didn't have the slightest idea where to begin, or whether I would even be allowed to begin.

Had it not been for my brother Pat, and for Pamela, I most probably would have fallen back into my typical pattern of marshaling more facts, seeking more counsel, intellectualizing nuances, and wrestling with all possible consequences before taking any action. But the luxury of time and the security of indecisiveness were suddenly ripped away on February 7, 1985, when Pat called and said, "I just got back from UCLA hospital. They took X rays because I've lost thirty-five pounds in the last three weeks. I have a large tumor on my lung. It's malignant, inoperable, and terminal."

M y brother Pat was one year older and a half inch taller than I. It was because of him that I first heard the expression *black sheep.* Up through high school and beyond, Pat was always getting into trouble. At the military grade school we attended, Dudley graduated a major, I graduated a first lieutenant, Pat graduated a buck private. Whereas Dudley and I were honors students at Loyola High, Pat was kicked out of Loyola and four other schools. While Dudley and I spent summers and vacations working our way through high school, Pat partied, banged up Mom's car in eleven separate accidents, and boasted thirty moving violations in one month. But for all his rowdiness and his disregard for the hardships he was causing the family, Pat was fiercely loyal to his friends, generous, charming, and fun to be with.

During my first summer out of grade school Pat knew that I had never been to a party and that I did not know how to dance. He invited me to my first party and then sent his girlfriend over to teach me how to dance. He kidded me unmercifully about the fact that I was twelve years old and had still never kissed a girl; he would grab his bed pillow, hug and kiss it passionately and, sharing raucous laughs with Dudley, tell me that was how it was done. But when I was sixteen and asked him if I could invite his steady girlfriend to my high school dance, he said yes unhesitatingly and with a smile.

Pat was always "pushing the limit" on things, ideas, himself. If he was driving a car, he wanted to know exactly how fast it would go and how fast he could turn a corner without the car tipping over; he wanted to know how many consecutive speeding tickets he could get before his license would be revoked. He wanted to know how long he could hold his breath and how many laps he could swim under water. He loved taking risks, he loved to gamble. I remember one hair-raising Saturday night when he challenged "mad-man" Pablo to a surface-street race from Santa Monica to downtown L.A. Both drivers vowed they would win, no matter what. What I soon learned this meant was that both would race at top speed, weaving their way through midnight Saturday traffic and that neither would stop at red lights. After careening through several red lights, I vowed I would never race with him again.

Some of Pat's friends thought he had a death wish. Those who knew him best realized that, in testing his limits and in living life on the edge, Pat longed for a sense of importance, of being able to say to others that he had experienced everything life had to offer.

"It's been very confusing," Pat said. "The doctor wants me to go in for more tests tomorrow."

"Why is it inoperable?" I asked.

"Because of its size, and its position on the lung. He's saying I should think of starting chemotherapy or radiation therapy immediately. They're going to run more tests, but they want me to decide about this therapy business right away."

"What are your chances of remission with the therapy?" I asked.

"I don't know. There are a lot of unanswered questions. Things happened so fast, the doctors were talking in such technical language, I really feel lost. I would have gone to the hospital sooner, but I thought the weight loss was due to an outdoor tile job I was doing at a home on the Palos Verdes Peninsula. It was raining, and the winds were ice cold. I caught a fever."

"How's Rosemarie taking it?"

"A lot harder than me. Michael's been really quiet, like he doesn't want to think about it or talk about it."

"Does Mom know? Dudley?"

"I'm going to call them now. I wanted to talk to you first." His voice fell silent. I could feel his pain.

"There's a doctor at UCLA, Ed Amos. He's a friend of mine. I'll call him right now and get back to you."

"Thanks, Terry. I love you, Brother."

"I love you too."

It was the first time we had ever said that to each other.

The next ten days were frantic, not only with numerous practical decisions (financial, legal, medical) that had to be made, but also with the storm of emotions erupting over the immediate and fatal threat to Pat's life. Dr. Amos became Pat's personal physician and coordinated the UCLA diagnosis. He informed Pat that with radiation and chemotherapy he might have a six- to ten-percent chance of survival. Without therapy he could die as soon as two weeks, or perhaps live as long as a year. With such a slim chance of successful therapy, and in light of the brutal side effects, Pat thought it better to refuse the therapy. Rosemarie disagreed. Pat called and asked if I would come by and talk it over.

I called Dr. Amos twice and asked his advice. Then, knowing that Pamela's father had died of cancer and that her stepfather was a surgeon, I called her and asked if I could also get Bill's counsel.

"Of course. I'll call him right now and ask him to expect your call. Oh, Terry, I'm so sorry."

"Dr. Bergin, this is Terry Sweeney. Thanks for taking my call. I know it's almost midnight—"

"Don't worry about that," he said. "Sorry to hear about your brother."

"He has to make a decision whether or not to do chemo and radiation therapy or to forgo it and spend the rest of the time he has left with his wife and son."

"I generally don't comment on cases I haven't been involved in."

I sensed his hesitation. "I'm sorry to have to ask you this way. . . ."

"What's the diagnosis?"

"He has a large tumor on the lung. It's malignant and inoperable. The doctors say he has small-cell carcinoma of the lung, oat-cell variety, and that with therapy he has a six- to ten-percent chance of survival."

"How old is your brother?" he asked.

"Forty-one."

There was a long silence on the other end of the phone as I waited for Dr. Bergin to speak. Finally he said softly, "I'd tell him to buy a fishing pole and enjoy his family."

As I drove over to Pat's house the evening of February 12, 1985, the word *terminal* kept sounding in my head. I just couldn't believe Pat was dying—Pat the Invincible. He had survived forest fires, attacks by gang members, and numerous car accidents. Once he hit a telephone pole with such force that he split the pole in half, and regained consciousness with the car engine jammed in next to him on the front seat. I just couldn't believe that *terminal* could refer to Pat, not now, not at his age, not with all the times he could have died and instead had walked away clean with that luck-of-the-Irish grin on his face.

As I drove up his driveway, I remembered the conversation we'd had when Pat had first started to smoke. Pat was fourteen. We were sitting in Mom's car outside our Aunt Flay's house in Westchester. Pat was lighting up a cigarette. "Don't start, Pat, you'll get hooked." "Not me," he'd said. "I can handle it. If I get to a point where I think I need it, I'll stop."

When I opened the screen door and walked in, Pat was smoking.

"Hi, Pat."

"Hi, Terry. Thanks for coming."

Rosemarie walked in from the kitchen. I gave her a kiss. From her swollen eyes I could tell she had been crying. But I also knew from the many times that she had bailed Pat out of trouble and stood by him, that her own tears were the least of her worries. "Hi, can I get you anything? Something to drink?"

"No, thanks, Rosemarie." I looked over and saw Michael playing with his baseball cards. "Hello, Michael."

Michael whispered a greeting. He, too, could sense the tension in the room, the uncertainty, the desperation.

"Honey, we're going now. We'll be back later." Pat led me out the door to his car. "Hope you don't mind. I wanted to get out of the house for a while, talk to you privately. There's a tile convention going on downtown, I need to check with a few people, thought we could talk along the way."

"Fine with me."

Pat started up the car, drove out of the driveway, and headed southeast. "Rosemarie's really pressuring me to do the chemotherapy. She thinks I can beat the cancer even though the doctors say I have only a slim chance. I want the time I have left with Michael and Rosemarie to be quality time. I want to take Michael on trips. I want to die at home, not in some hospital bed with tubes stuck into me."

I could feel the tears starting to well in my eyes. I fought them back.

"I have to let Dr. Amos know tomorrow. Thanks for calling him, Terry, he's been great. The treatments just don't seem worth it if the best shot I've got is only ten percent. I don't want my hair falling out and my skin turning yellow. What should I do?"

"It's your decision," I replied.

"I know, but what would you do?"

"Since I've been at Loyola, four people in the Jesuit Community have had cancer. They took the treatments, their skin turned yellow, they lost their hair, and they died."

Pat listened intently, said nothing.

"Dad was told that if he didn't have his legs amputated, he would die. He preferred to die with his legs than live without them."

"I never knew that," Pat said. "Guess I just kind of wrote him off after he left us—the way he hurt Mom. I should have paid more attention to him, like you did."

"Dr. Bergin's advice was that you should buy a fishing pole and enjoy your family."

There was a long silence. I waited to see if Pat was going to say anything. He didn't. I realized he was still waiting for me to tell him what to do. "If I were in your place, I think that's what I would do."

Pat let out a huge sigh. "That's it, then—I've just decided. In my gut this is what I've felt I should do, but Rosemarie's been resisting it."

His voice was calm now, almost peaceful. "Hell, I'm not afraid of death. I've been close to death enough times before. It's just that I don't want Michael's last memories of me to be of some broken-down cancer victim dying in some strange hospital. I want to die in a bed I've lived in. I want to die in our own home, with my wife and son next to me."

I could no longer restrain the tears forcing their way from my heart. In that instant I understood something about my brother that I had never known before. I always knew that Pat was restless and reckless and loving, but now I knew that he was also coura-geous. I felt immensely proud to be his brother.

"Thanks, Terry, I feel like a great weight has been lifted."

After spending two hours at the tile convention, we drove back to the house. When Pat told Rosemarie about his decision, she burst into tears. She rushed over to me. "Tell him, Terry, tell him to fight, even if there's only a one-percent chance of survival. Pat's never been a quitter. Tell him not to give up now!"

"I'm not giving up, Rosemarie—it's my decision!" Pat shouted.

"What about us—Michael and me?" she cried. "Don't we have anything to say about it?"

"I told you, honey, I want to die here, not in some hospital bed—"

"You're not going to die—not if you fight!"

"It's my body!" Pat cried.

Rosemarie grabbed my arm, pleaded desperately with me. "Tell him, Terry. He's always been a fighter. He can beat this. Tell him!"

I saw the pain in her eyes and tried to say as calmly as I could, "As much as he loves you, it's his life, his body." I hated myself even more as I saw the tears streaming down her face and new levels of agony break her heart.

The air is gray, threatening. Overhead, seagulls are screeching and flying at strange angles in the sky. I am standing on a stretch of sand near the Santa Monica pier. Behind me are the high cliffs overlooking Pacific Coast Highway. People are trying to claw their way up the side of the cliff.

Others, on the beach near me, are running frantically toward the cliff.

From the ocean I hear a violent, thunderous wind. I look out. There, coming toward me is a massive tidal wave, growing in size as it rumbles toward the shore.

Its towering size will totally submerge the entire one hundred-foot cliff wall. I don't know whether to run with the others and try to scale the cliff or to dive into the water and try to swim toward the tidal wave, hoping to reach it before it crests and smashes against the shore.

I dive into the water, begin swimming toward the wave. The undertow from the shore draws me rapidly into the teeming wave. I see floating in the wave drowned human bodies and shattered pieces of boats and furniture.

Swimming as fast as I can, I strain to make it beyond the wave, but it is just now swooping up into a gigantic crest. It's about to crash over me.

The nightmare shook me awake. My body was drenched in sweat, my breathing short and heavy. As the potted plant in the far corner of my bedroom took shape in the darkness, I tried to let the silence of the night soothe the terror of the dream. I knew that the nightmare portended either death or an extremely profound disturbance in my soul. Pat's cancer was shaking me to the core, but at that moment on that night I could not know whether the nightmare foreshadowed Pat's death or a profound threat to something inside of me.

Too many times I had been called to the bedside of cancer victims. I had seen what this merciless disease could do to the human body. And now my brother was its victim. And I, the priest, the purported man of God, could not save him. Three times as a priest, people had begged me to intercede with God on behalf of loved ones terminally ill. Two of the three had lived, but the third person died—a beautiful, gracious woman who left behind her husband and nine-year-old daughter. At the mortuary the little girl, dressed in a knee-length navy-blue dress, walked past rows of flower stands and bouquets to touch her mother's casket. When she began crying, I felt the failure of my prayers. I asked God why, but there was no answer, only the realization that miraculous cures come only when God wills it. But how could God not want this heartbroken girl to be with her mother? I wanted to talk to her, to comfort her, but I had neither the faith nor the strength to do so.

And now death was calling my brother.

I needed to talk to someone who had stared death in the face, who had watched cancer steal away life, blood, love. I spoke to many in the Jesuit Community about Pat's illness. Several offered to keep Pat in their prayers. Only one took the time to visit him.

I called Pamela the morning of February 14th. Ellen told me she was going to be gone all day. I had just finished eating supper at the Community when Pamela returned my call.

"I don't believe it! You're finally off the phone. I tried lots of times between interviews to return your call, but your line was busy, busy. . . ."

"I was going to invite you to dinner, but it's too late. I've already eaten."

"Lucky you, I haven't even had breakfast yet."

"Then let me treat you to breakfast, lunch, and dinner, all in one."

"But you've already eaten," she protested.

"So what, you haven't. See you in twenty minutes?"

"Okay. You sure . . . ?"

"I'm on my way."

We went to a little café on the renovated Main Street in Venice. She ordered a grilled-cheese sandwich and ate a total of about three bites of it.

"Our family's decided to have a Mass and reception for Pat. It would mean a lot to me if you could be there."

"Yes, of course I'll be there."

"Good. Besides, I want to introduce you to Pat and to my family."

"I'd like that very much. Is there anything I can do to help with the reception—bring food or anything?"

"No, thanks. It's all taken care of."

We left the café. I drove north on Pacific Coast Highway, not toward any specific location. It was a beautiful, crisp night. The coastline was sparkling with lights, stars could be seen overhead.

"How long did your father have cancer?" I asked.

"Thirteen months."

"Did he know it was fatal?"

"We never talked about it with him in that way. All of us kept on hoping he would recover. But I think he knew. When I was asked to go on tour with *Generation,* I was really afraid of leaving him. But my mother told me that if I didn't go, Daddy might suspect he was dying. It was a dumb thing to do, not to talk about it. My dad was a brilliant man. In his silence he was trying to protect us. We were all trying to protect each other. His illness became the focus of our lives. Mom had set up a hospital bed in the guesthouse on our property, and she wouldn't leave his side. She rarely ever left the house. She gave him his shots and took care of him when the nurse was off duty. Nothing else in our lives was as important as Daddy getting well. Did you know that Bill was my father's surgeon? I don't know what we would have done without him. I remember how he described my dad to his partner, Dr. Gooel, before they operated on him for the first time. Dr. Gooel walked into my dad's hospital room, extended his hand and said, 'Bill told me I was going to meet a man with a smile on his face.' Bill loved my father. As he saw the end getting close, Bill just stopped eating. He got thinner and thinner himself as he tried to stop my dad from wasting away. Finally, as a surgeon, there was nothing more he could do. They tell me that after Daddy died that night . . . Bill went over to the guesthouse and just held my father in his arms for a long, long time."

Her voice trailed off into silent memories. We drove around the hills in Rambla Pacifica and found a private road overlooking the shoreline. I stopped the car, turned off the engine, and rolled down the window.

"It's so beautiful up here," she said as she rolled down her window and looked out at the ocean.

"What do you think death is?" I asked.

"I don't know. What do you think?"

"A veil, a thin, fragile veil that separates this life from the next life."

"What do you mean?"

"I don't know exactly. As Christians we're taught to believe that the resurrection of Jesus foreshadows the resurrection of all who live in faith and love. It's an extremely promising, hope-filled notion, and most of me believes it. But when my father died and I stood next to his casket, I didn't feel hope or life. I felt darkness. Perhaps we wouldn't be so terrified if we could just be certain that on the other side there was life."

She lay her head back against the open window, looked up at the stars. For a long time we sat there silently. It seemed as though we were lingering on feelings too secret for words. I followed her gaze up to the heavens, wondering if she were finding there some secret to life and death, some answer to that simple but most dreaded of all questions: Is death the end? Somehow, at that moment, with the sound of rhythmic waves washing against the seashore, and the tiny, but brilliant stars lighting the night sky, and this woman sitting so calmly and trustingly only a few feet away, I felt instead of the terror and dread of the nightmare a tranquillity, a peace. I felt, even though our bodies were not touching, that our spirits were soaring past the same stars, searching, laughing, hoping.

On February 17th, the morning of Pat's Mass, the restlessness and the dread had returned. The memory of the pain in Rosemarie's eyes kept forcing its way into my heart. I had seen that look before, many times, mostly at bedsides in intensive care units or standing next to caskets at gravesites—that look of panic, of utter helplessness and anguish when love is shrouded by death. But I felt powerless to help her. I remembered the biblical story of Lazarus's sisters crying out to Jesus, "Lord, if you had been here, my brother would not have died!" Wasn't that a power Jesus had given to His disciples, to cure diseases? Hadn't He said, "If you had faith the size of a mustard seed, you could say to this mountain, 'Rise up and throw yourself into the sea' "? And Scripture said that the disciples "set out and went from village to village proclaiming the Good News and healing everywhere." Was I not a disciple? Was my faith so weak that God would not hear prayers of healing for my own brother?

As I crossed the road leading to Huesman Hall, I saw Pat's car pull up in front of the chapel. He, Rosemarie, and Michael got out. Pat looked so pale as he put one arm around Rosemarie, the other around Michael, and walked slowly to the chapel entrance.

I couldn't face Pat right then. I was afraid he would see my dread and that I would break down. I slipped into the side door behind the chapel, pleading silently with God to help all of us get through this. I was the priest, I was supposed to bring hope, but the only thing I could feel as I fought back the tears was utter helplessness.

I walked into the sacristy, began vesting. A memory of my father's funeral Mass flooded in. Father Lavery had left the church with Dad's casket. Everyone had been getting up to leave, but Father Lavery's words lingered in my mind: "The Mass is ended." *So is Dad, so is love, so is life.* I'd wanted to get up and follow the others out, but I could not move. Therese was telling me it was time to leave, but I could not speak. I wanted my body to stand up, I told my body to stand up, that it was time to bury my father, but it would not move. Suddenly Pat was there, standing over me. He didn't say anything, he just reached down, took my arm, placed it over his shoulder, and guided me to the waiting hearse.

The memory brought more tears as I put on the yellow patchwork chasuble made by the handicapped children belonging to Mary Melanson's catechism class. My glance fell on the patch, which had a cloud, a sunburst, and a rainbow. I touched the patch, as though hoping to draw from it some strength. Family and friends had gathered in the chapel now. They needed me. My mother needed faith deeper than her sorrow; Rosemarie needed grace stronger than her anger and her hurt; Pat needed healing; Michael needed his father, alive. And I knew from my failures, from the many times I had pleaded heart-and-soul for others to be healed, that my prayers now would not answer their needs.

The entrance hymn began. I wanted to crawl into a hole and hide. I felt shame and embarrassment at my total spiritual impotency. Twenty-two years of religious life, thousands of hours of prayer, twelve years of priesthood, and still, at this most critical moment, I was at an utter loss. Now Pat would know, the family and everyone waiting in the chapel would know my nothingness. I wiped the tears from my eyes, walked to the chapel entrance.

So be it—faith or fear, healing or death, all I could do was beg.

10

PAMELA

As I drove into the parking lot at ten o'clock Sunday morning, I was very nervous. I had no idea what to expect. It was true that I'd never met any of Terry's family, nor did I know any of his friends. But it was more than that. I knew I was going to meet Pat. And Pat was going to die. Although I'd heard how bravely he was accepting death, I was frightened. I was frightened in the way anyone is when death is nearby. I was frightened of the pain of past memory and fear of future loss. And I was frightened for Terry. I knew how difficult this was going to be for him.

I shook aside these grim thoughts and focused on the love and joy behind this family gathering. So often people are reluctant to share their grief. How beautiful it was that this family had chosen to gather all their friends around them for a very personal, private farewell while Pat was still alive to enjoy it. Not only was Pat Sweeney loved, but those who loved him were welcomed to share with him one of the last, most precious moments of his life. I was very grateful to have been included.

The parking lot was full, and I was surprised to see so many people piling into the tiny chapel. Every seat was taken, practically all the standing room was filled, and still they continued to come.

As I looked around, I could see Terry near the back, hidden partially by a door, hugging people as they took their places. Guitars strummed, and I glanced down at the song sheet I had been handed: "Praise the Lord Who Heals the Brokenhearted." Psalm 147. That's what we were. The Brokenhearted.

Every heart here bled for Pat . . . for the imminent loss of a brother, a friend. We wept silently for loved ones long since passed, whose memories were suddenly with us once more as if time were standing still. Memories of funerals and pain and loss stung in eyes all around the room—watchful eyes. As we waited, I could sense the caution and the reserve. It was an unusual situation, to celebrate life in the face of impending death. Pat was meeting his future—our own futures someday. We wondered how it would feel, and why there must be separation from those we love so much.

I saw the Sullys sitting across the room, and I was terrified that they would see in my eyes all that I felt for Terry. He mustn't know; no one must know.

At last the door beside me opened and a small family walked in. Could that be Pat and Rosemarie? He was tall and extremely thin. His cheeks were drawn, yet it was easy to recognize how handsome he had once been. And there was that unmistakable Sweeney smile. He wore a simple sweater and glanced warmly at a small, fragile woman by his side. He threw a protective arm across her shoulders. She looked so tired and frail in her grief, and I was struck by the sweetness of her face and the tender looks that passed between them. Tentatively they walked down the aisle, almost as if afraid to look around them. They seemed completely surprised and overwhelmed by the number of people who were there. Alongside them was their son, Michael, a ten-year-old version of Pat with huge, expressive eyes.

As they took their seats up front in the row that had been cordoned off, the room fell silent. Those who had been chatting stopped, instantly aware of why they were here. They were witnessing death and love and courage. I'm sure each one of us secretly wondered whether we would be able to meet our own deaths without bitterness, with such gratitude for life. Though it was an intrusion upon their privacy, with a mixture of curiosity and respect, we wanted to look at this family . . . somehow to learn from them, to understand their courage. Yet they, themselves, had welcomed us all here to share in this precious moment, giving us each a gift to treasure long after Patrick Sweeney was gone.

A moment later a woman with a shawl over her shoulders entered with a slender young woman. That must be Terry's mother and his sister, Therese. They were followed by Terry's brother, Dudley; his wife, Dori; and their three daughters. Their son, "Little Michael," was cradled comfortably in his father's arms.

When the music stopped, I could hear footsteps outside the chapel. As I turned, I saw him and couldn't believe my eyes. My first thought was, *Well, we're both in yellow!* I had chosen a spring-yellow silk dress, opting for a cheerier appearance for this occasion—and there stood Terry in the same bright-yellow vestments.

The musicians began a new song: "I am the Light of the world says the Lord. He who follows me will have the light of life." We all stood, and Terry smiled as he walked into the chapel. A tentative silence hung over the room as he greeted his family and took his place at the altar. As we waited for him to speak, I could feel a prayer forming in my heart, "God, be with him."

"When we first learned of Pat's terminal cancer, the family got together to try and decide what to do. I suggested, in the true Irish tradition, let's have a party! My brother, Dudley, thought we should have a Mass."

Laughter! Release!

"So, to keep everybody happy, we're going to have both: a Mass and a party. But if during the Mass I sometimes stop speaking and my eyes fill with tears, please don't feel uncomfortable—they are tears of sorrow, yes, but also tears of joy—joy at having Pat for my brother, joy that he is alive with us, joy that he has brought something good to each one of us here. Tears of joy. In the name of the Father, the Son, and the Holy Spirit. May the grace and peace of our Lord Jesus be with each one of you."

Therese read the first passage from Scripture, and Dudley, the second, with Michael still cradled in his arms, his head nestled against his father's chest. Terry read the Gospel and then began his homily.

"I don't know why God heals some people and others die. When I was a chaplain at UCLA hospital, there was a four-year-old boy who had contracted spinal meningitis and had been given twenty-four hours to live by his doctors. At the same time there was a woman in her thirties who had contracted cancer. She had a nine-year-old daughter. The parents of the little boy and the woman's husband begged me to ask God to heal them. I prayed with my whole heart and soul for them. The mother died; the boy lived.

"I don't know what the power of faith is, and I don't know why God makes the choices He does. Jesus could heal at will, and He asked His apostles to go out and heal the sick, comfort the afflicted. But I know from my own experience that sometimes the afflicted die, even though we beg God to keep them alive.

"I want my brother to live. And your being here today is a sign of your love and affection for him. I wish I could say to my brother, Pat, as Jesus did, 'Be healed.' I don't know what God's will is for him. All we can do in our prayers is to place our love for Pat in God's hands."

Terry's voice was hoarse. I sat there, helpless, longing to rush up and hold him. But of course that was impossible, not only today, but perhaps for always.

"Let's all stand now, join one another's hands in a circle and sing together the 'Our Father.' " As we sang, Terry never took his eyes off the floor. His body moved back and forth as he swayed rhythmically in time with the music, constantly swallowing his tears. I don't remember whose hand I held on my left, but privately I pretended that my empty right hand was squeezing Terry's and giving him strength.

I'm not sure exactly when it happened, at which precious moment along the way. It may have been during the Prayers of the Faithful, when Pat's mother stood before us and prayed aloud: "That God will give my son the strength he needs, that He will help Rosemarie and Michael, we pray to the Lord." Maybe it was during the Consecration, when Terry held up the Host and said with a breaking voice, "This is my Body, which will be given up for you." Or perhaps it was during the Greeting of Peace. One by one each member of his family moved to embrace Pat, and then one another. Friends crossed the room to cling to him tightly, if only for a second. Perhaps it was seeing the grateful smile on his face then. As I stood by myself and watched, I wasn't sure exactly when it came. But it did come. Gradually a deep, warm, healing peace came over us all. The tension and uneasiness which had permeated the room only moments before was gone, leaving us only a thoughtful, quiet peace. Each of us who had retreated into his own self-conscious world suddenly felt the presence of everyone around him. We met each other's sorrow face-to-face, and looking into strangers' eyes, found comfort there. And then we looked to Pat. Did he feel it too? The uncertainty seemed to have melted away, and as we watched him walk ever so slowly to Communion, his face was filled with light. This Mass, born of heartbreak and tragedy, had become for us all a testimony of love.

After the service there was to be a buffet at a charming little cottage on campus called the Bird's Nest. It seemed an endless walk to me, walking alone, filled with emotion. There was so much I wanted to say to Terry. But it would have to wait. One by one they sought him out, longing to draw some strength from him or to offer their gratitude. For hours he was surrounded. Moist eyes were masked by smiles and embraces. So much love poured out. After what seemed like an eternity, Terry tapped me on the shoulder.

"I want to introduce you to Pat."

I felt nervous. We crossed the room, and there he sat, surrounded by love. He turned to Terry.

"When Rosemarie and I first arrived, we felt very awkward. We didn't want this whole thing to be a downer, maudlin. We didn't want Michael walking away with feelings of sadness or pity." He looked around the room at his friends, then again at Terry. "This has been the happiest day of my life. Thank you."

Since there was no place for me to sit down, I crouched on the floor at Pat's feet, and we began to talk.

"It's such a grace and gift to have all these people around who love me. I don't want to leave Rosemarie and Michael, but I'm not afraid to die. What comes after this life has got to be an evolution. Better."

There was peace in his voice. I tried to understand. I asked questions, and he asked some of me. But so many people wanted to speak to him that he offered, "Why don't you come over to the house and we'll talk more?"

Just then Pat's wife walked up. With an Irish twinkle, he smiled up at her. "Have you met Rosemarie?"

Her soft brown hair fell across her blue cotton dress and she smiled a knowing smile at her husband. There was a lifetime behind her eyes, and she masked her sorrow well. As I stared up at her, I felt immediately her loss, her pain, her terror, her desperation, her courage. This woman was to become, in time, my treasured friend.

Later in the day Terry took my hand and led me into the center of the room where his mother was standing. He put his arms around both of us, pulling our heads close together in a circle. He whispered, "Mom, I want you to meet Pamela. She's been a tremendous help to me in all of this. Her stepfather, Dr. Bergin, was the one who gave some crucial medical advice that has been most helpful to Pat."

Angie said, "Well, thank you, and thank your stepfather for me."

"I will. It's good to meet you. Terry has told me so much about you."

Angie looked back at me with a gleeful twinkle in her eye, "Well, don't believe everything he says, even if he is a priest!"

I was impressed by her joyful spirit. "Wasn't the Mass beautiful?"

"So many people have said that. I don't know how Terry got through it. I would have choked up. It's great to have a priest in the family, but I can't give him all the credit." She gave Terry a reassuring hug. "The One up there should be given His due."

A while later, when people finally began to leave and the Sweeneys started taking family pictures, I slipped out the side door without saying good-bye. I knew Terry would know where to reach me if he wished to.

11

TERRY

After the Mass the cancer continued to ravage Pat's body. He couldn't keep food down any longer, and his weight continued to drop at an alarming rate. Even though he was exhausted, he was seldom able to sleep the whole night through. His bones felt brittle, tender, and he winced in pain when bumped into or touched too hard. There were days when he did not have the strength to walk. He realized it was only a matter of time before he would be totally confined to his bed. But in the midst of this deterioration and pain, Pat was peaceful. In fact he was more than peaceful, he was joyful.

Something had happened that day of Pat's Mass and reception, certainly not the physical healing I had hoped for, but something else. Before then there had been shock, disbelief, panic, resistance, tension, sorrow, and bitterness. These prevailing feelings in Rosemarie and in Pat now seemed to give way to a kind of stark and profoundly spiritual realization that since death was such a certain and imminent reality, it was a waste of precious time and energy to curse it. Far better to live the remaining precious moments of life to the full, with family and friends, in celebration and in love. This realization was not just the result of logic, nor of emotions beaten down to the point of exhaustion and unwilling acceptance.

It took place suddenly, spontaneously, during that Mass and reception. Death had been faced, and love was not crushed or broken. On the contrary, it had become more powerful.

But the thought of Pat's leaving created a vacuum in my soul. I could not understand why God was allowing him to die when Michael and Rosemarie needed him so much, when we all needed him. Uncontrollable feelings would rush through me, bringing with them a kind of sweet pain—sweet because Pat was alive, peaceful, and experiencing love; pain because he was dying, and there was nothing in faith, in prayer, in the Eucharist, in Christ that I could do to stop it.

I had always been taught that God's mercy and compassion were infinite and that Christ could heal at will, regardless of the measure of faith in those afflicted or petitioning. Why, then, was Pat dying? As often as I asked that question, the answer was a painful silence.

Though I believed in Jesus' resurrection and the promise that held for all Christians, I longed for certainty. If I could only be sure that Pat's death was leading to a happier life with God. But how could I be certain, when there was no proof that any Christian had risen from the dead? Yes, there were biblical accounts of prophets, apostles, and Jesus bringing dead people back to life, but to life on this earth. And even the Gospel accounts of the risen Jesus were brief narratives of his interactions with his disciples; they did not fully reveal "heaven" or what "oneness with God" in the next life really means. This fundamental uncertainty made me acutely aware of how utterly fleeting and fragile life is and how inadequate faith can become in the face of death. Saint Paul was able to see with conviction and enthusiasm beyond the veil of death. He was certain that neither life nor death could ever come between us and the love of God. I wanted to believe that, I longed to have Paul's certainty, but it was in me as a hope, not a conviction.

Witnessing the way Rosemarie loved Pat: caring for him, cooking for him, cleaning up his vomit, keeping him warm, supporting him when he needed to walk, letting their house become a constant stream of visitors, arranging for legal and medical appointments, hospice care, watching over him long after he dozed off, I came to realize that the threat of death can either crush you or make you intensely aware of how precious a gift love is.

Rosemarie already knew this and was living it. I knew it mostly in theory and only partially in act. The more I struggled through the emotions Pat's cancer stirred up in me, the clearer it became that death strips life down to the most radical of human choices: either to love or to hate, to accept or to reject, to trust or to fear. It is as though death is the final courtroom in which the human will judges itself, a judgment that will carry its life to the grave, or beyond. Pat's dying was forcing me to decide what choice I was taking to the grave, and his own example was inspiring me to choose love. I knew I was a priest and a Jesuit and that whatever love I offered should reflect that, but I also knew that the celibacy laws were dubious and that Jesuit "obedience," and indeed obedience throughout the Church, was becoming more constricting, and more difficult for me to accept.

On the other hand, who did I think I was? I realized also from my many confessions as a Jesuit that I had sinned, sinned against God, against faith, against love. I knew that others had been hurt by my failures. I was fallible and flawed. This awareness of my weaknesses made me all the more hesitant to challenge the Church. Even this quandary was resolved by the threat of Pat's death. Not that I became suddenly aware of the truth of things hitherto unknown. Rather, the love between Pat and Rosemarie and Michael made me aware that in the end, in the face of death, all that matters is love, whether for another human being or for God. Their relationship, and its beauty, was giving shape in my soul to a choice, a course of action, an interior principle: *Do what is right and most loving.*

I considered the principle for several days, prayed about it, and struggled with its radical consequences, because I knew that even in the highest echelons of the Church, with all its proclamation of truth and love, there was human pride, there was abuse of power, and there were sometimes erroneous teachings presented under the mantle of "divinely inspired tradition." To challenge these teachings, however erroneous they were, was to invite severe reprisals. Yet I could not escape the realization that the Church and the priesthood were suffering gravely because of these teachings. If I did not speak out about these injustices now, how would I feel facing God at the moment of my death? Pat and Rosemarie had already made their choice, to live the remainder of their lives from a place of love, not fear. I should do no less.

I asked God's grace to live my life doing what is right and most loving. As soon as I made this interior choice, it was as though a heavy weight of indecision and confusion had been lifted from my heart. It was not at all clear to me what this choice would mean in the future, nor down what path it would take me. What was clear was that blind obedience and mandatory celibacy would no longer be foundations for my actions; rather, with God's constant help and an abiding awareness of my personal sinfulness, I would try as much as possible to live doing what was right and most loving. Even as I felt a deep calm and strength emanating from this decision, which had taken all of my life to make, a cold chill swept through my body, causing me to shudder. Intuitively I knew that this choice was going to cost, and cost dearly.

Sometime later I picked up the phone, called Pamela, and invited her to campus.

We sat in my office at McKay Hall. I tried to tell her how grateful I was for her helping Pat—and me—that it was really comforting to be able to talk to someone who had "been there," who knew what it was to witness the dying of someone you loved. Through her I was coming to understand friendship to a depth I had never before experienced. I tried to explain to her Aquinas's three kinds of love: love of desire, love of friendship, love of benevolence. I was trying to tell her how much her friendship meant to me. Even though she listened very attentively, I knew my attempt was awkward and sounded too much like what a professor might say during a lecture on love. I tried again, saying there was a song I really wanted her to hear, a song sung by Placido Domingo and John Denver called "Perhaps Love."

As the song finished playing on the cassette, I looked across the room at her and said with a cheerful, happy voice, "I just have to tell you something. I love you, I really love you." She got up from the floor, sat down on the edge of the couch. Her eyes were radiant as she answered with a broad smile, "I love you too."

As we listened to the song twice more, I became aware of how much I was enjoying just sitting there with Pamela and listening to music. There was comfort in it, safety, mystery.

Suddenly I felt an emotional warmth permeate my whole body like an enveloping sweetness. Something deep inside of me was telling me to let the warmth be, not to check it, analyze it, or try to confine it to the bounds of guarded reason and emotion. It was like a warm, soothing wave enfolding me. I looked down at Pamela's left hand. Her fingers were long and graceful, her skin a soft white. Another voice, deep inside of me, was telling me not to touch her hand, not to pick it up.

But that voice was as powerless to stop me as I was to stop Pat's cancer.

The warmth led me to stretch out my hand and touch hers. I lifted her hand, held it, caressed it, placed it against my cheek, kissed it, placed it against my heart. It was strong yet gentle, cool yet warm, inviting yet hesitant.

"I know you probably want your hand back—but you can't have it. I don't want to let it go."

"You can have it—it's yours. It's yours!"

I looked into her eyes. There was wonder, excitement, laughter, tenderness, vulnerability. She was smiling through her tears. I placed her hand against my lips and my cheek, again and again. Hours passed that I did not know. Somewhere in the background the music played on, but I could no longer hear it. I heard only the warmth and her silent joy.

12

PAMELA

Shanghai Reds. A mysterious name. It calls to mind a back-water bar somewhere in a busy section of Hong Kong. In fact, it is a modern restaurant on the water in Marina del Rey with better-than-average food and lovely surroundings. The entrance welcomes you with a waterfall and tropical fish swimming beneath a tiny bridge; and if you are fortunate enough to have a table by the window, you can look out at boats moored in the harbor while you enjoy your meal. Thinking back to this important evening, I always refer to it as Shanghai Reds. It was the beginning of a confusion that would take two years to unravel. Whatever I had expected that night, what happened certainly wasn't it.

The slow ride down in the elevator from Ellen's apartment seemed interminable. My heart pounded wildly with anticipation, and I felt shy excitement. I wanted to scream at the top of my lungs with the sheer delight of knowing that this wonderful person was walking through the world at the same time I was. I was comforted simply by his mere presence on the planet. He was here. I had found him. And if it had to be, that would be enough. I was so grateful that God had let us meet, had let us love. In the last two days it seemed as though my feet hadn't touched the ground even once. The moments of tenderness shared with Terry in his dorm room played over and over in my heart. Nothing I had ever experienced in my life had been so powerful. He had held my hand, stroking it, kissing it again and again, with such adoration in his eyes. He had seen into my heart and soul, and, more incredibly, had allowed me to see into his. We hadn't felt the need to talk. The pure contentment of being close, looking deeply into each other's eyes, spoke more in the silence than the night has ears to hear. We loved each other . . . it was so simple, so pure, so tender. We never kissed. He just held my hand, as if drawing life from my fingertips. Never have I felt more loved, more acknowledged, more appreciated than I did in those five hours. But years of restraint and caution drew a line he would not cross. He was still a celibate priest—but he was also a man filled with longing and desire. It was the purest love I have ever known.

At last the elevator doors opened. As I bolted through the lobby, I could see Terry through the glass doors waiting for me by his car, his hands shoved deeply into his pockets. He laughed as I skipped off the curb, and we hugged. As I slid into the passenger seat, I noticed a gorgeous postcard of a Hawaiian sunset on the dashboard in front of me.

"That's for you," he said.

My heart thrilled as I turned it over.

Dear Pam,

This card reminds me of the kind of "presence" you have been in this last most important week—a presence that is at once calming, beautiful, understanding, radiant. Thank you for being alive, for blessing me with your friendship. I feel so incredibly fortunate to know you, to be your friend.

Love,
Terry.

So, he felt the same way I did! Yet there was a nervousness in the silence as we drove to the marina. Terry hardly spoke, and I began to feel apprehensive as we crossed the bridge into Shanghai Reds. The hostess seated us at a table overlooking the harbor.

"This is so lovely. You continually amaze me!" I laughed.

"I wanted someplace quiet where we could talk."

There was an unmistakably serious tone to his voice. I knew something was coming, but I wasn't sure what it would be. After we had ordered, he looked at me intently.

"Look, I meant what I said on that postcard—but I really want you to be careful. I really do love you, but there's a big difference between loving someone as a friend and falling in love. And there's just too much going on in my life right now, there are just too many obstacles for me to fall in love."

I could feel the color drain from my face. Suddenly I was freezing cold. My fingers went numb. I stared across the table. What was this man telling me? Had I been a fool two nights ago? Had I imagined those five hours? Had I somehow created this fantasy for myself out of my own desire? Surely not. What was happening?

"Pam, you could really get hurt. Priests aren't supposed to fall in love, and this could all be terribly painful for you. You are a wonderful friend in my life, and I don't want to lose that friendship. I just don't want to hurt you."

Terry continued to talk, to explain. I could hear his words, but they seemed to whiz right past me and circle somewhere above my head. I looked out at the boats, trying to put it all together. I had been so sure of my feelings—and of his. He had said he loved me. I fought to understand. Perhaps he'd had time to think it over and changed his mind. Perhaps he didn't think I had the fortitude to deal with such a complex situation. I tried to focus on the boats. Suddenly I was furious!

"Excuse me."

With an icy glance I got up and found my way to the ladies' room. I threw cold water on my face and paced back and forth for a few minutes. I just didn't understand any of this. Had I acted improperly and somehow embarrassed Terry the other night? Instead of the bliss of our previous meeting, I now sensed an unflattering criticism. Perhaps the intensity of my feelings had far surpassed Terry's, and his recognition of that fact was somehow demeaning to me.

There are few things more painful than realizing you love someone more than he loves you. Suddenly the word *friendship* had an empty, hollow sound. But whatever was going on, I was determined to maintain my self-respect.

When I returned to the table, our supper was waiting. I ate silently and looked out the window, avoiding Terry's eyes. He was obviously very worried about my feelings, but I wasn't about to beg for his love. When occasionally I did look at him, I could see his distress. His face was pale, and he looked as if he were going to cry. Terry told me later that as he looked across the table at me, he became acutely aware that he was in danger of losing something very precious to him. He knew he had to make a decision, and that with it would come a great deal of pain for both of us, no matter the outcome.

By the time Terry walked me to Ellen's front door, I was beginning to feel a little better. Our conversation took a lighter tone as we rode up in the elevator.

"Would you like to come in for a few minutes?"

"Sure."

As we sat on the couch and talked, we couldn't help but let down our defenses once again. When we were together, it seemed impossible to pretend or ignore the closeness we felt. Eventually we were laughing.

"You look as though you'd like to hit me and hug me all at the same time," he said tentatively.

"You're right," I admitted, "but I guess I'll settle for a hug."

Ever so shyly Terry's arms went around my shoulders. As he hugged me, he began to kiss my cheeks in the same sweet way he had kissed my hand two nights before. There was gentleness and respect and gratitude in his kiss . . . and there was relief in the tender hug he gave me before he left. He told me months later that he had made his first crucial decision that night. He knew in his heart he did not want to lose me.

The next afternoon at around six o'clock the phone rang.

"Would it be all right if I come by in a little while? I could bring over a pizza and we could just talk. Would that be okay with you?"

Terry's voice was trembling.

"Yes, of course it is. I'm just here cleaning up. Tomorrow I'm moving to another apartment in Beverly Hills for one more week of house-sitting. Then I get to move back into my own apartment! The tenant who sublet it is leaving unexpectedly. Good timing, huh? I can't believe I've been living out of a suitcase since December! If you don't mind a little mess, come on over."

When I opened the door, I could see the strain on Terry's face. He looked pale, and his cheeks were hollow. There were dark circles under his gentle eyes, and his manner was soft and quiet.

I felt hesitant, still confused by the mixed signals from the night before. But I could sense that Terry's mind was far, far away.

"I went to visit Pat and Rosemarie today."

He got up and moved slowly to the couch.

"It was their wedding anniversary, and they wanted to renew their vows. They asked to go to Confession first. That's the first time Pat has ever confessed to me. For the vows they asked their son to be their 'best man.' It was so beautiful. I just can't . . . I can't help him. I'm a priest and I can't help him. What good does it do? My brother's going to die, and I can't save him!"

At last the sobs came. The mask that protected Terry from the outside world—the priestly mask worn to shield others from pain, to comfort and support them yet never to receive their comfort— was shattered by his anguished sobs. For a minute or so he would stop crying, and then it would begin again.

Terry's sobs were coming from a place so deep in his soul that they frightened me. I felt lost. I felt as powerless to help him as he did to save Pat. I knew there must be more, much more locked within his heart that he could not share with me. I could do nothing but hold him and stroke his head and hand him tissue after tissue. At last, exhausted, he lay on the couch in silence while I sat on the floor beside him holding his hand. I wondered how he could survive without anyone to share his burdens. Would the mask return as he faced the world, his smile hiding his rage and fear? And what could I do? *Oh, God, let me take away his pain!* All I could say was, "I know, I'm here, I understand."

He lay quietly for some time, and when his strength returned, he walked slowly to the door.

"Thank you," he murmured. "Thank you."

———

My mother looked so pretty in her navy-blue suit as she added one final pump of hairspray to her sunny red hair. I looked up at her from my cross-legged position on the floor of my brother's house, where my parents were visiting for a few days. I had been looking forward to some time alone with my mom. There were so many things I wanted to share with her, so many conflicting emotions that needed an attentive ear. How thrilled she would be to know that I had found what I had been looking for, that my heart was bursting with so much joy that I could barely contain myself. I longed to tell her that I had met a handsome, loving, compassionate man. I had found my soul mate at last! I wanted to shout that the world was a wonderful, wonderful place to be.

But how could I? My soul mate was a priest. I needed to hear what she would say to that. I needed to ask her if I was being selfish or if I was offending God. Was I committing a terrible sin, one that would blacken not only my name, but my soul? Should I walk away or follow my heart's lead? Discussing Terry at all filled me with apprehension. I had no desire to compromise him or to hurt my mother. I began haltingly to talk about my "new friend," this priest who was helping me . . . the priest whose brother had cancer and to whom Bill had offered advice . . . the priest who had talked to me about God. My mother leaned against the doorjamb, looked at me seriously, and exclaimed, "Pam, he's probably going to try to convert you! It's nice that you're friends, but that's what Catholic priests are supposed to do, convert people! You know what they say: If you're not baptized a Catholic, your soul won't go to heaven. For some reason they want everybody in the world to believe exactly as they do, and if you don't, they think you're somehow not connected to God."

My mother was totally distressed!

"Honey, you know how much your religion has always meant to you. I love my Christian Science, and so do you. I may not go to church every Sunday now, but I did most of my life. And my faith is very strong. Everyday I say my little prayer:

" 'Fear thou not, for I am with thee. Be not dismayed, for I am thy God. I will strengthen thee, yea, I will help thee. Yea,

I will uphold thee with the right hand of my righteousness. For I, the Lord thy God, will hold thy right hand, saying unto thee, fear thou not, for I am with thee.'

"I feel surrounded by God's love everyday of my life.

" 'For I am persuaded that neither death nor life nor angels nor principalities nor things present nor things to come nor height nor depth nor any other creature shall be able to separate me from the love of God which is in Christ Jesus, our Lord.' "

My mother's eyes were filled with the peace and serenity of those words.

"I believe all those things, too, Mom. But Terry's not trying to convert me. He's really not like that. He's so nice, and he listens to me, Mom. We talk about religion and Christian Science all the time. He's even read *Science and Health* cover to cover." *Science and Health With Key to the Scriptures* by Mary Baker Eddy is the textbook which accompanies the Bible in Christian Science. What had tentatively begun as a conversation about love had turned to religion. Now was not the time to go further.

"Terry asks me all about what I believe and who God is to me. He asks me so many questions. It seems he's really searching to understand who I am. Besides, he's going through a terrible experience watching his brother die."

"Oh, honey, I'm so sorry to hear that." My mother's eyes grew sad. "He must be in a great deal of pain. We certainly know what that's like. Maybe you can help him."

"You'd really like him, Mom."

"Just be careful, honey," she said.

I walked happily beneath lavender jacaranda trees through the quiet courtyard filled with brightly colored spring flowers. As the key turned in the lock, I breathed a sigh of relief. I stood in the center of my own living room, listening to the creak of the hardwood floors and feeling the warmth of the old friends I'd collected over the years. I said hello to my old English wall clock and my antique hanging mirrors, to my Morris chair and my Handel lamp. People always said that walking into my Beverly Hills apartment was like taking a step back in time. I've never cared for anything modern, and my home has always been a reflection of my love for the old-fashioned. As one looked through the sheer lace curtains and an abundance of weeping jacaranda branches, the sidewalk was visible to the front, and to the side, the peaceful courtyard. After months of living out of a suitcase, I was home at last.

I unpacked in a hurry and then settled on the couch with a cup of tea, and Devon, who was ecstatic to curl up beside her mama and rest her head in my lap. Feeling guilty for all the months I had been without her, I kissed her nose. With the licks she gave me in return, I knew she had forgiven me. On the coffee table in front of me I spread out a new script, *I Had Three Wives.* I had already auditioned for the producers twice, and now I was going back in for another "dreaded" network reading. Though I had made it down to the last few girls for *Family Honor* a few weeks ago, I'd lost out. But here I was again. I took a soothing sip of tea and plunged in. Though I already knew the lines backward and forward, I decided to start from scratch, looking for some new colors to add to my character. I was tired. Basically I'd had a rough week. Between my auditions for the new series, I was also filming an episodic TV show, and we were in the middle of night shooting. Last night I hadn't finished until three A.M. We'd been out in the valley shooting outdoors, and I was wearing a sleeveless silk dress. It was freezing, and between takes the crew would warm me with blankets and a portable heater. All the guys were wearing heavy jackets. When it came time to do a scene, off would come the blankets. I found it practically impossible to keep my teeth from chattering during my close-ups. I prayed I wouldn't get a cold.

The alarm rang early the next morning. The readings were to take place at twelve noon at CBS, and I wanted to allow plenty of time to get ready. I always like to get to an audition at least half an hour before my actual call so that I can spend some time calming down from the frenzy of traffic and think about my character. And today was going to be much worse than usual. A decision would be made today.

When I walked into the waiting room, I was happy to see my old pal Lee Purcell. She's a terrific actress, and I felt myself to be in good company. But then the nerves began. We all sat quietly looking at one another, thinking, *Why didn't I wear something like that?* or *She's got on more makeup, maybe I need some eye shadow!* It's really tough not to second-guess. One by one we were ushered into the audition hall to read with the star, Victor Garber, for the network heads and the director, Bill Bixby. During the reading itself I felt fairly relaxed, and walking back to my car after it was all over, I was pleased. The rest of the day would be spent in waiting.

It didn't take long for the phone to ring. My agent's voice held a happy tone.

"Well, I've got good news and bad news. You didn't get the series regular role—they went with a brunette who was more 'mother-looking,' they said. However, they want you to play the guest starring lead for the pilot episode starting Thursday. Your wardrobe fitting is tomorrow."

I wasn't sure exactly how to feel. At least I would be working. But always a bridesmaid and never a bride! How many times I had been cast in guest roles in pilots, just missing out on the series regular role. *How shall I feel?* I took a deep breath. *Good. I guess I'll feel good.*

That night as I tucked my pillow under my chin, I considered my situation. I knew that the pit in my stomach would have to be reckoned with. I could not continue to support two apartments— and New York was awaiting my return. The Christmas tree would still be up, certainly dead by now. Closing my eyes, I could visualize pine needles lying all over the floor and my lonely panda on the mantle. I was behaving irresponsibly by remaining in Los Angeles, and I realized that I had to make a decision very soon. Friends were beginning to question me. I knew in my heart that I had a reason for staying in Los Angeles, but not one that could be shared. How could I say, "I've met a priest. His brother is dying of cancer, and he needs me. I don't want to leave him." How could

I ask others to understand what I could barely fathom myself? For now it was best to let them think what they wanted. But a decision had to be made, and soon.

The urgency of these thoughts was uppermost in my mind as I sat across the table from Terry at a tiny Italian restaurant. Christmas decorations covered the walls and ornaments hung from the ceiling. Apparently this is the decor all year-round.

"But you're working here. You've had three jobs already. Aren't you pleased?"

"Of course I am. But that's not the point. Terry, I can't afford two apartments, and if I don't go back, I'm just going to be in the same position professionally I was in before I left."

"Look, if you go back," he said quietly, "we won't be able to see each other very often. I don't want that to happen. You've come into my life like a ray of sunshine, and I don't want to lose you. If you go back, I'll miss you."

I looked at his face, knowing all too well exactly what he felt. Softly I replied, "Terry, I don't even know if it's appropriate for me to be in your life."

He reached over and took my hand in his.

"Pam, a friend is an incredible treasure. I know that whether you are in New York or L.A., we will still be close. If you need to go back to New York, then you should go. But I just want you to know something. I'm going through a difficult time—a very dark time, especially with Pat. It's as if your spirit is the one happy light in all of this. It's like the prism in your window that scatters rainbows all over the wall. I need you."

Terry held my hands very tight. I couldn't read the look in his eyes.

"I've never said this to anyone before, but I'd like to explore our relationship. I'd like to see if there's any possibility of a future for us together. If you go back, we'll never know."

As I heard his words, I knew in my heart that a future together was exactly what I believed we should have and would have. But my sense of logic wondered how in the world this would ever come to pass. A thousand reasons to turn and run back to New York were obliterated by this one simple, impossible dream. But now there were two of us dreaming the same dream together. And I knew that for this man I would give up everything.

"Okay," I said. "Let's see what happens."

13

TERRY

A United Airlines attendant smiled, checked my boarding pass, and sent me down to a window seat in the nonsmoking coach section. I was relieved to be headed home and looked forward to the return flight to L.A. The flight would give me time to read, to pray, to reflect on the many images and feelings demanding my attention.

This New York trip had been productive, yet disturbing. I had met with Franco Zeffirelli, Anne Grant, and an investor, to discuss initial plans for Zeffirelli's directing *Hamlet* for select theaters on both coasts. Anne's father, Philip Scharper, had recently suffered a stroke, and when we visited him in the hospital, the doctors indicated that the brain damage had been far too extensive to warrant any hope of recovery. Her father, a warm, brilliant man, was editor of Orbis Books and had been the person most responsible for introducing the writings of progressive Latin American theologians to U.S. readership.

At the hospital Bede Scharper had pleaded with the doctor to recognize that his father was indeed "responding" to Bede's repeated questions: "If you can hear me, Dad, just squeeze my hand. Just squeeze my hand. Dad, it's Bede, this is really important now. If you can hear me, squeeze my hand. . . . There, it moved! Did you see that, Doctor? He can hear me, I know it!"

The doctor gently but firmly disagreed. Pat's illness made me all too aware of what Bede was feeling—helplessness, resistance, desperation, grief. Now, in the quiet time before takeoff, I whispered a silent prayer for Philip, his wife, Sally, for Anne and Bede.

I opened up my carry-on bag, took out Laeuchli's book, *Power and Sexuality: The Emergence of Canon Law at the Synod of Elvira,* and Daniel Callam's article, "Clerical Continence in the Fourth Century: Three Papal Decretals." As the plane taxied toward the runway, I sensed this was the last time I would see Philip Scharper alive. *Life—how fleeting and fragile,* I thought. *"Man's days are like grass, he flowers like the flowers of the field; the wind blows and he is gone, and his place never sees him again."* Sobrie estote et vigilate—*Be sober and vigilant. "Death comes like a thief in the night. You do not know the day or the hour." How many more hours does Philip have? Pat?*

I had seen Pat just before my trip to New York. Pamela, Rosemarie, and I were sitting on their bed, looking at Pat's and Rosemarie's wedding pictures. Pat was now so weak that he rarely left his bed. His face was hollow, bone-thin. His skin was pale, his eye sockets dark. He had been lying perfectly still with his eyes closed as the rest of us had chatted and laughed about the wedding pictures. We couldn't tell lately whether or not he was sleeping. He would have long periods where his mind just seemed to drift off to another place, oblivious of everything around him. As I sat on the bed next to him that day, I felt as if death were hovering over his body, watching him, just waiting for the moment to claim him. Suddenly and unexpectedly Pat's voice had interrupted our conversation:

"Honey and Pam, can I talk to Terry alone for a minute?" We were all startled to hear him speak. Rosemarie and Pam left the room.

"Terry, there's something that I've felt bad about from the time we were little kids. It's bothered me my whole life. I think I should get it off my chest. Remember that time in Griffith Park when we were coming out of the swimming pool and those four gang members started chasing us?"

"Yes, I remember."

"Well, I ran faster than you and got away. Two of them started beating you up. Well, you never knew this, but I was hiding in the bushes. I saw them beating you up, but I thought they would be a lot less hostile if there was just one of us. I figured they would beat you up a little and let you go. If they started hurting you real bad, I was ready to jump in."

There were tears coming down his cheeks. "I'm really sorry, Terry. I could hear you crying from my hiding place. I've felt bad about that ever since. Will you forgive me?"

"Yes," I said. "Forget it. They didn't hurt me that much anyway."

"I love you, Brother," he said.

"I love you too."

Rosemarie walked in from the kitchen, set the glass filled with wine on the coffee table in front of me. Therese had left her home in Austin, Texas, and had moved in with Rosemarie to help with the shopping, cooking, cleaning, and the steady stream of visitors who had been coming to see Pat. Even so, Rosemarie's face was furrowed and pale, her eyes tense and darkened from lack of sleep.

"Thank you," I said.

"You're welcome. Is Racha bothering you there?" she asked.

"No, she's fine."

"She doesn't want to leave Pat's side." She turned and walked away.

I opened the Missalette to the readings, then looked at everyone. Thirteen of us had gathered at Pat's house for Holy Thursday Mass. Pat was stretched out on the couch, a blanket over him, a pillow under his head. Michael was seated on the floor close to him. I was on the couch, too, at Pat's feet. Across the room Mom looked over at us and smiled tenderly. Pamela glanced shyly around the room.

I was aware that only a few miles away my Jesuit confreres at Loyola Marymount University were putting on their vestments in preparation for the Holy Thursday liturgy—full choir, beautiful music, foot washing, formal candlelight procession of the Blessed

Sacrament from Sacred Heart chapel across campus to Huesman Chapel. Being in Pat's crowded living room, seeing the bread and wine in front of us, realizing that we were here because Pat's body was being broken—all these things reminded me of that Last Supper two thousand years ago when Jesus said to his friends, "How I have longed to eat this Passover meal with you before I suffer." I felt that the heart of all religion is not found in ritual or in rule, but in people bonding together in the face of life, death, despair, hope. Then, when pushed to the limits of human agony and ecstasy, one is either most open or resistant to the divine.

It struck me that the Crucifixion is far more than a past event, suffered by the Son of Man. Everyone born of Eve can be a sign of the Passover Mystery, that suffering and death can lead to the resurrection if only the choice is made: "Not my will, but thine be done. . . . Into your hands I commend my spirit."

During the homily and the Prayers of the Faithful, various family members shared their feelings, their truth about Pat's cancer, their struggles of faith in light of his pending death, their admiration of his courage. In that sharing, because the words were spoken from the heart, a peacefulness came over the room, a sense of family bound together by pain and by love. During the Kiss of Peace everyone embraced Pat and each other.

After Communion Rosemarie squeezed in on the couch next to her husband and son. They were smiling, with tears in their eyes.

Father Ray Bluett, pastor emeritus of Saint Francis of Assisi parish in La Quinta, had asked if I would help him with his Easter Sunday Mass. He had a heart condition and was expecting an overflow crowd.

I told him I'd be happy to, but that I had already promised to spend part of that day with Pamela Shoop. He hadn't met her before, although he'd heard me mention her name several times previously.

"Bring her down. Come down Saturday night. If she doesn't mind roughing it, she can stay in one of the two guest rooms. I'll be out for dinner. I'll leave a key under the mat."

The drive to La Quinta from Los Angeles was a little over three hours. All the way down, except when I was shifting, I held her hand.

She smiled, "Penny. . . ."

"Penny?" I asked.

"For your thoughts."

"I was just thinking of the word *companion*."

Her eyes lit up brightly. "It's a beautiful word."

"I'm glad you're coming down here with me," I said.

"So am I," she answered.

We got to Ray's house, left our things there, and went to the Sand Bar restaurant about a mile away. During dinner Pamela excused herself to go to the ladies' room. She returned with a huge smile on her face.

"Well, you see, I really had to go, but the ladies' room was filled, so I had a guy check to see if I could borrow the men's room for a sec. On the way out who comes walking in but Andy Williams! I could have died! He was just a little surprised to see me!"

She had a funny way of saying and doing things sometimes. I found myself laughing a lot when I was with her.

After dinner I asked her if she'd like to go for a walk.

"I'd love to," she answered.

The streets around Ray's house are at the base of the La Quinta hills. The night temperature was pleasantly warm. The moon was full. Stars crowded brilliantly into the sky.

"Pamela, I know I've asked you to stay in L.A. to see if there might be a future for us. But I want you to be aware of the risks. I love being a Jesuit priest, but not if that means being obedient to superiors even when they're wrong. Eight years before I met you, I started doing research on the priesthood. What I'm learning is convincing me that there are serious disorders threatening the Church. Before I can make any decision about us, I have to complete this work."

"How long will that take?" she asked.

"I don't know. If the conclusions warrant it, I might have to write a book about it."

"Are you talking another eight years?"

"No. I'm working as hard as I can on it. Probably another year or so. The research I am doing is highly sensitive and most likely will get me in trouble."

"Why?" she asked.

"Because it has to do with the very nature of authority, and the priesthood. I'm researching the historical origins of the laws that forbid priests to marry. I'm learning things, shameful things, that were never told us in the seminary. How Church laws violated God's law in breaking up marriages. How married priests and their wives were abused, scorned, imprisoned—"

"You're kidding!" she said incredulously.

"I wish I were."

"But why? I didn't even know there were married Catholic priests."

"Yes, for over a thousand years. Most of the parish clergy were married, more than forty popes, and most of the apostles, including Peter, the first pope."

"Are you saying that Jesus didn't ask his apostles to be celibate?"

"That's correct. He didn't. He could have selected all of them from the Essene community, which vowed celibacy. But he didn't. In fact, contrary to the impression conveyed by Church teaching, there is no scriptural evidence whatsoever that suggests Jesus ever made a vow of celibacy. People assume that if Jesus had a wife, she would have been mentioned in Scripture. But even if Jesus had no wife, this would not prove that he had *vowed* never to marry. Many people would like to marry but haven't done so because they haven't found the right mate, or perhaps because they're too busy caring for a widowed parent."

"Well, if Jesus didn't expect his disciples to be celibate, where did the practice come from?"

"Some say it began with the apostle Paul, who strongly advocated 'in these times of stress' and because 'the world as we know it is passing away' for a married man to stay married and for a celibate man to remain celibate. Saint Paul also felt that an unmarried man was more free to devote himself to prayer. But according to I Corinthians 9:5, Paul was married. And Paul himself stated that those who taught that marriage was forbidden were uttering the doctrine of demons."

She looked at me intently. "So, what caused the change?"

"The first mandatory celibacy laws date from the fourth century. Any priest who had sex with his wife or who fathered children would be dismissed from the clerical state."

"Why would anyone dream up such a law?"

"Several reasons, not all of them good. Some popes and some very prominent Catholic theologians had assimilated from pagan philosophies the concept that sexual intercourse, even in marriage, was impure. They argued that because a priest touches the 'pure' body of Christ in the Eucharist, he must therefore refrain from the 'impurity' of marital intercourse.

"Further, under Constantine the Church evolved from being a persecuted church to being the officially recognized religion of the empire. With that recognition came endowments, land, wealth. Various leaders in the Church did not want this wealth to pass from priest-father to son. These factors were accentuated by the moral collapse of the Roman empire and by a reactionary asceticism that glorified virginity while denigrating all human passions."

"Well, why would the married priests accept such ridiculous laws?" she asked.

"They didn't. For seven hundred years they resisted, but the papacy became too strong. And with the help of the princes and European monarchs, celibacy was finally able to be imposed during the Second Lateran Council in 1139. At that point all current or future marriages of priests were ruled invalid, and no man could become a priest unless he first promised not to marry."

"Incredible!" she exclaimed.

"Yes, it is. The Church has always taught that marriage is indissoluble, yet, for over a thousand years the Church has enforced laws that divorce and nullify the marriages of priests. For twenty-three years the Church has been telling me what a great virtue celibacy is; now I'm learning that the laws requiring priestly celibacy were based on a misinterpretation of Scripture, a distorted notion of human sexuality, and a brutal disregard for priests and their wives."

"Your seminary didn't teach you anything about where the celibacy laws came from?" Pamela asked.

"No," I replied.

"Well, how did they expect you to make a vow, not knowing what it was all about?"

"I imagine that our seminary professors didn't know the origins of the celibacy laws, so they focused not on the canonical history of celibacy, but on its virtue and on those saints in history who best exemplified it. No professor even hinted that the celibacy discipline might be wrong."

"So, what are you going to do?" she queried.

"I don't know. The Catholic Church has nine hundred million members and a two-thousand-year history. Change doesn't come easily."

We walked for several minutes in silence, each of us thinking about what had been said, trying somehow to see into the future.

After the Easter Sunday Mass Pamela and I drove back to L.A., to Forest Lawn Cemetery so that we could visit her dad's grave. Pamela asked me to stop at a flower shop a block down from the cemetery entrance. As she wandered through the shop looking for a bouquet, I thought, *This is a woman who knows what it is to watch helplessly as death ravages your family. This is a woman who knows agony and who does not run from it. This is the woman who held you in her arms when you finally broke down and sobbed like a child. She's strong, she's comforting, she's beautiful. She makes you laugh and just happy to be alive. You want to know everything there is to know about her—feel her heart, her spirit, her body. Are you in love with her, Terry? You're a priest—first, last, always. You're not free to fall in love. You're supposed to love others and bring them closer to God, not closer to you. Detached, spiritual love—not mutual, interpersonal love. The Church is your spouse. All you could offer Pamela is a divided heart. You've told her that, but you also asked her not to go back to New York.*

We drove through the gates of Forest Lawn up the long hill to the Court of Freedom.

———

"Thank you for doing this," she said.

I pulled the car over to the curb. We got out and started walking past the rows of headstones.

"Here he is," she said, pointing to his gravestone. "Oh look, there are already flowers on his grave." Pamela looked pensive. "It's amazing," she said. "So many times over the years I've come out here and found flowers. I ask my family, but no one ever seems to know who's left them."

Just then a gentleman approached us. "Excuse me, but are you General Shoop's daughter?" he asked.

"Yes, I am," Pamela replied. "Did you leave the flowers?"

"I did, yes. My name is Milton Wallen, and my father was a friend of your father's. I knew your father at Hughes many years ago, and I served under him in the Air National Guard out at Van Nuys. I was just a kid then, but I'll never forget his kindness to me. One afternoon, he asked me if I'd like to go flying with him. I couldn't believe it! He took me up in the A-26 as his copilot. It was just the two of us, and we flew for about three hours together. What I didn't realize at the time was that your dad had found out that my military orders had come through and that my guard unit would be the first ever to be called to active duty. Of course he couldn't tell me that at the time, but when I got my orders the next day, I realized what had prompted him to take me flying. Your father was a very kind man." Milt's eyes filled with tears. "It was a pleasure to meet you."

"And you." After they had exchanged numbers and the gentleman had departed, Pamela sat slowly down on the ground near her father's headstone. We were both silent for a few minutes before she spoke again.

"One of my father's best friends is a man by the name of John Myers. At a dinner party recently, John told me about an incident that happened out at Muroc Flight Test Center before it became Edwards Air Force Base. My dad was in charge of Flight Test out there, where Johnny was also a pilot.

"They flew a lot of experimental types of aircraft. This one day, Johnny was testing the XP-56, a tailless plane made by Northrop that they called the Silver Bullet. The plane was made of magnesium, which is highly flammable, and it was carrying 130 octane gasoline. They didn't have ejection seats in those days; instead they had a ring of dynamite around the propellers so that, if the pilot had to, he could blow the props and get out quick. Well, on this particular day, even though everything they did at Muroc was secret, there were about a hundred people watching John make the test flight. When he came in for a landing, his landing gear failed. The plane was careening down the runway at about one-hundred-fifty miles an hour when the engine started to come apart. The plane went end-over-end two and a half times, shedding parts. In those days they didn't have crash helmets and he was wearing what he always called his 'polo helmet,' which didn't provide much protection. Well, after the crash, everyone was terrified that the plane was going to explode because of all the dynamite and everything. As Johnny tells it, he looked up and saw ninety-nine of the one-hundred people running in one direction away from the plane, and one man running toward him. His legs were broken, his teeth were all gone, his tongue was split and his lips were bleeding . . . and he was really frightened. He says he didn't know whether he was going to live or die. When my dad reached him, he looked up and asked, 'Shoopy, . . . how do I look?' My dad looked at him quickly as he was pulling him from the wreckage and replied with a grin, 'No worse than usual!' . . . In that moment, John says, he knew he was going to be okay."

Pamela sighed. "He touched so many people's lives. Seventeen years later, and people are still laying flowers on his grave. I wonder how many others there are who come here, people I'll never see."

She handed me the flowers, then reached down and pulled out from the grass the metal cylinder that served as a vase. "I'll put some more water in it. . . ." She walked to a water spigot some twenty yards away.

I bent down and touched my hand to the stone slab. It was warmed by the Easter sun. The inscription read:

SHOOP

MAJOR GENERAL CLARENCE A.

1907–1968

HE GIVETH WINGS

I wondered: *How do you carve a whole life, a person, into a slab of stone?*
I wished we could have met.

Pamela placed the metal vase into the ground. Some water spilled out onto the surrounding grass. She looked over to me as I handed her the gladiolas. As she arranged them neatly in the container along with the others, she asked, "What were you thinking?"

"Thoughts," I answered.

"What thoughts?" she asked.

"Ask your father."

She looked at me curiously for a long moment, then extended her hand to mine, "Would you say a prayer for my daddy?"

As I prayed, she rested her head against my shoulder. Tears drifted down the center of her cheek and over her lips. Afterward, we just sat silently for several minutes. She reached over to the gravestone, ran her hand gently across her father's name.

Pamela's heart ached to embrace her father again. As she stroked her hand over the silent headstone, I could feel the chasm separating them and the emptiness it left in her heart. During that moment I felt words forming inside me—words I wanted her father to hear: *Don't worry, I will take care of her. I will protect her.*

14

PAMELA

I kicked off my tennis shoes, crossed my legs in the passenger seat, leaned back, and closed my eyes. The cassette boomed out Camarata's "Let the Trumpets Be Triumphant, For They Are the Voice of God!" and I was ecstatic. My mountains were calling me, and I couldn't wait to get there. Terry and I were on our way to Idyllwild, a small village nestled six thousand feet in the mountains above Palm Springs. Every year I would go up there with Devon for a weekend, just to pray and get back to nature. But today was different. Today Terry was driving up with me, and my heart was dancing. I'd hardly believed it when he'd accepted my invitation! I smiled to myself, remembering his words.

"Well, it sounds terrific. I could really use some peace and quiet right now, and this sounds just great. But, you know, I'm a little confused. Where would we . . . I mean, I'd love to go with you, but I'm not ready to . . . well, where would we sleep?" His face had turned Irishman red.

I didn't want him to be uncomfortable. So, spending much more money than I should have, I reserved a three-bedroom cabin with lots of room, a huge kitchen, and a living room where I thought we both would have enough privacy. I hoped everything would be okay.

"Here it is—Hargrave Road. Make a right at the next exit."

Even Devon sitting in the backseat was excited.

"This is spectacular!" Terry exclaimed.

"I'd hoped you would like it."

Our little car wound up and through the trees past a small lake till suddenly we came upon the tiny village.

"Oh, look," I pointed, "Jan's Red Kettle! It's the breakfast hangout. Great pancakes! Pull over here."

The sign read, "Idyllwild Inn."

"Is this it?" Terry asked.

"Nope. This is just where we pick up the key. I'll go in." I signed the register and hopped back in the car.

"Okay, now just hang a left and turn another left between those two trees." We entered a small circle of log cabins set among the pines—very private, yet cozy. We continued to the farthest cabin in the back.

"This is it."

"You're kidding!" Terry exclaimed. "This isn't a cabin, it's a house!" He started to laugh, and I took him on a tour.

"Do you think you'll be comfortable here? Enough privacy?"

"Of course! I'd pictured a little cabin. This is just fine."

"Great! Here, why don't you put your things in this bedroom and I'll take the one down the hall."

"Okay."

We unpacked the car and headed to the village market for "supplies." We stocked up on potato chips and ice cream, marshmallows and wine—and of course some real food, which was incidental to me.

"How about spaghetti? I think I can manage that."

"Okay, but tonight let's go out."

After stocking the fridge, we decided there was still enough light left to take Devon for a walk. The air was magical, with the scent of pine needles filling our nostrils. We walked hand in hand, as Devon romped up the road.

"She just loves this place. Wait till you see her tomorrow on the hiking path! I'll show you Hummer Park and Tahquitz Mountain."

"You know, I was here once before with a good friend, Jim

Brown. Back in 1972 we drove across country together, updating his dissertation on the U.S. Catholic Church and broadcasting. He lived at Loyola until the late seventies, then left the Jesuits. We came up here because he was giving a talk at a conference center nearby, but I'd forgotten how peaceful and beautiful it is."

"It's healing. It always gives me strength. It's as if I need this place. I come here every year, and when I go back to L.A., I can cope with things better."

Terry smiled. "I can understand that."

We showered and changed for dinner and, leaving Devon to her own devices in the cabin, walked through the forest to the closest restaurant, the Gastronome, a few minutes away. We were seated at a table in front of the enormous roaring hearth. It was cozy and warm, and I could tell that Terry felt a sense of relief being away from the pain of Pat's illness and the confusing decisions facing him. We talked and laughed. From time to time, however, I found myself looking uncomfortably around the room. I wondered if anyone I knew might be here. Occasionally I caught Terry looking too.

"It's strange, isn't it?"

"What is?" I asked.

"Well, I shouldn't be sitting here with you. Here I am, forty years old, and I feel like a kid playing hooky from school, afraid of being caught."

"Yeah, me too." I knew what he meant.

"You know, a priest isn't even supposed to ride in a car alone with a woman. *Non solus cum sola:* not a man alone with a woman alone. In the seminary we were taught never to walk into town alone or go to the dentist alone or travel alone. The idea was that if we had a Jesuit companion with us, it would help us avoid temptation. You'd think they'd trust a priest to follow his conscience no matter where he is or who he's with."

"Maybe they're afraid because they know they're asking priests to do something unnatural. Why else would they lay down so many laws and restrictions?"

"We were constantly reminded never to form emotional attachments to women or to men. They called them 'particular friendships.' We were forbidden to think, feel, or do anything that could lead to physical or emotional intimacy or encourage falling in love. Even the counseling-room doors had windows in them to remind us that we should never have total privacy with a woman. The only exception is the confessional."

Obviously, being here with me in this remote village would have been completely unacceptable.

"The greatest Christian commandment is to love one another. As priests we were taught to love others for themselves, but never for anything that love might mean for us. Our role is to help others find God in whatever way possible."

"That's a very beautiful and selfless love, Terry."

"It is. And when we were going through seminary training, it all seemed to make sense." Terry sighed. "But when you get out into the real world of helping people, it's a very different story. So much of the time priests deal with people during huge crises in their lives. We're there to help and to give unconditional love and support during their most emotional and vulnerable periods. We're not asking for anything in return, we're just there to help. But then it's only natural that people respond to that kindness. Some respond with gratitude, others become emotionally dependent. Detached love can be extremely attractive to some people. Many times priests find themselves in the position of having a counselee fall in love with them, and it can be a really huge problem. On the one hand, you're trying to love this person and help, but when that person turns around and responds to that love, you have to shut down. It's extremely difficult because priests don't usually have the social or psychological skills gained through intimacy experience to deal with it."

"It sounds a lot like what therapists go through with transference."

"Yes," Terry said, "it's very much the same principle. There's a big difference, however. It's true that therapists are not supposed to have intimate relationships with their patients, but they are not forbidden to fall in love with someone else."

I thought about this dilemma for a few minutes. "How do priests deal with all of this, then?" I wondered.

"It's easier for some than for others. If a priest is really comfortable with celibacy in his heart and is also a loving person, he can do a lot of good for the Church. But if he has repressed his sexuality because that's the only way he could become a priest, then that can be extremely destructive. Repressed sexuality can cause real problems."

"Like what?"

Terry looked down at the table in silence for a little while. Finally he spoke sadly.

"Some escape into the bottle; some have multiple affairs with women, some with men; some molest altar boys; some just shut down emotionally and die inside long before they're buried."

. We were on very difficult ground. This discussion was a painful one, both for Terry to say and for me to hear. I sat back in my chair.

"I can imagine what they'd say if they knew we were here alone together. How do you feel?"

Terry's eyes glistened in the candlelight.

"Since I was seventeen years old, I've been taught that it would be wrong to fall in love. I've been taught that I could not serve God as a Catholic priest if I fell in love. But now, after all I've read, I'm not sure it's wrong at all, Pam. Church law says it's wrong, but I'm not so sure God does."

We walked back to the cabin in silence.

"How about a fire?" Terry suggested.

"Great," I said, "I'll pour some wine."

I parked myself on the floor in front of the fireplace, while Terry sat on the couch across the room. As we chatted, I looked at his face in the firelight. I loved this man. When at last it was time for bed, we said good night and went to our separate rooms. I lay awake for some time longing to be in his arms.

The next morning we awoke early, donning our jeans and hiking boots. After a light breakfast we headed up to the state park at the base of Tahquitz Mountain. The path wasn't crowded at all as we began our trek up into the wilderness. Devon charged out in front of us, disappearing into the distance. Eventually she would come racing back as if to say, "Hurry up, you guys, what's taking you so long?"

The views were spectacular, and often we would stop to take

pictures of each other and the mountainscape. Up and up we went, following switchbacks until, at last, the sheer face of Tahquitz Peak came into sight. Two mountain climbers could be seen perched precariously on the sheer, jagged rock.

"Isn't it amazing how they do that?" I panted.

"It sure is. Listen, Pam, do you mind if we walk in silence for a little while? I'd like to pray, if you don't mind."

This was fine with me. I was beginning to find it difficult to hike and talk and breathe all at the same time! I let Terry get up ahead of me on the path so that he wouldn't notice how often I had to stop and catch my breath. We were up seven or eight thousand feet by now, after all! He looked down through the branches at me. *This guy's in great shape*, I thought as I waved up at him nonchalantly.

That night the hot water in the shower felt better than ever before. Dressed in clean jeans and a turtleneck, I busied myself in the kitchen while Terry set up chips and dip on the porch. We sat outside as the sun set, listening to the wind and watching Devon play with the squirrels. So serene. So healing. So close to God.

When finally the sky had filled with stars and the chill of the night mountain air enfolded us, we moved inside to the warmth of the fire, spaghetti, and roasted marshmallows.

"Do you feel comfortable here with me?" I asked as we settled on the couch.

"Yes, Pam, I do." He paused. "I'd like to hold you. Would that be all right?"

"Yes," I whispered.

Terry pulled me close to him and put his arms around me. He stared into my eyes and smiled. He caressed my face and my hair. My heart was bursting with joy. He held me in the firelight and silence for a long time.

"It's as if I love you with a divided heart, Pam. I know this is hard for you," he said at last, "but I'm just not ready yet. I love you . . . but I'm not ready."

Alone in my bed that night, I wondered if Terry Sweeney ever would be ready for my love.

15

TERRY

The ringing of my phone jarred me awake. The alarm clock's digital numbers glowed in the dark, tracing out the numbers: 1:50.

"Terry, it's Rosemarie. Sorry to bother you so late."

The tone in her voice made me instantly alert. I tried to sound calm, but a choking feeling was grabbing at the base of my throat: "No problem."

"It's getting close. . . ." she said.

"I'll be right there." I hung up the phone and jumped out of bed. Thoughts, feelings, and images started rushing in, screaming for attention. *Is Pat still alive? Will I get there before he dies? Where are my holy oils? Yes, good, they're in my car. Pat, don't die. Rosemarie needs you, Michael needs you, I need you. Yes, die, you've suffered too much already. No one should feel so much pain.*

Why did Jesus heal the sick, raise the dead, and tell his disciples, "All these and greater things shall you do"? Is my faith so weak? Is His promise not true? Why was God's will so difficult to accept?

While driving past Huesman Chapel, images of Pat's Mass and reception flashed through my mind—his arms around Michael and Rosemarie, the embraces he received from all his friends, the trusting look in his eyes as he received Communion. The words he

---

118

said to me at the reception resounded again in my head: "Thank you, Terry, for the happiest day of my life."

Were Mom and Dudley there yet? Would we all watch him die? Was he still conscious, or had he drifted off into another delirium? Would he hear us calling his name? *Pat, Pat, we love you. . . .*

The light at Loyola Boulevard and Manchester turned green. I turned left toward Inglewood. *How is Rosemarie taking it? God, what she's been through, watching him waste away, trying to keep him alive with her heart. And Michael?* I remembered the look in his eyes when his father had taken him in his arms and said, "Michael, listen to me very carefully. I have cancer and I'm dying. And even though I won't be around much longer, I'm never going to stop loving you and Mom. Do you hear me, Michael?"

"Yes," Michael had answered.

"Good. I want you to take good care of Mom. You're going to be the man of the house now."

Maybe that's why Pat had asked Michael, three weeks earlier, to be his "best man" during the renewal of his marriage vows. To prove to Michael that maturity is shaped by suffering, not age—to prove to Michael that nothing makes you grow up faster than death.

There were cars parked in their driveway, so I pulled over to the curb in front of the house. I took the holy oils from the glove compartment, then walked up the driveway and through the un- locked door.

Death is here, I thought. *I can hear it in Rosemarie's voice.* She was talking to Dudley, Therese, and Dan in the kitchen.

I forced myself to look toward the couch. Racha lay on the floor, her black tail curled up under her body, her eyes opened wide, staring up at her silent master.

Pat was dead.

I sat down next to him, looked at his closed eyelids, the slight parting of his lips, the terrible stillness of his face.

Oh, Pat . . .

I reached for the vial of holy oil, removed the cap and the cotton, stuck my thumb into the oil, touched his forehead: "By this holy anointing, may the Lord grant you eternal life, happiness, and peace. And may our Lord Jesus Christ grant you pardon and absolution from all your sins, and I absolve you from all your sins in the name of the Father, the Son, and the Holy Spirit."

With the holy oil I made the sign of the cross on Pat's forehead. Rosemarie and Therese, Dudley and Dan stood by quietly, watching. I pulled back the blanket that was covering Pat, lifted up his hand, began anointing his palm.

You did it, Pat. You looked death in the face and laughed. Cancer took a hundred pounds from your flesh, it hovered like a vulture over you, taunting you. Death ravaged your body, but your spirit won. I really thought it would break you, make you fold into anger or beg for mercy—but you laughed and smiled. You knew so much more about life than I realized.

Oh, Pat, I am so proud to be your brother. I hope, when I die, to have half your courage. I love you, Brother. Lord, welcome him into your kingdom. Embrace him. Let him feel your peace, your joy, your love.

Pat's hands and feet were cold as I finished anointing him. Racha was standing now, sniffing the oil on Pat's hands. I patted her on the head. She looked at me, then back to Pat. She whimpered and curled up again near his feet.

Rosemarie's eyes were filled with tears and grief.

I walked over to her and hugged her.

Mom came in the door, went immediately to Pat, held him in her arms, and cried softly. "Oh, son, dear son, my baby—Pat."

Dudley went over to her, put his arms around her, comforted her.

I embraced Therese and Dan. "Did he die in his sleep?"

Rosemarie shook her head. "He was in a lot of pain. About midnight he became delirious, started saying things I couldn't understand, like, 'My hands, get it off my hands! Turn my hands inside out!' "

Rosemarie wiped the tears from her eyes. Therese hugged her.

"Therese and I didn't know what to do. After about two hours he grew very calm. Suddenly he came out of his delirium, looked at both of us, called us by our names, and then said, 'I love you.' He died right after that."

Rosemarie embraced me silently for a long moment. "I'm going to wake Michael," she said.

———

I walked over to Mom and took her in my arms. She was wiping tears away from her eyes. "He was so brave. Are you okay?"

"Yes," I answered.

Dudley turned to me. "Who should we call first—the coroner? or the mortuary?"

I picked up the telephone and dialed McCormick Mortuary. "Hello, this is Father Terry Sweeney, I want to report a death in my family."

Rosemarie brought Michael to the couch. She held him tightly with one arm; with the other she hugged Pat, kissed him on the lips. They were crying as Rosemarie said, "You must say good-bye now."

Michael said, "Good-bye, Dad." Then he put his face against his father's and whispered something in his ear. Rosemarie pressed her face in close to Michael's. It was a private moment, very tender, very painful. I could see from the tears streaming down Rosemarie's face that Michael's pain trebled her own anguish.

Left open on the coffee table in front of the couch was a diary Pat had promised to keep when he first learned two and a half months earlier that he had terminal cancer. The diary was a spiral notebook with a blue cover. I picked up the notebook, flipped through the pages. They were all blank, except for one page, which had only one line on it—a line that was an unfinished sentence. It said:

On having received the tremendous grace of advance notice . . .

During the funeral Mass Michael, dressed neatly in dark suit and tie, read three farewell letters written to his father by his cousins Michelle, Aileen, and Lisa. One of Pat's closest friends, Jeff Pasternak, played a musical eulogy he had composed in Pat's honor. He called it "Sweeney's Anthem." Dudley talked about what Pat meant to us, and he ended his words with, "We will miss you, Pat. We love you."

While reading the Gospel from John 14—"In my Father's house there are many dwelling places. . . . I am indeed going to prepare a place for you, and then I shall come back to take you with me"—my heart was flooded with images of standing at this very pulpit before, first for Dad's funeral, then for my ordination, and now for Pat. Pat, the invincible.

I looked down at Pat's casket. The small cross placed at the head of the casket was perfectly still. For a moment I heard nothing but silence.

Rosemarie, standing in the first pew, also looked at the casket, then back at me. She waited. I saw it in her eyes. The Absence. The Emptiness. The Void. I knew she longed to have Pat again in her arms, no matter how emaciated, no matter how sick or delirious— if only for a few seconds more, just to see Life again in his eyes, to hear him say, "I love you."

The graveside service was at Holy Cross Cemetery. Pat had asked to be buried on the same hillside as Dad. The plot he had selected was near a fledgling tree, on a hillside that looked back toward Marina del Rey.

Several weeks after the service, with Pam's help and encouragement, I returned to the gravesite. It was Father's Day. Balloons and fresh carnations had been placed in the flower holder above Pat's tombstone. Resting unopened below it were two envelopes, one in Rosemarie's handwriting and the other in Michael's. The gravestone was emerald green and had, carved in it, mountains, a pine tree, and a stream flowing across toward the inscription:

BELOVED HUSBAND AND FATHER

PATRICK JOHN SWEENEY
1943–1985

EXPLORED LIFE WITH
COURAGE, DIGNITY,
FAITH AND LOVE

TILL WE MEET AGAIN

For several minutes Pamela and I stood over his grave, saying nothing. Finally she asked if I wanted to say a prayer. Prayers were crowding into my heart—*Father, hold him, keep him, comfort him and*

Rosemarie and Michael, fill their hearts with your love, not pain, not emptiness, not silence; Lord, grant me his courage, help me to do what is right and most loving—but I could not speak the words. Pain was choking my throat and flooding my eyes with tears.

A soundless breeze swept through the carnations, shimmering them. The balloons flapped out and away from the sticks anchoring them to the grave. They wanted to break free, but couldn't.

16

PAMELA

I stood at the side of the airstrip looking up toward the sky. A soft drizzle and gusts of wind danced across the English countryside. The runway blended unobtrusively with the farmland outside Oxford, silent and still.

During the Second World War my father had been commanding officer of the Seventh Photo Reconnaissance Group of the Eighth Air Force. At dawn's first light forty years ago, the first planes had taken off in the thick English fog headed for the beach at Normandy. My father had led the reconnaissance mission that morning—D day—armed with cameras in place of guns, his only weapon his skill as a pilot. The headlines back stateside had read, SHOOP—FIRST MAN OVER, FIRST MAN BACK. It seemed as if the nervous energy still hung in the air over the now-peaceful airfield. And here I was, after all the stories I'd heard as a kid, standing on the runway, hearing the roar of his engines in my mind and feeling his excitement in my heart.

Daddy, what were you thinking? Were you afraid?

My mother walked up to me, "That's the farmhouse over there, honey."

She pointed across the fields to an old farmhouse in the distance standing alone against the sky. I'd heard about it all my life. That's why they called it Mount Farm—an airbase hidden in the farm-lands. Mom, Bill, Steve, and I jumped into a Jeep and headed across the meadow. Someone still lived in the beautiful little cottage. Graciously they allowed us to wander up the tiny staircase to the attic room where my father had lived during his time in England. The next room had been occupied by Elliott Roosevelt, who had become a good friend. I could visualize them sharing breakfast over the giant hearth in the kitchen and remembered the crazy stories I'd heard about Roosevelt's antics at the base.

My family and I had flown to England to attend a dedication of a war memorial to Mount Farm in honor of my father and the other men who had served there during the war. For a week we attended all sorts of functions in celebration of this event, and had the opportunity to talk with men who had flown reconnaissance missions along with my father. "He never asked anyone to do anything he wouldn't do first himself." Some told of having been shot down, and still others described how frightening it was to fly into the thick of battle without any guns to defend themselves.

At the final banquet something very beautiful took place. There was a piece of the runway to be auctioned off as a memento. To our amazement, Bill bid higher and higher until, at last, the coveted chunk of cement belonged to us. "This should belong to the family," Bill said. With tears in his eyes, Bill walked to the podium. It was a few seconds before he spoke.

"I want to thank all of you for welcoming me here. As some of you know, I flew B-25's over in China during the war. It's been great to share so many interesting stories about those days with all of you. But . . . what I wanted to say was . . . that this family means everything in the world to me. And Shoopy . . . Shoopy wasn't only someone I admired—he was my friend."

I was crying as Bill returned to the table. I put my arms around him and held him very close. "I love you," I said. We sat that way for a long time, and I realized how very lucky we all were that such a courageous, wonderful man had come into our lives.

The next afternoon, while the others were napping, I went for a stroll through the gardens of Oxford University. The scent of flowers fresh from the rain caressed my senses as I gazed about me at the old stone buildings. Church bells chimed just across the way. Tentatively I entered the chapel and sat quietly listening to the Eucharistic service in progress. Gazing up at the beamed ceilings, I felt a sense of history all about me. As the priest's voice echoed through the old English chapel, my mind wandered back to Terry miles and miles away. How I longed to tell my family about this wonderful man I'd met. My mother had already intuited that what I felt was more than friendship. I had hoped that this vacation would be the occasion to explain, but somehow it just wasn't. Sometime in the very near future, however, I would need to offer some sort of explanation. They'd heard me mention his name so many times, and it wasn't normal behavior in our family to keep things from one another. They were as confused as I. And often-times out of confusion, suspicion is born. Somehow I had to allay their fears. But this trip, with all its memories of the past and the happiness of the present, just wasn't that time.

Back home in L.A. the summer of 1985 passed as a tapestry woven of wonder and the joy of falling in love. On Sundays, after Terry's priestly duties were over, we would hike to the top of Franklin Canyon, a state park situated, amazingly, in the heart of Beverly Hills. One can literally hike for hours over a mountain trail overlooking a peaceful reservoir. It is country quiet, complete with stream, grassy lawn, and the most lovely bandstand beneath an enormous oak tree. Basically, it was a time for talking and just being quiet together. After our hike we would head for El Coyote Mexican Café on Beverly Boulevard, which I'd been going to since I was eight years old. It is open 365 days a year, the parking lot is always filled, and despite the low price you see everything from BMWs and Mercedeses to beat-up vans and Jeeps. Yes, Sundays were wonderful.

I found myself longing to understand Terry's vocation. Who was Terry Sweeney, the priest? We talked for hours on end about God, the final vows Terry had put off taking, and Saint Ignatius of Loyola. What did Terry's personal conflict really mean? I needed to know more about what had drawn him to priestly life.

"Have you ever seen an ordination?" Terry asked.

"No. You're the first priest I've ever met, remember?"

"Well, actually this Saturday is the anniversary of the day I was ordained, and at Sacred Heart Chapel four more Jesuits will be ordained. I can't be there, but you could probably walk into the chapel and watch if you wanted."

Saturday came, and at two o'clock I entered the beautiful chapel on the Loyola campus and took a seat in the back. The powerful music lent an air of intense majesty to the ceremonies. Nearly a hundred priests filled the side altar, and behind me a few rows back were about twenty priests sitting in the pews. I turned around and was surprised to see Terry sitting among them. He nodded a private hello. When, a few minutes later, I turned around again to look, he was gone.

The service lasted about three hours, and as I watched, I felt that I grew to know each of the four men who were embracing the priesthood that day in June. At one part of the ceremony each man walked down the long aisle of the church and lay prostrate on the floor, arms outstretched, face to the ground, humbling himself before God. I looked at the man lying on the floor next to my pew. I felt in some way that through loving Terry I could understand and share in the pain of this man's sacrifice. And I couldn't help but wonder if he really knew how difficult it might prove to be in years to come. I wept for him—for the personal companionship he would never share, for the children who would never call him Daddy—and yet I loved him for his faith. I tried to imagine Terry at his ordination: his exhilaration, his joy, his sense of accomplishment. How God must have loved him that day! Had Terry known when he'd entered the Jesuit order at age seventeen what it would all mean? I felt small and insignificant amid the grandeur all about me. Unworthy and ashamed, I prayed, *Dear God, please don't let me take him from you. Don't let my love be sinful.*

As the weeks passed, my desire to be part of Terry was growing to such an intensity that I was afraid even to consider the alternative. I wanted to crawl into his arms and lie there, contented and safe, forever. But I was afraid. More afraid than I had ever been in my life. Each day I drove my little car to Good Shepherd Church to sit in the empty pews. Sometimes I would kneel at the altar until my knees gave out. Each day I prayed . . . I sat quietly in the empty church . . . and I listened.

What, dear God, do you want of me? What can I do? I love this man, how I love this man!

I doubted myself, I hated myself. I loathed the longing within me that could take Terry from his call to serve his God.

Oh, God, I'm not a bad person. Please tell me I'm not!

My conscience replied, *You're evil, Pam. Your spirit is sinful and impure! God finds you disgusting and unworthy.*

I felt at times that my heart was dying. How? How could this love I believed in be wrong? How could Terry's sweet soul, which seemed to need love so badly, be hurt by my loving him? The dreams I dreamed alone in my bed at night were beautiful, gentle, tender dreams. I believed that my love was pure and good, but everything around me cried out, No! I hadn't even slept with Terry, and yet I felt like an adulteress. The Catholic Church said that to love a priest was a sin and a disgrace and that my soul would be condemned to eternal hell. I wrestled and fought and prayed that God would lead me Home.

Day after day I would sit in the silent church, my loneliness and despair a blanket around my shoulders. At times the pain was so great, I felt I could not take even one more breath. As my love grew deeper, so, too, did my torment.

Gradually, however, emotion began to give way to clarity. I knew that I was in love with Terry Sweeney. The confusion and torment I was now experiencing came from somewhere far outside the boundaries of my heart. I had no wish to compromise Terry's priesthood. If it was his choice to remain a Jesuit priest, then I could not, would not remain in his life. Whether or not he remained a priest was not my decision to make, for it was his vow, his vocation. This realization led to great personal frustration and the feeling that I was at the mercy of forces over which I had no control. But finally I saw clearly that I, too, had a choice. I could stay or leave. I knew that in truly loving this man, I wanted only what was best for him. If that meant walking away, I would do so. I could not live a half love, half life. If it were inappropriate for me to be in his life, even as a loving friend, then I would go.

What about loving Terry in secret? The sense of isolation that would occasionally overcome me during Mass as I sat unnoticed in the pews, one woman among hundreds of faces, was enough to tell me that I could not hide my love for Terry as if it were something of which to be ashamed. I could not allow myself to become a mistress in the shadows. I would not hide my love, nor would I hide from it. If it was wrong for people to know about my presence in Terry's life, then it was clearly wrong for me to be in his life at all. And if friendship were all that would be left, I knew that I would not be able to share only snatches of borrowed time with him for the rest of my life. The pain would be too great, and the diminished emotion would destroy me. I began to realize that I might have to cut the cord cleanly. With that calm realization, frustration gave way to sadness. And I told Terry how I felt.

As the days passed, however, a new and unexpected awakening took place. With the ambiguity I had felt newly resolved in my mind, I began to find the Church a haven instead of a place where my conscience did battle with my heart. Peace and warmth would descend on me as I would pray—and ever so gradually I began to believe that I was Home. It was God who had put this love in my heart, and I came to realize that I was exactly where God wanted me to be. He had brought our lives together at precisely this moment for a reason. My conscience and heart began to breathe in harmony once more. Although it wasn't clear to me what purpose I was to serve, I truly came to believe that there was very definitely a purpose for me in Terry's life.

With Terry's retreat drawing nearer, so, too, was his decision regarding final vows. His Provincial was urging him to make up his mind, and I was well aware that with whatever choice Terry made, my life would be changed forever. It seemed to both of us that there was nothing incompatible between our love and Terry's ministry. I loved his work and the fact that he could help people. For now, though, it was his world, his mission, his priesthood, and his decisions that were all-important. I told myself that whatever my concerns, they were lesser and that I would live with the outcome.

A relationship between equals, of course, cannot survive long with this kind of imbalance. In the coming months my role in Terry's life would become a source of grave tension, not only between the two of us, but within my own soul. Yet, beneath it all, in the stillness of the deepest part of my being, I still believed that somehow things would work out and that we could be together forever.

As if my life weren't complicated enough, I was diagnosed at this time with endometriosis. My physicians recommended exploratory surgery to see the extent of the disease. Unfortunately, my surgery was scheduled for the day before Terry was to leave on his retreat. I was horrified at the prospect of saying good-bye to him with filthy hair from a hospital bed! However, there was not much I could do, so I resolved to make the best of it.

My parents were in town from Mendocino, and they naturally intended to be with me at the hospital. As yet they had not met Terry, which was one more challenge with which I had to deal.

It was arranged that the night before my surgery we would all have dinner at Trader Vic's in Beverly Hills. Terry and I were shaking as we entered the private-key elevator in the new wing of the Beverly Wilshire Hotel. The owners of the hotel at that time were two of my parents' best friends, and Mom and Bill often stayed with them when they were in town. We were to have drinks there first and then go on to dinner.

I'd been nervous all day. It was an unusual situation, to be sure. Although it wasn't uncommon at all for Terry to go to dinner with various families and parishioners, it certainly was unusual for my parents to be going to dinner with their daughter and a Roman Catholic priest!

The elevator doors opened onto a plush hallway with beveled-mirrored walls.

"Ready?" I asked as we paused to take a deep breath.

"Sure, Shoop—I'm looking forward to this!"

We knocked on the heavy, wood-paneled doors. They opened right away, and Bill shook Terry's hand firmly as he said with a twinkle, "Well, I've certainly heard a lot about you!"

From the time they greeted Terry with warm smiles and genuine interest, I knew that, for now, everything would be all right.

At the restaurant the conversation was casual.

"Bill, I want to thank you for your advice about Pat. You have no idea how crucial it was. It really helped him to make his final decision."

During the evening Bill was able to talk to Terry about his brother's illness and about Bill's own personal decision to leave the Catholic Church. Occasionally, under the table, Terry would reach over and squeeze my hand reassuringly. Eventually, over coffee, my surgery became the topic of our conversation.

"Pam, a laparoscopy is a simple operation—absolutely nothing to worry about."

"But, Bill, my doctor says that I have endometriosis, which can interfere with my getting pregnant in the future. He says he doesn't know what he's going to find, or how serious it might be."

Medically, Bill was right—the procedure was an easy one. But it wasn't just the surgery that was frightening me, it was the possible outcome. I was not looking forward to tomorrow.

That night at home, before Terry left, I could contain my fears no longer. Realizing that Terry was under tremendous pressure leading up to his retreat, I had kept these fears to myself. But tonight, with so many unknowns facing me, everything suddenly gave way. The tears wouldn't stop. Would the option ever to have a child be taken from me? Would I lose Terry to the Jesuits? Yes, I was frightened . . . really frightened.

17

TERRY

She looked beautiful and vulnerable in her white hospital gown as she fidgeted with the sheet covering her body. I reached over, grasped her hand. She was trying to sound cheerful, upbeat, but her eyes couldn't hide her fears. We both knew that her operation might reveal any number of complications that might lead to the same conclusion: no possibility of children. I had shared a dream with her: that if we were to marry, we would have children. She had asked that if we could have only one child, would I prefer a boy or a girl? Girl, I'd answered, because then there'd be two of you.

"If I can't have children, will you love me anyway?" she asked.

"Yes."

"Are you sure?"

"Yes."

She smiled, squeezed my hand, then brushed away some of her tears. "We haven't even made love yet, and here I am worrying about children!"

A nurse walked through the doorway pushing a small cart in front of her. "Good morning," she said. "The anesthesiologist wants me to get you ready for him." The nurse pulled up the sleeve of Pamela's hospital gown and began inspecting the vein in her arm.

"You're sure I'll be asleep during the entire operation? Trust me, you wouldn't want me waking up in the middle of surgery."

The nurse laughed, "You'll be just fine."

"If I woke up in the middle of surgery, I'd scream so loud, the whole operating room would go into cardiac arrest—and we wouldn't want that, now, would we?"

"You won't feel a thing," the nurse reassured her as she prepped the needle and IV hookup.

"Do you really have to stick that thing into my arm?"

"I'm afraid so," the nurse answered.

"As you can see, my veins are the smallest in the history of life. Three weeks ago I tried to donate blood for a friend. Two different nurses tried to put the needle into my vein. They couldn't do it. Are you sure you have to do this? Couldn't you just give me a pill or something? If I start to scream, it's nothing personal—just ask every doctor who's ever given me a shot!"

They were both laughing mildly as Pamela closed her eyes and averted her head. The nurse pierced Pamela's arm with the needle. Pamela took a deep breath, and I could tell from the way the nurse withdrew the needle from Pamela's arm that she had missed the vein. She held Pamela's arm more firmly and plunged the needle in a second time.

Pamela stiffened, "Ouuucchhh!"

The nurse pulled the needle out a second time. Beads of sweat were forming on her head as she pushed the needle in a third time, then withdrew it quickly. "Sorry, this isn't working."

"That's what I was trying to tell you," Pamela said.

The nurse swabbed and bandaged her arm, then did something with the IV needle. It was difficult for me to see exactly what it was because I was paying more attention to the pained expression on Pamela's face.

The nurse placed Pamela's hand, palm down, on the cart, then drove the IV needle into one of the veins in the top of her hand. Pamela let out a short scream as her blood filled the IV connector.

I felt the color drain from my face. My head was suddenly very hot. Pinpoints of light were bursting out everywhere. My legs began to buckle underneath me, so I quickly found a chair and sat down.

"Terry, you're pale as a ghost," Pamela said. "What happened?"

"I don't know. I just got queasy all of a sudden."

"You look positively horrible!"

"Thanks."

"Nurse, I think you'd better forget about me and take care of him."

The nurse walked over to me. "Keep your head between your legs and breathe deeply."

By the time the orderly arrived a few minutes later with the gurney, I was feeling okay again.

Pamela got out of bed, stood up next to the gurney, and winked at me. "Sure you don't want this? I could walk by your side down to surgery."

"No, thanks. I'm fine."

"Then why are you the one fainting?" Pamela lay down on the gurney. The orderly began wheeling her out of the room. She looked up at me. "Maybe Doctor Francis should be operating on you! That'd be just fine with me. Do you want to take my place? Do you think he could tell the difference?"

The orderly was laughing now.

"If he can't, you're in deep trouble," I said.

Some three hours later the doors to the surgery area flung open and a tall, handsome man dressed in surgical scrubs walked up to me. "You Terry Sweeney?"

"Yes."

"Rodney Francis," he said, extending his hand. "Pamela will be fine. She's in recovery now. Her brother came in during surgery and wanted me to check back with him. Do you know where he is?"

"Yes, I'll show you." I led Dr. Francis to the X-ray room where Steve was answering questions from another physician about the chest X ray on the lightboard in front of them. Steve asked Dr.

Francis detailed surgical questions about Pam's laparoscopy. Their medical vocabulary sounded like a foreign language. After they shook hands and said good-bye, I asked Steve for a translation. The news was favorable.

Manresa is the name of the Jesuit Retreat House located in the foothills of Azusa, California. It was named after the cave in Barcelona, Spain, where Ignatius of Loyola spent thirty days and nights in prayer and fasting trying to achieve a more perfect union with God. From this soul-wrenching experience Ignatius laid the foundations for his Spiritual Exercises and Rules for the Discernment of Spirits. In their enthusiasm for extolling Ignatius's virtues and the profound spiritual insight of the Exercises and the Rules for the Discernment of Spirits, most biographers fail to mention that Ignatius's Manresa "retreat" also brought him to the brink of suicide.

While a senior in high school I had come with several classmates to make a retreat at Manresa, and it was here that I had finally decided to become a Jesuit. Now, twenty-three years later, I was finally to decide whether I was going to spend the rest of my life in the order. Eight days of prayer, memories, discernment, and a decision. The Provincial had said, "Make it a priority, Terry. You've had long enough to think about final vows. Put aside your work, make a retreat."

I picked up the phone, called Pamela, and told her I had arrived safely.

"Good," she said. "I miss you already."

"I miss you too. Are you feeling any better?"

"Still very sore. I can at least walk around a little now. Mom's been just great. What's Manresa like?"

"I'll tell you when I get back. Pray for me, will you?"

"Oh, Terry, I'm afraid my life might end in eight days."

"If you're doing what God wants, and I'm doing what God wants, there's no way we can lose—no matter what decision is made."

"But how can we really know what God wants?"

"Ask."

"And if He doesn't answer?"

"Ask again. And if He still doesn't answer, do what you think is right and most loving. That's why God gave us minds and hearts, to think for ourselves."

"When I look into my heart at my love for you, I can't imagine it's not from God. I love you so much, Terry."

"I love you too. I really need this time alone. I won't be calling. Don't call me unless it's an emergency, okay?"

"Okay."

"Good-bye."

" 'Bye."

I hung up the phone, then walked out the front door of the main house. To the left, to the right, and immediately behind the house were rows of single-room lodges that could accommodate some sixty retreatants. Immediately in front of this two-story building was a lawn, a swimming pool, and a tree-lined garden interwoven with a pathway leading to fourteen wood-carved Stations of the Cross. Instinctively I shied away from the garden and walked down the road.

Tall palm trees lined this half-mile driveway stretching from the retreat center back down to the main road. The driveway itself was separated into entrance and exit roads by a center divider filled with a colorful variety of flowers and shrubbery. Flanking both sides of this drive was a multiacre nursery consisting of dozens of greenhouses and long rows of neatly potted trees.

It was soothing just to hear the steady, rhythmic sound of the tall sprinklers spouting light sheets of water over the center-divider garden. It was a relief to have the noise of McKay Hall, the constant barrage of phone calls, and the rush of my daily work schedule behind me. And it felt good, after the long, freeway-congested drive from Westchester to Azusa, to stretch my legs and imagine eight straight days of no driving and no traffic jams.

But the sense of relief passed within seconds as I became aware of why I had avoided the garden. Unconsciously I hadn't wanted the very beginning of the retreat to be filled with images of suffering and death. I felt ashamed of my attempt to block out the poignant reminders of Christ's agony. I knew all too well that there was no place I could go, no matter how peaceful, where I could forget Him, or what He suffered two thousand years ago, or what He suffers now in those He loves. I thought of Pat, of his pale, silent face as I traced the sign of the cross on his cold forehead.

It wasn't necessary to look back two thousand years to feel Christ's suffering. All that was needed was not to run away or shut myself off from the suffering around me.

I asked God to give me the strength not to turn away from the pain that Pat's death had caused or to run away from finally deciding which of two opposing notions of obedience I was going to live by. I asked for the grace to really know what celibacy meant and whether my love for Pamela was telling me that I could not live a celibate life.

Pat's death was making me acutely aware of the fragility of life; it made me understand with much greater clarity what Ignatius (in his Meditation on the Two Standards) had advised those about to choose between the banner of Christ and the banner of Satan: to imagine ourselves on our deathbed and intuit what choice it is we wish we would have made. Faced with death, Pat's love for his wife and son became all the more precious. Faced with Pat's death, I realized how important it was to live whatever years, months, or days I had left as best I could. Surrounded by this aura of death, I felt an inner urgency to clean up my life, to try to dispel the evil in me and around me.

It was already twilight as I made my way back up the long road to Manresa. I was filled with shame as I thought of my sins, of the people I had hurt, of the people I had failed to help. Conversations with superiors were still ringing in my head, counsel about "prudence" and "discretion." I was still weighing the good that could be accomplished as a priest against the folly of jeopardizing my priesthood by speaking the truth at the wrong time or to Church officials who might punish me. It had been all too easy to rationalize my silence regarding the Humanae Vitae Encyclical, the Church's punitive actions against those priests and religious who had openly protested the Vietnam war, and the Declaration on the Admission of Women to the Ministerial Priesthood (a strange title for a document that explained why women couldn't be ordained!).

The priesthood and religious freedom were suffering to the point of death, and to protect my secure place in the vocation I loved, I had kept silent. *"Qui tacit, consentire,"* Thomas More had said. I had valued my exercise of priestly ministry more than the truth and the good of the Church.

The cement walkway leading to my living quarters was bordered with tall, multicolored rosebushes, their brightness now muted by the orange hues of twilight. The roses reminded me of my friend Mary Melanson's wedding bouquet and her radiant smile as she had walked down the aisle to meet her groom. Would Pamela ever walk down the aisle to me? No, she couldn't, because that is what celibacy means: helping others, even your closest friends, to marry and find happiness. Celibacy means always saying good-bye. Celibacy means always helping others to love God, but never allowing them to fall in love with you.

Even if I had wanted to leave the priesthood in order to marry Pamela, this pope would not have allowed it. He was making it nearly impossible for priests to resign with dignity.

The Vatican had already instructed canonists that there were only three conditions under which a priest would be granted permission to be "laicized with freedom to marry": (1) if the priest admitted that at the time of his ordination he seriously lacked the freedom of will and the necessary maturity; (2) if the priest confessed that he so lusted after women that he could not live without one ("better to marry than to burn"); (3) if the priest was dying (and his illicit marriage would therefore be placing his eternal salvation in jeopardy).

A priest falling in love and wanting to marry was treated with more scorn than a priest who had multiple but "repentant" affairs, or a priest who had molested children. Affairs and child molestation were considered sins of weakness and deviant behavior. Falling in love and wanting to marry was treated as a sacrilege, a sin against Sacred Orders, against the Church.

The desk inside my room was stacked with books I had brought along to read. That first night I didn't open any of them, not even the Psalms, which had been a constant source of comfort. Instead

I got ready for bed, turned out the lights, and worried.

In the darkness the feelings and images, with no apparent logic or direction, continued to crowd their way through my heart and mind. Pat's cancer and suffering had generated emotions in me I could not control. I no longer tried to direct every thought and feeling—now I let them be, listened to them. Pat's death made me realize how much of my life had been spent living from my head; the love he showed made me realize that knowledge alone is only half a life. The discomfort of being assaulted by random feelings and images lasted for hours. Then a voice I had heard twenty-one years earlier sang its way through the confusion. It was the voice of Jim Reites, as he stood in the choir loft of the Jesuit novitiate during a vow Mass, singing the prayer of Ignatius: *Suscipe, Domine, universam libertatem meam*—"Take, Lord, all my liberty. Accept my memory, my understanding, my entire will . . . Give me only your love and your grace, with these I am rich enough and desire nothing more."

I fell asleep asking for the grace and the strength to live that prayer. For a long moment I imagined the end of my last breath and finally standing face-to-face with the God who had so eluded me throughout my entire life. In the silence and nakedness of that moment what I felt was not judgment or reproof, but embrace—and the depth of the love emanating from that merciful embrace made me burn with regret that I had not lived more, sacrificed more, loved more, that I had so little to offer One so incredibly tender and loving.

The next morning while getting ready to celebrate Mass, I wondered why the Vatican was so obstinate in refusing to allow optional celibacy for priests. It seemed contradictory for the Vatican to defend the right to marry as one of the most fundamental of all human rights and yet to deny that same right to priests. The continuing imposition of celibacy seemed such folly. In 1971 the U.S.-based National Federation of Priests' Councils, by a vote of 193 to 18, had urged, "We ask that the choices between celibacy and marriage for priests now active in the ministry be allowed and the change begin immediately." The highly respected Jesuit psychiatrist James Gill had said, "There is every reason to suspect that sociological surveys will continue to reveal, as they have consistently been disclosing all over the U.S., that the majority of priests prefer that celibacy be made optional. It will continue to be dangerous for the Church not to give serious official consideration to their wishes." Since Vatican II over fifteen thousand U.S. priests had resigned. From 1968 to 1983 seminary enrollment at the high school and college levels had declined seventy-four percent, and at theologates fifty percent. No wonder the world-renowned Jesuit theologian Karl Rahner had concluded, "If the Church in a concrete situation cannot find a sufficient number of priestly congregational leaders who are bound to celibacy, it is obvious and requires no further theological discussion that the obligation of celibacy must not be imposed."

After breakfast I walked down to the garden and began walking the pathway of the fourteen Stations of the Cross. While looking at the statue of the skeptic Pilate washing his hands after condemning Jesus to crucifixion, I felt welling up within me a truth: God has already proven His love for me. His love does not hinge on whether I am a Jesuit or not a Jesuit, a priest or not a priest, whether married or unmarried, a sinner or virtuous. Becoming aware of this truth filled me with a radical freedom that enabled me to face the decisions of this retreat and whatever future might be born from them.

What was human sanctity or vice compared with the One who is, who was, and who shall be Love? What was one single vocational decision compared with the sufferings of Jesus? Publicly betrayed, mocked, paraded through the streets, stripped, nailed to a cross, abandoned by His apostles, abandoned by God—*Eloi, Eloi, lama sabacthani!* That cry of despair, uttered with so much love, changed the destiny of the universe forever. And my heart.

All I had wanted to do, from my earliest days as a Jesuit, was to become part of His cry, part of His love, if He would have me. But this desire was so easily obstructed by pride, ignorance, and the countless other means we invent to confuse love with passion, authority with power, tradition with truth. How, at that moment when we had nailed Him to the cross, could He say, "Father, forgive them, for they know not what they do"? Far easier to call down twelve legions of angels and end it all. Far easier for us to complain that He expects too much, that He dreams too much, that His visions of all being equal under one Abba were those of a spiritual madman. Far easier, like the betrayer Peter, to run into the darkness and hide: "Lord, I am a sinner." And in that hiding do nothing but dwell in our own misery. Jesus warned us that the path to God was narrow: Love God with your whole heart, mind, and soul and your neighbor as yourself—as I have loved you. But religion, using God's name, taught us that the path to God was broad, filled with laws, commandments, rituals, precepts reaching into every aspect of human conduct. By your morality will you save your souls, by your virtue. Thus religion became an ethic, not a relationship grounded in and defined by love. "Simon, because she has loved much, much has been forgiven her. . . . You did not wash my feet, but she has not ceased washing my feet with her tears, and drying them with her hair." Jesus taught us that the law was made for man, not man for the law—and for that teaching we crucified Him. His death proved the world is not yet ready for a God of love.

As I looked at the statue of Mary holding her crucified Son, I fell silent for a long time. What agony she must have felt. Ignorance and hatred and fear had taken her Son's life, her Son whom she had nursed and cuddled and taught to walk and speak and love.

It struck me that priests in love are also condemned to die. They must abandon either the woman they love or the priesthood and community they love—or else watch their love degenerate through guilt, secrecy, and turmoil into hypocrisy. They must deny either the woman and children of their love or the ministry and Church they love. They must suffer the opprobrium of judgmental bishops and scandalized family members and parishioners. They must stand by and have their love called a sin and the woman they love called a temptress. If they accept the burden of the laws excluding marriage from the priesthood and choose marriage, they must admit that their priesthood was never a call from God. They must accept the notion that priestly love and conjugal love are mutually and radically exclusive, when they know in their hearts they are mutually enriching. At the very moment they choose either their priesthood or the woman they love, the other has to be buried, thrust into a psychological tomb lest the crucifixion of the choice, or of not choosing, destroy everyone. How is it that the priesthood, supposedly a messenger and symbol of Christ's love, could be so cruel to conjugal love?

The question forced its way into my awareness: If I were totally free at this moment to marry Pamela, would I? The question unlocked a storm of conflicting emotions. But you are not free, Terry, you have a vow of celibacy.

But you made that vow because you were taught that celibacy was the best way to love God and the Church and that it was the only way you could become a priest. Now you've learned that priestly celibacy is a man-made discipline that was founded on a reckless disregard for the marriage bond and on a destructive concept of human sexuality. Jesus' married apostles and the thousand-year tradition of a married priesthood have proven that priesthood and marriage are not mutually exclusive, so why are Church laws making them so? Suppose the Church passed laws *requiring* that all priests marry? Or that anyone wanting to become a priest had first to promise to marry? Who would accept such preposterous impositions?

And yet we have tolerated the imposition of celibacy on the priesthood for over a thousand years! Why?

You still haven't answered the question, Terry. Are you willing to give up your priesthood for Pamela? Do you love her more?

I love both.

You're avoiding the question. One has to go. Which is it? Which one are you going to deny?

No! It isn't right!

I left the Stations of the Cross and walked back down the main road.

Again the question forced itself from my heart: *If you were totally free to marry Pamela, would you?* Again, I resisted: *But I am not totally free.*

BUT IF YOU WERE . . .

Finally I stopped resisting it and simply attended to the thoughts tumbling out.

Well, if I were totally free (which I'm not) even to consider that question, I would say that the decision to marry is an extremely serious one and should be based on a lot of things—mutual love, mutual understanding, knowing each other's strengths and weaknesses.

I love Pamela, but whether or not I love her enough to marry her is something I can't answer right now. Loving, being in love, and being in love enough to marry are three different degrees of love and commitment. There have been just too many things happening now for any major decision about Pamela to be given the attention it deserves.

Even if I were not a Jesuit and not a priest, I would still need time to get to know Pamela better before deciding whether to ask her if she would marry me.

I've been a Jesuit for over twenty-three years; I've known her for less than one. I just do not know her well enough to say, "Pamela, I'm leaving the Jesuits because of you."

Besides, Pamela would feel guilty if I left the Jesuits for her sake only.

She knows the turmoil of loving with a divided heart. She knows this would be destructive for both of us. She doesn't want that any more than I do.

That's it, then. I will spend the rest of the retreat addressing the same issues I was researching before Pamela came into my life. Can I live with the obedience the Society expects? Do I accept and desire the celibacy the Church requires of her priests? I will remain a Jesuit if it is the right and most loving thing I can do.

If it isn't, then time spent with Pamela will tell whether marrying her would be.

I felt a sense of freedom, both emotional and intellectual. Even though I still had to face the painful decision about whether to remain a Jesuit, it was reassuring to know that Pamela would not want me to leave the order if I really wanted to stay.

For the next four days I continued reading and praying about celibacy: its meaning, its origins. Some books, very much in line with what we had been taught in the seminary, praised celibacy as an exemplary virtue, modeled after Jesus himself, whose love for God and zeal for proclaiming God's kingdom were all consuming.

But there were other books I read, books never recommended or ever mentioned throughout my eleven years of seminary training, that presented a very different and very disturbing picture of the historical origins of celibacy. During our four years of theological and historical studies at Berkeley, we had read about many of the dark sides of the Church—the greedy, lustful, or power-corrupt popes; the Crusades; the Inquisition; the papacy's nurturing of the worldwide conquistador spirit of Spain and Portugal; the injustices and brutalities of the Reformation. But at no time during theologate or any other period of formation was there even the slightest hint that the celibacy laws themselves had dubious origins.

Thus it was all the more disturbing when, over the last few years, through personal reading and research, I had become aware of a radically different, and ethically suspect, foundation for the vows. In essence what I had been gleaning was that the vows originated not only from pure motives of imitation of Christ and total availability for the kingdom of God, but also from a philosophy that regarded human nature as evil and from an institutional dynamic that perceived in the vows a way for Church leaders to gain more control over the clergy. The monastic tradition, with its emphasis on learning, self-denial, and zeal for perfection became a standard for holiness. Many popes were themselves monks before being raised to the papal throne. The monastic vows of chastity and obedience were perceived as a norm that should apply to all priests, not just monks.

Most important, the vow of chastity assured that a priest's loyalty went exclusively to the Church, not to a wife and children. An unmarried priest was far easier to support, direct, and assign than one with wife and children. Furthermore, the vow of chastity precluded even the possibility of a priest having a son to whom he would entrust his benefice, his parish, and whatever income they supplied. The vow of poverty, even though professed by monks and not by secular priests, makes it far easier for the Pope and bishops to claim that all Church-related donations, income, and bequests belonged to the institution (meaning the bishop, the Pope) and not to the individual priest. The vow of obedience assured that only one person's will and voice (that of the bishop, the superior, the Pope) was the voice of Christ, and therefore absolute. All others in the monastery, the clergy, or the convent were bound to obey.

Thus what originally had been practices of virtue intended to unite the soul more fully to God became mandated disciplines whose purpose was to bind the soul more fully to church "authority." By legally mandating poverty, celibacy, and obedience, church authority grew wealthy and powerful.

Nowhere was this "dark side" of the vows more evident than in the beginnings of the laws of continence and celibacy.

Canon 33, which prohibited bishops, presbyters, and deacons from having sex with their wives or fathering children, initiated seventeen hundred years of strife between those popes who demanded that the clergy be celibate and those clergy who believed that priesthood and marriage were wholly compatible.

But why was the institutional Church so insistent on a celibate clergy? Because conjugal intercourse was considered tainted, stained, unworthy of the purity of Christ. "Faced with the purity of Christ's body, all sexual union is impure," said Saint Jerome. Pope Siricius argued that marital intercourse is contaminated by "carnal concupiscence" and that if the laity are willing sometimes to abstain for prayer, how much more should bishops and priests, who are always to be ready for ministry, be always continent.

Saint Augustine regarded marriage as a concession to human lust and looked upon marital intercourse as degrading and ignoble. Origen was so adverse to even the notion of intercourse that he castrated himself. Saint Ambrose looked upon marriage as a "galling burden." Saint Gregory of Nyssa termed marriage a sad tragedy, while Tatian regarded sexual intercourse as an invention of the devil. And these same "Fathers of the Church" proclaimed the holiness of virginity and the baseness of marital love.

To maintain the purity of the Eucharistic sacrifice, priests were ordered to abstain from the impure act of conjugal intercourse—and wives were expected to honor all the various papal decrees and laws demanding this.

By enacting laws forbidding intercourse to married clergy, the institutional Church bought into the age-old wiles of the Tempter that pitted man and woman against each other, against nature, and against God. The most sacred of all loving acts—creation itself—was condemned as defiling.

Several times prior to this retreat I had read about the distorted sexual attitudes of these "Fathers of the Church" and the many injustices married priests and their wives had suffered. This knowledge had sounded in me a kind of intellectual alarm. But during this retreat, as if the barriers of time and space had been lifted, I began to feel in my heart the cries of those wounded families, the injustices they had suffered, and the depraved attitudes of those who had believed they were doing a service to God by breaking up clerical marriages.

In her book *Married Priests and the Reforming Papacy*, Anne Barstow quotes Peter Damian, an eleventh-century papal legate, and one of the most zealous enforcers of the celibacy canons. He had this to say of married bishops:

> I have wanted to place locks on their sacred thighs. I have attempted to place the restraints of continence upon the genitals of the priesthood, upon those who have the high honor of touching the body and blood of Christ. . . . We extort from them, however, a meagre promise to observe the ruling, a promise postponed with trembling backslidings. (They do not do this secretly but publicly, everyone knowing the names of their concubines, even of their fathers-in-law!) Finally, when all doubt is removed, the bellies are swelling, the children running around.

But Damian reserved his most obstreperous tirades for the wives or concubines of priests:

> I speak to you, charmers of the clergy, appetizing flesh of the devil, that castaway from paradise, you poison of the minds, death of souls, venom of wine and of eating, companions of the very stuff of sin, the cause of our ruin. You, I say, I exhort you women of the ancient enemy, you bitches, sows, screech-owls, night-owls, she-wolves, blood-suckers, [who] cry "Give, give! without ceasing" (Proverbs 30.15–16). Come now, hear me, harlots, prostitutes, with your lascivious kisses, you wallowing places for fat pigs, couches for unclean spirits, demi-

goddesses, sirens, witches, devotees of Diana, if any portents, if any omens are found thus far, they should be judged sufficient to your name. For you are the victims of demons, destined to be cut off by eternal death. From you the devil is fattened by the abundance of your lust, is fed by your alluring feasts.

You vipers of madness, parading the ardor of your ungovernable lust, through your lovers you mutilate Christ, who is head of the clergy. . . . You snatch away the unhappy men from their ministry of the sacred altar, in which they were engaged, that you may strangle them in the slimy glue of your passion. . . .

Moreover just as Adam desired among all the fruits of paradise precisely that one which God had forbidden, thus you from the entire multitude of humankind have chosen only those who are utterly prohibited from any alliance with females . . . the ancient foe pants to invade the summit of the church's chastity through you. . . . You suck the blood of miserable, unwary men, so that you might inflate into their parts a lethal poison. They should kill you . . . for is there any hand with sacred chrism that you shake with fear to touch, or oil that you do not defile, or even pages of the gospels and epistles that you do not use familiarly (in an obscene way)?

So angry did this last passage make me that I slammed the book closed, cursed, and rushed out the door. For hours I wandered around trying to calm down. I felt betrayed. I felt my mind and heart had been deceived. The vow of celibacy had been presented to me as a preeminent, Christ-like virtue, but in fact the vow was symbiotically bound to error and filth.

Damian's misogyny, and the sexual antipathy of several popes and Church Fathers, were not confined to words and opinions. Their attitudes were given shape in laws, and these canons had been forced on married clergy with cruel and often brutal punishments. Priests and their wives had been fined, flogged, imprisoned, separated, divorced, and murdered.

When I thought of those priests' wives who had been turned

into slaves of the Church, I wept. I wept for them, for their sons who had been declared bastards, and for their husbands whose "mortal sin" was that they loved their wives and children. My soul was filled with grief over those church leaders who, in the name of sacramental purity, had destroyed families. And I wept for myself, because my ignorant and trusting assent had condoned the injustices of the celibacy laws.

For the first time in my life I felt more than disappointment and shame over the Church's failures. I felt outrage.

Part of me wanted just to walk away and never look back. But as a priest I had grown to love the Church and to look upon it not as an institution, but as people struggling to believe, to forgive, to love. These people I could not abandon.

Days later, when the tears stopped and the hard reality of truth lingered silently in my soul, I knew that I was now bound to speak what I knew—no matter what the cost.

But how could I, as a Jesuit, even begin to question the Vatican's decision to maintain the current priesthood policy? Ignatius had written, "For the Superior is to be obeyed not because he is prudent, or good, or qualified by any other gift of God, but because he holds the place and the authority of God, as Eternal Truth has said: 'He who hears you, hears Me; he who despises you despises Me.' "

Ignatius regarded obedience as the cornerstone of Jesuit life and felt that union with Christ's will and with the Pope were absolutely essential to combat Satan and his followers, who were assaulting the Church with heresy, disobedience, armed revolt, and schism.

But another Jesuit, John L. McKenzie, had written,

Imposition of one's will is a strange form of diakonia. Equally strange is the application of the line, 'He who hears you hears me,' to the command of obedience; in the context the line clearly refers to the proclamation of the gospel. . . .

The acts of authority cannot be considered the acts of God, for if authority commands something sinful, the subject is bound to disobey. . . .

The teaching office is not empowered to control either the world of learning or the world of morality.

These two conflicting interpretations of obedience reminded me again of the dilemma that had kept me from final vows. But how could I finally resolve this? I knew how the first and the second Vatican councils defined authority: that Christ gave Peter supreme authority over the other apostles and over His mission of salvation; that the Pope is the successor to Peter and the bishops are the successors to the apostles; and that the authority of the Pope in matters of faith and morals is infallible.

But these assertions, to have validity, had in some way to be founded in the life and teachings of Jesus. I searched the Scriptures and the early history of the Church, asking the following questions: Did Jesus, in selecting the apostles and commissioning them to proclaim the Gospel, intend that only the Twelve, and those appointed by them, would possess his authority? Did Jesus give Peter authority over all the other apostles? Did Jesus intend to establish a hierarchical, infallible authority?

The more carefully I probed these questions, the clearer it became to me that Jesus did not entrust an authority based on apostolic succession, primacy, and infallibility. The authority Jesus entrusted was His spirit of faith and love. Inerrant, irreformable definitions offend the humility required by faith—a radical open-ness to God who is both revelation and mystery. As to primacy and hierarchy, in the ministry of Jesus, who fed the hungry, clothed the naked, healed the sick, and gave sight to the blind, the only primacy was that of love.

With alarm I started to recognize the stark possibility that the entire model of authority now governing the Roman Catholic Church was an authority never intended by Christ.

The implications of this notion were staggering. If true, the Church would have to redefine its entire governing structure radi-cally. Even if it was only partially true, I now had a responsibility to research further and to communicate what I had learned con-cerning this vital issue affecting the entire Church.

No sooner had this awakening come than I begged God not to ask me to speak publicly about the wrongs the Church was committing under the guise of obedience and celibacy. Who was I to be casting stones? Pick someone irreproachable, who did not have such serious failures. To critique the vows and the priesthood in an honest and scholarly fashion would occasion severe enough reprisals, but to talk about these as a priest in love would provoke rancor, censure, and exclusion.

I pleaded with God to pick someone stronger, someone not so afraid of rejection and ridicule. Even as I uttered this prayer, I realized its motivation was self-protective and selfish. Once again I was trying to tell God how to act and what to ask. Typical. So much for Ignatius's Third Degree of Humility—so much for choosing the way of humiliations and rejection because this is the path Jesus chose.

It struck me that it might be very illuminating to find out first if the bishops themselves agreed with the papacy on the exclusion of marriage and women from the priesthood. It was already proven that the majority of priests and laity were not in agreement with the current policy, but what if the bishops also disagreed?

What if many of the bishops discerned that Christ's teachings and the pastoral needs of the faithful would be better served by a priesthood that included women and marriage? How could the faithful be expected to "assent with sincere mind and ready will" to Vatican policy if the bishops themselves disagreed? What would such a disagreement reveal about the nature of hierarchical authority? How could so many Catholics be so wrong about what was good for the Church? While still on retreat, I sketched out a four-question survey and cover letter that I would later send to the U.S. bishops to determine their attitudes on these issues.

On the last day of the retreat I was again filled with fear. Who was I to question Vatican policy or to challenge Ignatian obedience? Who was I to presume to question the hierarchical model of authority? Perhaps I was being excessively zealous, or had an exaggerated notion of my responsibility. I doubted that I had the courage, the strength, or the intelligence to enter into what might

ABOVE: Angeline Sweeney asks her son's first blessing as a priest. Terry was ordained by Bishop Juan Arzube at Saint Jerome's Church in Los Angeles, California, on June 15, 1973. (*Photo by Therese Sweeney*)

LEFT: Father Terry Sweeney leads the Prayers of the Faithful during Michael Sweeney's First Holy Communion Mass, celebrated at Saint Jerome's Church, May 16, 1982. (*Photo by Rosemarie Sweeney*)

ABOVE: After moving out of the Jesuit Community at Loyola Marymount University into his own apartment, Terry wonders whether any bishop in the United States will allow him to minister as a priest. Terry resigned from the Jesuits rather than follow Rome's directive to destroy his research on the hierarchy's attitudes on married clergy and women priests. (*Photo by Mark Sennet*)

RIGHT: Pamela in front of her parents' home in Beverly Hills before they moved to Mendocino. Pamela's parents allowed the house to be used in many films and television shows. It was Carol Lombard's home in *Gable and Lombard*, and Joan Crawford's home in *Mommie Dearest*. (*Photo by Ian Vaughan*)

ABOVE: In *Dead on Arrival*, Pamela costarred opposite Jack Palance, who taught her a great deal about combining instinct and imagination in creating a character. (*Photo courtesy of Cal Am Productions, Inc.*)

LEFT: Pamela Shoop is seen here with Alex Cord in a two-part episode of "Murder, She Wrote" in which she played a high-wire circus performer. Pamela not only had to learn how to walk a tight rope for the part, but also how to somersault from the net and fall into an airbag. (*Courtesy of Universal Pictures*)

Having just received the Distinguished Flying Cross for his heroic mission over Normandie on D-Day, Pamela's father, Major General Clarence A. Shoop (here a Colonel), is awarded the Distinguished Presidential Citation by Elliott Roosevelt at Mt. Farm (Berinsfield, England) in 1944. (*Photo courtesy of Raymond Korczyk*)

ABOVE: In May of 1979, Pat and Rosemarie Sweeney celebrate Michael's graduation from Rogers Park pre-school in Inglewood, California. With them is their dog Racha. (*Photo courtesy of Rosemarie Sweeney*)

BELOW: Pamela's brother, Dr. Stephen Shoop, offers a toast at Terry and Pamela's engagement dinner on Easter Sunday, 1987. Speaking of their commitment to their love, Steve said, "I've learned a lot from them about what the word 'sacrifice' means." (*Photo by Stephen Paley*)

ABOVE, LEFT: Pam and Terry after a rousing snowball fight at Ginger's ranch before Christmas. *(Photo by Stephen Shoop, M.D.)* RIGHT: A rare moment of tranquility during the tumultuous months between their engagement and their marriage. *(Photo by Mark Sennet)*

A family portrait—Pamela, Terry, and their black Labrador, Devon. Of Devon, Pam and Terry say, "She is more to us than just our dog; she is our friend." *(Photo by Mark Sennet)*

ABOVE: On the arm of her step-father, Dr. William Bergin, Pamela starts down the aisle thinking of all those women who were unable to marry the priests they loved. *(Photo by Mark Sennet)*

LEFT: Pamela's mother, Julie Bishop Bergin, dances with her new son-in-law at the wedding reception. Julie's care and attention to the details of the reception earned her praise from a close friend from Denmark, who remarked that it was like the grand old weddings in Europe. *(Photo by Mark Sennet)*

ABOVE: Father Terrance Sweeney and his bride married publicly in 1987. "I love God, I love the priesthood, and I love this woman. They are not incompatible. Love is not a sin; it is a grace." *(Photo by Mark Sennet)*

BELOW, LEFT: Just before their entrance into the ballroom for their wedding reception, Pamela and Terry take a private moment to gather their strength in a tender embrace. *(Photo by Mark Sennet)* RIGHT: Gregory Peck offers his congratulations to Terry and Pamela on their wedding. *(Photo by Mark Sennet)*

As husband and wife, Terry and Pamela descend the grand staircase into the Crystal Room of the Beverly Hills Hotel. *(Photo by Mark Sennet)*

all too easily prove to be a confrontation with the power structure of the Church.

Damian's insults against women rang again in my ears, and their injustice reminded me that silence would be cowardice.

Following Ignatius's advice on making an election, I decided to reflect on the reasons why I wanted to remain a Jesuit and the reasons why I did not want to remain a Jesuit. Under the reasons for remaining a Jesuit, five items were listed:

1. Ignatian vision of service—*Ad Majorem Dei Gloriam*
2. *Contemplatio ad Amorem*
3. Jesuit vision of faith and justice
4. Friends and companions in the Jesuit order
5. Apostolic effectiveness

While praying about these things I felt dedicated to the Jesuit vision of faith and justice and to the Ignatian ideal of striving always to do that which is most conducive to furthering the greater glory of God. But even while considering these positive reasons, spontaneous provisos would crop up, such as the exaggerated notion of papal loyalty Ignatian obedience encourages; my unhappiness over the dissolution of Jesuit Media Associates; and my recognition that Jesuit community, in practice, centered mostly around the cocktail hour.

The reasons I listed for not remaining a Jesuit were:

1. Jesuit obedience has become more papal-centered than Christ-centered and prompts me to fear that my will and thinking will be controlled or crushed.
2. Biased, myopic seminary formation regarding the vows has led me and is leading others to uninformed decisions regarding priestly life.
3. Requiring celibacy by law is wrong and therefore must be challenged. As a Jesuit I would be expected to support, not challenge the celibacy laws.
4. The prevailing notion of obedience and loyalty to

authority threatens individuality, freedom, and equality of expression.

I closed my notebook and walked out of my room and down the main road. The sprinklers in the center-divider garden were on. The sun and the spray of water carried by the breeze formed a huge rainbow right next to me. Over the years I had seen a few rainbows, but they had been in the clouds or over some distant stretch of land. Rainbows, to me, are exquisitely beautiful and mystical. At that moment during the retreat the rainbow from the sprinkler reminded me of the covenant God had made with Noah after the flood. It seemed to me that the Lord was asking me to be faithful to what I was learning about authority and love. Though I did not understand clearly what this faithfulness might entail, I asked for the grace and courage to live it.

As a kind of gesture to show my desire to be faithful to whatever the Lord might ask me to do, I walked through the sprinklers and the rainbow. As the water poured over me, and as I walked through colors that disappeared, it felt as if God was smiling in my heart.

I sensed that I would be dismissed from the Jesuits if I were to publish my thoughts on authority, mandatory celibacy, and women priests. I wondered whether I should let this happen or resign first. It seemed to me that as a Jesuit I would be forbidden to discuss these issues honestly. Dreading that probability, and worn out from the retreat, I tried to go to sleep early. The words on Pat's gravestone burned into my heart: "Explored life with courage, dignity, faith and love." Although my soul wanted to live like this, my mind felt buried in confusion and fear.

At three-ten A.M. I was awakened from sleep. Something very deep inside told me it was time to start writing a letter to the Provincial. It was not yet clear to me what I should write nor what thoughts or decision should be presented in the letter. I asked God how it was even possible to write such a letter. In the darkness and silence, I felt that all God wanted of me was that I listen to my heart and trust whatever might emerge. If I lived to do His will and to serve His people as lovingly as I could, He would show me the way.

18

PAMELA

Gazing about me at all the life-saving equipment in the interior of the ambulance, I wondered if this constituted an emergency. Terry had been very clear that while he was on his retreat, I was not to contact him unless it was a real emergency. I lay on my back, strapped to the gurney, my neck in a brace. On this, my first day out of the house after my surgery, my car had been broadsided by a car rented by a pair of Japanese tourists! The jolt had really scared me. When the ambulance attendants arrived, I immediately told them that I was recovering from abdominal surgery, and they very gingerly loaded me into the ambulance. The siren began to blare.

In the emergency room of Cedars-Sinai Hospital, I was examined and X-rayed for a couple of hours. Though every part of my body ached, they determined that I could be released. Cautious and unsteady, I made it home and crawled back into bed. Unsettling, yes. I sighed. Emergency, no.

The rest of the week passed uneventfully. I spent many hours lying in my apartment playing John Denver love songs over and over. I tried to imagine what Terry was doing. Was he distancing himself from me? Was he wearing the Super Bowl T-shirt I'd given him that he said he was taking with him so that I wouldn't feel insecure? All those books he had taken with him on the history of the Church, and only one little reminder of me!

Lying in bed with Devon at my feet, I began to worry. Days passed in the silence of prayer and the deep realization of the magnitude of Terry's decision. Decisions have always been difficult for me. Being a Gemini, I tend to weigh both sides of everything, and, seeing the value of both options, I frequently never make any decision at all! It's annoying. But the gravity of Terry's situation froze my mind and heart so that I could think of nothing else. The consequences would be devastating no matter which choice he made. If he chose to remain with the Jesuits, our love would become a memory. If he chose to leave the Jesuits, so many questions remained unanswered. Could he remain a priest? How would it affect his mother, his family, and all those who sought comfort from him? Would Terry have to leave the priesthood altogether in order for us to have a life together? Would others blame me and hold me responsible? Suddenly I became frightened by the enormous responsibility this could place upon my shoulders.

There is a lovely boardwalk along Santa Monica Boulevard that runs the length of Beverly Hills. Each day Devon and I would take a long walk among the flowers, she enjoying the activity, I lost in thought. Up until now I had believed that Terry's solitary life had left him unfulfilled in many ways. I had believed that I could enrich his life and fill those empty places in his heart. Terry had lived the life of sacrifice demanded of priests, and I had seen in him a preoccupation with the negative. His work so often revolved around helping people through their moments of tragedy and darkness. There were lighter times, of course, such as baptisms and weddings. But for the most part, people seem to turn to their priest in times of trouble. This selfless life was one to be proud of. And I was proud of Terry, but I couldn't help feeling that it left him with an imbalance in his own life. I remembered once having reminded him that God, in creating the world, had blessed mankind with so many riches. He had given us beauty and sweetness and harmony, the magnificence of nature, the joy of companionship. All were precious gifts to be cherished. Life was more than pain and suffering; it was also beauty and happiness, laughter and contentment. Just because Terry had chosen to be a priest and to help others with their problems, God hadn't intended him, I believed, to ignore all the rich blessings of His creation. I had never wanted to diminish Terry's responsibilities, but I did believe that if there were more balance in his own personal life, it would greatly enhance the quality of what he could give to others.

But now I began to worry about Terry in a different way. What if happiness with me was only temporary? Could our relationship fill a lifetime? Could it fill the void left by fellow priests and parishioners? If only we could get to know each other without the pressure of our unusual situation hanging over us. The last thing I wanted was for Terry to be unhappy. What was best for him? That was something only he could answer.

Saturday at last. I was almost afraid to pick up the phone when it rang.

"Hi! I'm back. How are you feeling?"

"Oh, I've had my ups and downs." I relayed a little of my accident. "How about you? How did it go?"

"I have a lot to tell you, but not right now. I started a letter to the Provincial last night and I want to finish it. I'll see you at church tomorrow, okay?"

"Okay."

I couldn't tell. I simply couldn't tell. Was Terry avoiding me? Was his letter to notify the Provincial that he was ready to take final vows and he didn't want to break the news to me over the phone? I would have to wait one more day.

When Sunday afternoon finally came, I still wasn't ready for the answer.

"Here, sit on the couch," Terry said. "I want you to read this."

He moved across the room and stood quietly by the door. I held the letter in my hands and read it through. But my heart was pumping blood through my body so fast that I just couldn't assimilate it. I read it again.

"Dear Jack: Greetings and Peace

"I am a sinner, but one aware of God's personal, redeeming love. Thus I am able to write to you informing you of my decision to leave the Jesuit order, and of my continuing hope to live and die as a priest."

A cold sweat broke out over my body as I read.

"Twenty-four years ago, while making a high school retreat here at Manresa, I decided to seek entrance into the Society. My principal motive at that time was that it seemed likely to me that being a Jesuit priest was the best way I could help people find happiness and God. . . ."

As I turned page after page of his letter, I read how his seminary training taught him that the best way to attain perfection was to become a celibate and obedient priest.

" . . . Good decisions are based on sound knowledge and goodwill—if the knowledge is incomplete, so are the decisions. If vital knowledge is lacking, the decisions, choices, vows are vitally lacking.

I say this because I am now convinced, after years of prayer and reflection, that vital information concerning the vows was not presented to me. The vital information I refer to here might all be found in this honest question of a good man: 'What good reasons might a person have for not taking vows?'

Strange as it may seem, in my twenty-three years as a Jesuit—except in very infrequent personal conversation—the vows have never been taught or presented from the perspective of that question. The vows have always been presented as the answer to the question: 'Lord, what must I do to be perfect?'

Stated more precisely, my entire formal education concerning the vows has not been objective.

I was not taught that the scriptural texts cited as the proofs and foundation for the vows are, in their interpretation and application, contested by many scholars.

I was not taught the multicentury struggle of the papacy and the hierarchy to impose continence and later celibacy on an unwilling married clergy.

I was not taught that obedience and chastity were imposed on the secular clergy as a means of gaining control over them and church property.

I was not taught that the chief motive for the earlier legislations imposing clerical continence was 'cultic purity.'

I was not taught that the wives of priests were called 'whores,' 'prostitutes,' and 'snares of the devil.'

I was not taught the implications for obedience of Pope Boniface's bull 'Unam Sanctam,' in which he claimed that the authority of emperors and kings came directly from the popes.

I was not taught that theologically and psychologically other states in life might be as perfect or more so than the vowed life of a religious.

Had I been taught these things, or similar reservations, during my novitiate formation, I would not have promised perpetual poverty, chastity, and obedience. Given my substantial reservations concerning the vows, it is evident that I cannot, in conscience, ask to be solemnly professed in the Society."

With a deep sigh I looked over at Terry, who was still standing by the door. Our eyes met for a long moment before I continued reading the letter.

"After considerable prayer, study, reflection, and dialogue, I have come to the conclusion that life in the Society, and the 'praxis' meaning of the vows (particularly obedience) as defined by the Pope no longer present to me personally the 'more perfect way' to help others find happiness and God.

The current climate of religious life in the Society no longer presents to me that 'perfect freedom of the sons of God' or that inner assurance of God's covenant, which should not be obscured or threatened in the name of obedience, by any pope or person in authority—'I will place my law within them, and write it upon their hearts; I will be their God and they shall be my people. No longer will they have need to teach their kinsmen how to know the Lord. All, from the least to the greatest, shall know me. . . .' "

When I had finished the nine-page letter a second time, I looked up at Terry and asked quietly, "Are you sure?"

"Yes, Pam, I am sure. You have no idea what I realized on my retreat, the things I read. I lay in my bed at night and cried for the priests and their wives whose marriages had been destroyed. If I had known that these laws were created by men and not God, I would never have taken my vow of celibacy in the first place. And in my opinion it was wrong of the Jesuits even to ask such a thing without first giving us adequate information."

Why was I crying? Terry was resigning from the Jesuit order. Perhaps there was a future for us ahead. I should be elated. Then why couldn't I speak? Suddenly the realization of what Terry was doing hit me, hit me hard. I felt responsible. What if he were making a mistake? What if he were merely infatuated with me and it didn't work out? What then? After he had closed all the doors behind him, where could he turn?

"No, Pam. It isn't because of you. Don't you see? Read the letter again. We have drifted so far away from what Christ intended for the Church, what Ignatius hoped for the Society. There are so many things happening now that are just plain wrong, and I must do something about them. I'm not sure right now exactly what, but I know God wants me to do something, say something. If I don't do what I believe in my heart is right, a part of me will die."

Terry's eyes were passionate and sincere. We held each other for a long time.

Over the next few weeks my heart grew lighter as I recognized in Terry a freedom of spirit I had not seen before. On long walks in Franklin Canyon he described more of what had finally started to come into focus for him during his retreat. He began to discuss with me his growing belief that the imposition of the law of celibacy was immoral.

"Immoral? Terry, you can't mean that! How could the Church be immoral?"

"Laws which violate God's law or human nature are unethical.

Church laws which separated and divorced married priests from their wives violated both. If a person freely and lovingly chooses celibacy, that's a beautiful decision, and that choice should be praised and protected, even by law if necessary. But laws that forbid priests to marry, or that forbid married priests to have children— these laws violate one of the most fundamental of all God-given rights: the right to marry and to found a family."

I could see that Terry was wrestling with a far bigger issue than just our love. "There's something I don't understand. The Church didn't actually force you to become a priest, and you knew before you were ordained that celibacy was required."

"Yes. I knew what the seminary taught me about celibacy, that it was a great virtue. But I didn't know until long after I had vowed celibacy that the very laws requiring celibacy of priests were born in error and injustice. These terrible facts had been obscured by over a thousand years of history, and by the Church's suppression and punishment of those who objected to the celibacy laws."

"The Church really did that?" I asked.

"Yes, unfortunately. But you're right to say the Church did not force me to become a priest. But the Church did say that the only way I could be ordained was by first promising never to marry. For all those seminarians who would not have chosen celibacy unless it were mandated, this is coercion. Suppose the Church were to decree today that all priests must marry—or that anyone who wanted to marry must first promise to become a priest. Imagine the outcry.

"Priesthood and marriage are not slaves of the Church. These are sacraments, and the Church has the privilege and the responsibility to safeguard them. The Church does not have the authority to pass laws forcing anyone to be celibate, or to marry, or to be a priest. Nor does the Church have the authority to subordinate Christ's priesthood to the man-made laws of celibacy. But that is exactly what the Church does in its laws requiring that all priests be celibate!"

"What will priests do when they find out that the celibacy laws are unethical?" I asked. "What about those who have spent their lives struggling to remain faithful to their vow? Won't they feel they've sacrificed for nothing?"

Terry's face grew very sad. "Some will feel betrayed. Some might use this knowledge to rationalize their affairs. Some will be grateful to know that the choice to marry or be celibate is totally theirs, and cannot be coerced by Church law. But until Church laws regarding celibacy are brought into harmony with Christ's teaching, the priesthood will suffer."

Terry became silent, as though the future of which he spoke weighed too heavily upon his heart.

Days passed, but Terry did not mail his letter. He said that he needed to spend more time in prayer and reflection. He discussed his intentions with his mother, a number of his close friends, and his spiritual adviser. And he listened—he listened to those he loved, and to the inner silence, waiting to know when the moment was right. Some of Terry's closest Jesuit friends felt that he was doing the right thing. They knew that he had been through a difficult struggle and were glad that he had made a decision. Privately, some of them agreed with his position. Although it would be difficult to lose Terry as a Jesuit, they understood that following his conscience would bring him peace.

His mother had different concerns. "You're going to find that the world out here is very different from what you think. Nobody's perfect. Not the Jesuits or anybody else. You're going to find that in real life things are a lot less perfect. As difficult as your problems are in the Church, out in the real world things are a lot worse." But whatever distress the idea of Terry's leaving the Jesuits may have caused her, his mother never told him not to resign. I truly admired her for that. She didn't ever try to impose her own will. She simply cautioned him to weigh both sides before making his decision.

And I, as devil's advocate, asked him constantly, "Are you sure? What if you're wrong? You've had a relationship with the Jesuits for twenty-three years. What if you lose those friendships? Is it my fault? Is it me? It can't be me. You mustn't let me be your decision. Your decision must be yours apart from love. Are you sure?"

"Pam, if you ask me that one more time, I won't mail the letter!"

After four weeks I began to think he would never mail it. Perhaps after returning home to familiar faces and daily routine, he had changed his mind. Maybe he felt comfortable again. Maybe he did not want to leave the Society after all.

November 10th was a Sunday. Terry greeted me with a smile after Mass.

"It's time," he said. "I'm going to mail the letter to the Provincial today. I've talked to everyone I need to, I've prayed about it, and I feel now the time is right. Would you like to come over to Loyola this afternoon? I'd like you to be there."

I followed Terry in my car across town. I was glad to be in my own car; I didn't feel like talking.

I sat poolside at Loyola University watching Terry's even strokes as he completed his laps easily and gracefully. The six-lane, twenty-five-yard pool was beautifully situated on the peaceful campus. He was used to rising at seven A.M. and swimming a mile before breakfast. Then he would walk, as he still does today, for about forty-five minutes in prayer. Terry is definitely a creature of habit. Punctuality and ritual had been cultivated during his seminary training, where the novices answered to thirty-six bells a day. (On recreation days the number of bells would be drastically reduced to twenty-eight!) With such order in his life, how would he ever adjust to me, I wondered? Terry hopped out of the pool. "I'll just be a minute."

Terry's home was a campus. Everything he could ask for or need was at his fingertips: the pool, the library where he spent long hours late into the night, the chapel, the wonderful meals, the students . . . and the Jesuits. The campus held many memories, but more than that, it held friendships. I knew Terry would miss Wednesday-evening Masses in the dorm and the students racing through the halls, knocking on his door at all hours, their whole lives ahead of them. I knew he would miss Sister Agnes Marie and Sister Katherine. He would miss table conversation over delicious dinners in the Jesuit Community Residence. Here he was surrounded by scholars, teachers, those whose minds thirsted for knowledge like his own.

And Mario. And Curtis. Terry had known Mario Prietto since they were both thirteen years old. Curtis Bryant was two years older, but all three of them had entered the seminary together. They'd gone through the Jesuit training together, and though now all three worked in different cities, they had remained friends for twenty-seven years. Terry would be saying good-bye, not only to the Jesuit life, but also to the special bond between the three of them.

Clouds were forming as we walked out to the huge cliff behind Terry's dorm room. The wind was picking up as we wandered across the bluff gazing at the Santa Monica coastline in the distance.

"This is where I walk most mornings."

"Are you sure you want to leave all this?"

"Of course I don't. But a view isn't everything, you know."

By evening it was raining.

"I'm ready," Terry said. "I'm ready to mail the letter. Will you come with me?"

"Are you sure?"

We drove to the post office and sat in silence for a number of minutes. It was cold in the car. Terry moved to open the door.

"Terry, wait. Let's read it again, okay? One more time?"

We held the letter between us and read.

" . . . As I conclude this letter to you, Jack, with tears, I know the Society has given me graces in abundance—deep bonds of friendship, intimate knowledge and love for Christ, a thirst for faith and justice. I can only hope my life as a Jesuit, at least in some small way, has brought more love to the Society, and to the world we serve. As a man, as a priest, I continue my life-long desire to help others find happiness and God . . ."

I was trembling, perhaps from the cold. Terry was calm. "I have to ask you this one more time. You're sure it's not because of me? You're really, really sure?"

"I'm positive, Pam."

Terry opened the car door and stepped into the rain. He ran quickly through the puddles, carefully holding the letter next to his heart beneath his jacket to protect it from getting wet. I could hear the iron creak as he pulled back the arm of the mailbox. I watched as he said a private, silent prayer . . . and dropped his past and his future into the slot.

19

TERRY

The jet touched down on the runway and the wind roared against the lowered flaps, finally slowing the plane to an even roll. The forty-eight-minute flight from L.A. had been a smooth one, but inside, my stomach was churning. I was about to meet with the Provincial in order to formalize my resignation.

He had phoned two weeks earlier. "Terry, this is Jack Clark. I just got your letter. I'm stunned. We need to talk." The time since the retreat had proven very stressful. I had finally accepted, as a most unwelcome reality, that the Pope's and the Provincial's concept of obedience was irreconcilably different from mine.

As passengers disembarked the plane and moved into the terminal, I wondered again if I had been wrong about the Jesuits. Maybe the Provincial was right to be "stunned" by my reasons for wanting to resign. Perhaps I was being hypersensitive about this whole matter of authority and obedience. Had I submitted my resignation based on exaggerated and inaccurate perceptions? Questions had been gnawing at me with such intensity that I had lost fifteen pounds since the retreat, and my stomach was in so much turmoil that I'd gone to a doctor to see if I had an ulcer.

Passing through the tall iron gates leading up the long road to the Provincial's residence, I remembered a warning the Master of Novices had given our class twenty-three years earlier: that if we ever walked out those gates without permission, we would be dismissed from the Society. Six inches—the difference between being in or out—a Jesuit or an ex-Jesuit. The iron gates were a symbol of iron obedience. But the obedience demanded of me was not to God, but to man—an iron gate with hinges of clay.

The driveway wound past a massive oak tree at least three centuries old. Standing in front of the tree, encased in wood and glass, was a dramatic wood carving of Jesus crucified. I realized that this might well be the last time I would see that statue, which expressed such passion and helplessness.

At precisely two-thirty the Provincial, a tall, soft-spoken man, welcomed me graciously into his office.

"Hello, friend. Good to see you."

"You, too, Jack."

He motioned me to a corner in his office that had a coffee table and two chairs. On the coffee table was a Bible. The Provincial picked it up.

"Mind if I start with a prayer?"

"Please."

He read devoutly and softly a short passage from Saint Paul, then closed the book.

"I appreciate your coming up here. I've given your letter a great deal of thought, and I've sought the advice of some people here. You raise a lot of objections to your early training in the Society. However, there have been many changes in the Church and in the Society since then. Vatican II has changed many things. Sometimes, when the change is significant, even our way of thinking is altered. We have to be careful about judging the past in terms of present values. Before Vatican II, the Society put a lot of emphasis on ascetical spirituality. Now we don't emphasize that as much."

"Please don't misunderstand me, Jack. I'm glad to have experienced both pre— and post—Vatican II formation. It's enabled me to better understand the viewpoints of those who resist the changes and are threatened by them. What I'm objecting to is knowing that there are serious disorders threatening the priesthood and the

Church and being forbidden to discuss them. The most important point of my letter is something we have discussed several times: the meaning of loyalty and obedience. In my understanding our primary responsibility as Jesuits and as Christians is to be loyal to God and the truth; our secondary responsibility is to be loyal and obedient to the Pope and to superiors. If ever there is a conflict between God and the truth and what the Pope or Jesuit superiors are saying, our responsibility is to God and the truth."

The Provincial listened without comment, so I continued.

"Something does not become true merely because someone in authority utters it. If a bishop says the Vietnam war is a 'just war,' it does not become a 'just war' because he decrees that it is. And if I feel in my heart it is unjust, I am obliged to speak out. Or if the Vatican says women can't be ordained because it would be hard to see in a woman at the altar the image of Christ—and I think this is scripturally, psychologically, and theologically wrong—my vow of obedience obligates me to challenge that Vatican declaration."

"The Society's obedience is to see in the voice of the Pope or the Superior the voice of Christ," Jack asserted.

"But if the Pope says all forms of contraception are immoral, and he says this after his own pontifical commission has concluded that some forms of contraception would be morally acceptable, then we have a problem. A huge problem."

"The Church is a human institution," Jack said, "but one divinely guided. The Pope has access to information that a lot of us don't."

I tried to explain my dilemma with a different example. "You know that much of my work is in mass communications. I know the importance of a statement going out over world press. If the Vatican issues a statement declaring that women will not be ordained because 'there were no women among the Twelve,' and because 'Jesus was and remains a man,' and this statement goes out all over the world as representing the Catholic position while those who take issue with this statement are only allowed to express their opinions in scholarly journals that a few thousand people might read—where is the justice here? Hundreds of millions of people read that the Catholic Church won't ordain women because they are not made in the image of Christ, while those who disagree with this are told either to shut up or to express our opinions through journals that only other scholars read."

The Provincial shifted uncomfortably in his chair. "You're very angry, Terry, so is your letter. It would be important for you to seek help."

"My anger is not so much over the past, it's because the current problems indicate that certain mistakes are being repeated. Like the silencing of the Berkeley Jesuits when they wrote a letter protesting the Vatican Declaration excluding women from the priesthood."

"They weren't silenced," Jack replied emphatically.

"They were reprimanded for expressing their opinion through the *Los Angeles Times,* and they were told that this was not the proper forum for voicing their disagreement—that, at best, they could do it through scholarly journals. That may not be silencing in your view, but in mine it shows a massive imbalance when the Pope or the Vatican can express its viewpoint, whether right or wrong, over world press, and theologians, scholars, and priests who disagree are forbidden to do the same."

Jack's normally quiet manner had disappeared. What he was hearing obviously disturbed him. "There would be nothing but confusion in the Church if everyone went off expressing his own opinion—"

"Granted," I said, "but the solution is not to say that the only ones entitled to express an opinion publicly are Church 'authorities.' "

This was beginning to sound like instant replays of arguments we'd had before—opposite points of view, raised voices, totally different understandings of obedience. Still, I wanted him to understand why I was resigning.

"In research I've been doing I've learned that the two most frequent causes of U.S. priests resigning have been conflict with authority and difficulties with celibacy. The anger you sense in my letter comes from my feeling of being in a trap: The Church and the priesthood are plunging headlong into a crisis, and I don't even have the freedom to say so. There's no religious freedom of speech.

And you and other superiors define loyalty and obedience as repeating the mind of the Pope. I really feel our primary loyalty is to God and the truth."

"The Church is an institution. Order in any institution is basic. The deeper issue is whether you, Terry, see any value in another's will as representing Christ's."

"The deeper issue is the real meaning of loyalty and obedience."

Jack looked at me for a long moment. "The Church and the Jesuits say conscience is first."

"But then they turn around and tell you, when your conscience disagrees with their teaching, that your conscience is wrong and improperly formed!"

The Provincial's face turned red.

After a long pause he said quietly, "In religious life we try to live according to the teachings of Christ, and His words, 'He who loses his life shall find it.' "

"Yes, losing your life in doing God's will—not doing the will of some man who has preempted God's will! These things we're arguing about, Jack, are not simply theoretical, armchair abstractions. I feel them very deeply—they're very real. And I'll be very specific."

I reached down into my briefcase, pulled out the cover letter and Survey on Priestly Ministers that I had drawn up, and handed them to him.

"I'm doing research on authority and celibacy. Please read this."

The cover letter described priestly ministry as a vital extension of the mission Jesus had entrusted to his disciples. The letter detailed the massive departures from the priesthood and the huge decline in seminary enrollments. The four-question survey asked the bishops whether, "in light of the mission of the Church and the pastoral needs of the faithful," they would approve or not approve of: optional celibacy for priests; inviting married and resigned clergy to return to active ministry; ordaining women to the deaconate; ordaining women to the priesthood.

Father Clark read the two pages carefully, then handed them back to me. "Okay, I probably would have changed some of the wording."

I wasn't sure what he meant. "The conclusions of this research may suggest taking issue with current Church policy. These questions are very sensitive; some bishops will object to them. But as you can see, the shortage of priests has reached crisis proportions. Those four questions in the survey present some of the most frequently proposed solutions. I need to know from you: Am I being loyal and obedient in pursuing this research, or am I being disloyal and disobedient?"

"Fine, Terry. Go ahead. But I would expect any writing you would do in these areas to be submitted to the ordinary process of review in the Society."

Jack's approval dumbfounded me. "But, Jack, you told me that speaking out publicly on issues in a way that is at variance with the Vatican viewpoint is not being loyal. You said that during our meeting in Phoenix, and again at Loyola."

The Provincial replied, "The Society has always been on the cutting edge. Sometimes Jesuits say things the Pope and others don't like, and the Jesuit superiors are accountable. But we are not a Society that simply repeats what the Pope says. He expects us to challenge him."

"Now I'm really confused, Jack. I understood you to say that if a Jesuit disagrees with a papal or Vatican statement, he could express his disagreement, if at all, only through scholarly journals."

Clark looked at me and said calmly, "You have misunderstood my meaning and the Society's meaning of obedience. Rarely have Jesuits been ordered, under holy obedience, to do things."

I was finding it hard to assimilate what seemed to be a total turnabout in the Provincial's attitude. Had I somehow misinterpreted all that he had said? Had I wrongly judged his and the Society's understanding of obedience? I had to make sure I was hearing him correctly. "Then, if this research survey leads to it, I can take issue with the Pope on matters of celibacy and the priesthood?"

Clark replied, "Yes, but in accord with our normal process of review. Most of the Society's 'censorship,' if you want to use that word, is to improve, not to stop the writings."

His words struck me like a bolt of lightning, filling me with both confusion and elation—confusion because either he was totally contradicting himself or I had radically misunderstood him, even to the point of wanting to leave the Jesuits. Elation because I had so hoped the obedience of the Society was not blind, but wholly guided by the Spirit and by truth. This was a different picture altogether.

"If loyalty and obedience in the Society can accommodate speaking out publicly on issues, and if our primary loyalty is in fact to God and the truth, then this is an obedience I can live by."

Clark appeared to relax when I said this. His tone became cordial once again. "When you came in here, Terry, I thought maybe this meeting would end in your signing a few papers and starting the process of resignation from the Society. I am very pleased with our conversation. I think we should reflect on what was said here today and that there should be more thought and prayer before making a final decision about leaving the Jesuits."

"I agree."

On the return flight to L.A. I was totally perplexed. Could I have been so wrong in my understanding of the way the Provincial and others interpret obedience? Was my intuition all these years wrong? Could I really speak out freely and publicly the truth as I see it? Are God's will and the truth really the primary determinant of obedience, even for the Vatican and Jesuit superiors?

I felt really shaken—about my judgment, about my assessment of blind obedience, about deciding to abandon my vocation for fundamental interpretations of authority that, according to the Provincial, I had misunderstood.

How could I possibly explain all this to Pamela?

20

PAMELA

Rush-hour traffic in L.A. is not a good thing. Terry's flight would be arriving any minute, and I didn't want to be late. The Century Boulevard exit was only a mile away, but in the bumper-to-bumper traffic it would seem like forever.

The last few weeks had taken a toll on Terry. He had lost a lot of weight, he was pale, and there were deep hollows under his eyes. He had reached a major turning point in his life. In signing his release papers from the Jesuit order, he was closing a door on twenty-four years. When he had boarded the plane this morning, he had been apprehensive, yet confident. He was sure he was doing what was right. It would all be over in a matter of hours.

The day had gone very fast for me. It seemed as though I had been sitting in morning traffic just seconds before. But tonight I felt lighthearted as I pulled onto the off-ramp.

The moment I saw him come through the terminal doors, I knew something was wrong. There was a shyness in his smile, his greeting. He embraced me with hesitation.

"How was it? Is everything all right?"

"Let's get something to eat—I haven't eaten all day. I'll tell you all about it."

Something was definitely wrong. I could tell it had been a very difficult day. We drove to a coffee shop called Papayas, where Terry had had breakfast with his mom a few days before. He ordered a huge chocolate sundae. Sitting across from me, he started at the beginning, telling me almost word for word what had taken place.

"And Pam, the Provincial totally surprised me. I showed him my survey and asked if I was being obedient in pursuing this research, even if its conclusions might contradict the Pope's stance on certain issues. He said that I could pursue the research, that the Jesuits have always been on the cutting edge, and that the Pope expects us to challenge him. Isn't that great?"

I stared at him in disbelief. Suddenly the neon lights of the restaurant made me feel as if I were on display. I felt dizzy and sick. I could barely force the words from my mouth.

"You didn't sign the papers, did you?"

"No."

Silence.

"He said that I'd misunderstood him and the Jesuits' concept of obedience. I can have the freedom to think and speak out about the crisis facing the priesthood. Now that I have this freedom, it's a different story."

I felt as though a vise were squeezing the breath from my lungs.

"Terry, don't you see? He's not telling you the truth! He's already overruled you before. He's the one who shut down JMA. He's told you before that you can't contradict the Vatican. Now he's telling you that you can? How can you believe that?"

Terry was silent. He looked at me. Was it pity I saw in his eyes? He knew that he was hurting me . . . he had to know. I had said good-bye to him at the airport believing that he was going off to sign his preliminary resignation papers. I'd believed that it would be the first step on the road to our future together. He'd debated and prayed and researched. He had been convinced that he was right. And in just a few short hours he'd reversed a decision that had taken him eight years to make.

And I had believed in Terry's decision, not only because I loved him, but for the thousands of little details he had so meticulously and conscientiously reasoned out. How was it possible that the same man who had overridden him before had, somehow, convinced Terry that his reasoning had been flawed? That he'd made a mistake? That he shouldn't sign the resignation papers? I felt ill.

"How can you sit there eating a chocolate ice-cream sundae and tell me that my life is over?"

He looked ashamed.

"Pam . . . I've got to find out if it's true. If I've been wrong, it changes everything. I have to know for sure."

He said it so quietly. His hands began to shake. He was nervous and sorry—and I was angry. Angry and in tremendous pain.

"Pam, can we see you on your mark, please? Just a little to the left. Okay, let's see your look to Kate."

Kate Jackson and Bruce Boxleitner stood opposite me. It was the day before Thanksgiving, and the cast and crew of "Scarecrow and Mrs. King" were eager to get off the set and go home. The last three days of shooting had been terribly difficult. A set can be a haven at times. While you are on a show, it is easy to develop a real closeness with people, since you are together sixteen hours a day. For me it's usually my makeup man or hairdresser to whom troubles just seem to pour forth over coffee at six A.M. in the makeup trailer. This time it was the poor makeup man who held my confidence. He knew that I was easily upset, though I didn't tell him why. Frequently between shots I would be unable to keep my eyes from welling up with tears, and he was constantly making efforts to keep my mascara from smudging. Between scenes I would run to the nearest phone booth and call Terry. There was only time enough for snatches of conversation, and by the time I got home at night and learned my lines for the next day, there wasn't time for any in-depth discussion. We knew it would have to wait for the weekend, and the frustration was mounting.

"Ready, Pam?"

"Yep."

"Okay . . . quiet, please . . . we're rolling . . . speed . . . and action, Pam."

The dialogue felt comfortable, and even though it was my close-up, I found myself amused at Kate and Bruce. The scene tickled me.

"Cut. Okay, gang, that's a wrap. Have a good holiday. We'll see you back here Monday."

I hurried to my trailer and changed.

Thanksgiving had always been one of my favorite days, and this year I'd begun counting my blessings early. There had seemed so much to be grateful for. I had found a wonderful man. I was in love with him, and he was in love with me. And against an impossible situation, God was working a miracle so that the possibility of a future lay ahead. Terry's retreat, the ensuing weeks of reflection, the letter to the Provincial—all had indicated that the love in my heart would be blessed with fulfillment, that the quiet voice within me had not been wrong. My faith had been very strong.

But as I sat in my trailer on this night before Thanksgiving, grief overtook me. With each dab of cotton a layer of makeup was wiped away, until finally I stared at my naked face in the mirror. I pulled my hair into a ponytail on top of my head and looked at what I'd become. Where was my faith now? It had only been three days since Terry's return from his visit with the Provincial. Could faith be destroyed so quickly? What had become of that willing journey down God's path? Was my faith as easily washed away as my makeup, leaving a cold, embittered woman in its place? Outside it was beginning to rain. I was thankful for that.

The next morning I awoke heartsick. All I wanted to do was stay in bed. But it was Thanksgiving: a day to be grateful, to share with family, to rejoice. Terry and I were supposed to go to his mother's in the afternoon for a family turkey dinner. I didn't feel I could face anyone. Pain, disappointment, fear all came out in tears. How could this be happening to me? I'd believed, I'd trusted, I'd followed God's lead. And now it felt as though someone were playing a cruel joke on me. I began to doubt my heart, my instincts, my belief in God.

It was a difficult day. Sitting in the living room of Terry's mother's house, I felt like an intruder. Suddenly I did not belong there with them in the harmony and warmth of their family. I was an outsider once again.

The four-day holiday was spent in agony while the rain poured down outside and Terry and I fought to understand one another. How could we be so far apart?

"Pam, I told you a long time ago that my research into authority and the priesthood had started years before I met you and that whether there was any future with us or not, I had to go forward with it. The priesthood is in crisis, and I feel God is asking me to speak out about why. I also told you that if I were free to do this as a Jesuit, I would stay a Jesuit."

"But you know you're not free. You realized that clearly during your retreat."

"The Provincial says I am. If not, then time will tell—but I have to know."

"By then it will be too late for us! I can see you waiting for years, believing this man, only to find that you were right all along. By then what will have become of us?"

I felt as though I were fighting for my life.

"Pam, I don't understand. Why did you ask me over and over again, 'Are you sure?' Why did you do that? You said you wanted me to be completely sure and comfortable with my decision; you said you didn't want it to have anything to do with you. Why are you changing now?"

"Terry, I do want you to be sure. And if I believed that what you were being told was true, then I would tell you to pursue it. If only I believed the Provincial—but I don't. He's contradicted himself so many times. And I think he would have said anything to get you to stay."

"You think he was lying to me?"

"Not consciously. Maybe he wants to agree with you. He probably doesn't think it will ever actually get to the point where he will have to silence you. But he just keeps contradicting himself! Oh, Terry, look, please, look at what he has done, not what he says.

"Terry, people say anything at a given moment to accomplish a goal. Words mean so little sometimes. Please don't listen to his words, look at his actions."

———

But Terry couldn't believe that the Provincial, his superior, would mislead him. And maybe I was being too severe. Perhaps the Provincial was a loving individual with a good heart and good intentions who didn't know how to cope with a situation such as this. But whatever the truth was, in the end the result would be the same. I couldn't seem to make Terry see what I could see, and what I did say to him sounded critical rather than supportive.

"Pam, I have to find out for sure. I've been a Jesuit for almost twenty-four years. I can't close that door if there's any measure of doubt. I can't walk away from more than half my life on a suspicion that something might be true. I have to know for sure. I have to know."

"That could take years! Years from now you could be sitting right where you are, saying that you were right in the first place. Then what?"

I was frantic. The pain of losing Terry was overwhelming to me. Although I'd faced it many times in my mind, the reality was practically unbearable. Bewildered and disillusioned, I buried my face in the pillows at night and sobbed. My dreams were crumbling at my feet. I tried to imagine myself going on with my life— moving back to New York with Devon as I'd told myself I had the strength to do, never seeing or speaking to Terry again. I longed to become cold, callous, and hard, to protect myself from the anguish that seemed would never pass.

On the last afternoon of Thanksgiving weekend, as Terry sat on my couch with the rain in the windows, when reasoning seemed impossible and we were reduced to simply repeating ourselves over and over again, when mental and physical fatigue were at their limits, the worst of me came out. For this I am profoundly sorry.

"I can't believe in God anymore. If this doesn't work out, how can I ever trust in anything ever again? I've never believed in anything as much as I've believed in us, and now I feel betrayed. My instincts, my heart, my faith—it has all come to nothing, hasn't it?

Terry looked at me in terror.

"What do you mean, you can't believe in God anymore?"

"Terry, I believed in our love, that it came from God. I believed that with all my heart. I was willing to give up everything because I believed so strongly that this is what God wanted of me. If I was wrong, what can I believe in again? How can I trust myself? How can I trust what God is telling me?"

"But, Pam, just because we love each other doesn't mean the whole world revolves around us. There are some things more important than our love."

"Yes, but to lose you and our love over them . . . If I thought this would make you happy, then that is what I would wish for you. And if I thought this decision was based on sound information, I would welcome your choice and know that God is behind it. But I don't believe that. And I feel betrayed and terribly naive. How could I have been so wrong? How could God ask me to go through all this only to lose you? I'm sorry, Terry, I thought I would be stronger. When I said that I wanted you to be happy, please know I meant that. I think I could handle this better if I believed that what the Provincial was telling you was true. If I really believed that you could have the life of intellectual freedom you desire in the Jesuit Community, I could accept it. But I don't. I just don't believe it. And I'm afraid of the cost of finding out the truth."

After four days of talk and tears, I knew it was hopeless. Terry had chosen. The Jesuit order had won.

21

TERRY

It was Friday, December 13th. The Thanksgiving-weekend argument with Pamela had left such bad feelings that I wondered why she hadn't returned to New York after she finished shooting her TV show. Maybe because Christmas was coming up and she wanted to be with her family. I was sitting at my desk tabulating the bishops' responses to my questionnaire when the phone rang.

"Hello, Terry. Jack Clark . . ." His voice sounded upset.

"Hi, Jack."

He mumbled something to the effect that he knew what he was about to tell me was going to be difficult. Instinctively I reached for some paper in order to jot down as much as I could of what he was about to say.

"Your research is damaging to the Society of Jesus at this time. I am telling you to cease and desist all work on your survey and destroy the material you have gathered thus far."

"What?" I asked incredulously.

"You are to cease and desist all work on the survey and destroy the material you have gathered thus far."

"Why?"

"Archbishop Mahony is objecting to it, the apostolic delegate, some others," he replied.

"But I told you during our last meeting that the questions were very sensitive and that some bishops would object to them. And I specifically asked you if I was being loyal and obedient in pursuing this research, even if it might result in taking issue with current policy."

There was a long silence over the phone. It seemed as though the Provincial was trying to decide how much to reveal. "I'll be honest with you, Terry—this comes from the General. And he has asked that you 'Cease the investigation and that you destroy the material you have gathered thus far.' "

His words burned in my ears. My worst fears regarding obedience were now confirmed. I should have listened to them, and to Pamela.

Trying to think clearly, I argued, "But over a hundred bishops have already responded to my survey. You're asking me to destroy the written opinions of over a hundred members of the hierarchy. That's an extremely serious matter."

"In my best judgment, for you to continue your research would bring great harm to the Society of Jesus, and to the Society of Jesus in California. So, I'm going to ask you to forgo this."

I tried to say something, but my mind couldn't formulate the words. Clark broke the silence. "I know this has vocational implications for you, Terry. . . ."

"But what about the bishops who have responded?"

"I'm telling you, Terry, that your research will bring damage to the Society and that the General has asked, 'in light of the good of the whole Society to abandon the project.' "

"Why will it bring harm to the Society?"

"I can't say why or how. I have this on extrinsic evidence, not on intrinsic evidence. I talked with the Assistant, Joe Whelan, not with the General directly."

"You're asking me to do something extremely serious. It's one thing to ask me to destroy something I alone had written; it's another to ask me to destroy responses from over one hundred bishops on issues vitally affecting the Church. I need time to pray about this."

"Okay, Terry, we'll talk again. Let's say Wednesday—how's ten o'clock?"

"That's fine."

After hanging up the phone I sat at my desk motionless for several minutes. A shrill, high-pitched sound reverberated inside my head—the same sound I had heard when I got swept up into a ten-foot surf at Carpinteria Beach and almost drowned. Then, the ringing had been part of an adrenaline panic as my body, which had been twisted like a pretzel by a powerful wave, was straining to swim toward the surface, but I didn't know where the surface was. Now, the shrill ringing was caused by a different kind of threat— the realization that finally, after more than eight years of fearing and dreading the possibility, a superior, claiming to represent the voice of Christ, the voice of God, was telling me to do something I felt was wrong.

If I suppressed the survey, this would be an offense not only against those bishops who had responded, but also against intellectual freedom. What further disturbed me was that this command was initiated not by Jack Clark, the Provincial of the California Jesuits, but by Peter Hans-Kolvenbach, the Superior General of the Jesuit order, the largest and most influential order in the Catholic Church—and that others in Rome, even more powerful than the General, wanted the attitudes of the American bishops and the cardinals worldwide suppressed.

When the Provincial phoned on Wednesday morning, his voice was resolute.

"Terry, I'll tell you why it does harm to the Society. Because, one, it is now launched in the name of the Society when you put it on the stationery of the Jesuit Community, Loyola Marymount University. Two, as the Archbishop and others have told you, this is just a bad theological survey. Third, it's harmful to the Society because a copy of this did go to Cardinal Ratzinger, which you sent to him, and he has objected to it. And Father General, in looking at the situation over in Rome with regard to the Vatican, has judged that it's harmful in his broader view of the Society. I don't think he should be asked to go into great detail with you on that. That's his judgment. And the fact is the obedience of the Society asks you to abide by the judgment of a superior."

There was a long silence. I was waiting to hear the Provincial state his real reason for wanting the research destroyed. All that he had just said seemed to me to be a kind of prelude to whatever his real reason might be. He broke the silence: "These are our reasons. Now you have to judge, I think, whether or not you can do this."

I was astounded. When I had shown him the survey and cover letter twenty-three days earlier, it had been written on Jesuit Community stationery. He had not complained then that the research was being done on Jesuit Community stationery, nor had he said the slightest word that might indicate that he considered it an unprofessional study.

In response, I told the Provincial that I would not use the stationery any more in relation to the research, that I was willing to submit the research to any sociologist of his choice, and that if it was considered invalid, I would not use it. Also I mentioned that I was puzzled why the Archbishop and others thought it invalid when in fact, each of the four questions in my survey had been asked before by highly reputable social scientists and were considered valid.

"Terry, you are asking for the reasons why you're being asked to do this. I gave them to you."

"But, Jack, three weeks ago, when I showed you the letter and survey, you told me that you were not going to stop me from writing and researching this. Those were words from your mouth."

"I said that at that time, now I have changed. I didn't promise my future action. I just said at the time that I was not interfering. I did not tell you what I was going to do indefinitely into the future. Not because I planned to double-cross you, Terry, but because I didn't know the future."

"In fact, not only did you not interfere, you said, 'Look, Terry, all I'm asking you to do is to submit your writing and research to the normal process of review in the Society.'"

"I didn't promise you a future action," Jack said loudly. "I didn't promise you I wouldn't do this. I had no idea you were sending this to people around the world, and, well, that's my fault. I really wonder why you sent it to Ratzinger. I really do. If subconsciously down there somewhere you didn't want to bring about this kind of thing. Sending this to Ratzinger was an extraordinarily provocative kind of action taken on your part, and you're getting a response from that."

In fact, the sampling base for the cardinals to be surveyed were those listed in *The Official Catholic Directory*. Cardinal Ratzinger was one of the cardinals in that sampling base. Was I supposed to exclude his name because his opinion might differ from that of other cardinals?

"I see right now that people bigger than I am have made a judgment," the Provincial said. "And I can certainly agree with their reasoning. I thought it was going to be handled prudentially in a little different way, that is, by you submitting the results to censorship before publication."

"Right—" I said, and was about to add that the survey results were not yet finalized, no conclusions had been formed, and not one word had been written. But Father Clark wasn't finished making his point: "They're suggesting that there's another way to do it."

"They're suggesting to destroy it! I mean, this sounds like something out of Watergate or the Inquisition!"

"I don't think it does," Clark said. "I'm telling you the General has asked for the good of the Society that you cease this survey."

"I think that is a very important request, and I certainly have enormous respect for the General and for you, Jack. All I'm saying is I would like to know why there would be harm to the Society."

"Okay. All right, Terry, what you're saying is, basically, you don't accept the reasons."

"Well, I have to say, Jack, that I in no way want to harm the Society of Jesus or the Church. But with something as serious as this, I think I am entitled to a dialogue with the people—not you, because you changed your mind in three weeks—the people who are really asking me to stop."

"I am asking you to stop. The dialogue should be with me."

"Then I'll repeat what I said earlier. I am more than willing to submit this to any sociologist of your choice. If that person says this is an invalid study, I will throw it out. That to me is very reasonable."

"Terry, I'm not asking you to submit it to somebody for validation. I'm asking you to cease this project. That's what my order is as a Jesuit superior."

"But do you understand why it's important for me to know that my obedience in a matter as serious as this is not part of some power play?"

"No, I don't understand."

"If someone such as Cardinal Ratzinger is complaining, he represents a theological point of view that a lot of people in the Church take issue with. So, if Cardinal Ratzinger is saying, 'I don't like this survey,' and the General is saying, 'We don't want Cardinal Ratzinger against us'—and that's the reason for the 'harm' to the Society—that, to me, is a use of authority and power without reference to the truth. If more than one hundred bishops take the time to express their opinions on this subject, and only a few are vociferously against it, that's the human race."

"Well, I'm not able to assure you how that decision was arrived at by another man. My personal knowledge of the General leads me to believe that this is not just a power play. I think he would find that very offensive, just as if you told me that what I was doing was a power play, I would find that offensive. That is not in my gambit of thinking about this issue. Obviously it is in yours."

"Well, when over a hundred-plus bishops reply without complaint, I question what's going on. How can I honor what they have done by ignoring it or putting it aside?"

"You can write them a letter, say your religious superior asked you to put this aside and not to pursue it."

"And what if some of them ask me why my superior ordered me to abandon it? I wouldn't have the slightest idea how to respond." I took a deep breath, asked the dreaded question. "What will happen if I refuse to give up work on this survey?"

The Provincial's answer was slow, deliberate. It seemed that he was speaking with great difficulty: "I would ask you, having decided to put your own judgment as the criterion for your work and putting it above the judgment of myself, who says this is harmful to the Society, I would then suggest you ought to think about leaving the Society."

His words burned into my soul, bringing with them an overwhelming sense of dread and a deep, immeasurable sadness.

On December 21st the Provincial was visiting at Blessed Sacrament Church in Hollywood. I drove across town to meet with him face-to-face. He repeated his directive and asked if I was going to obey.

Each time I had asked myself that same question, I realized that if I obeyed, I would be offending the bishops, suppressing information vital to the future of the priesthood, and going against my conscience. All this in order to ensure that I could continue ministering as a Jesuit and a priest. But I knew in my heart that I would be a hypocrite if I suppressed the research just to save my own vocation. Something inside the very center of my soul, something related to identity and integrity, would die.

"It would be wrong for me to follow the order you are giving me," I said. "To do so would be to dishonor the virtue of obedience."

It was January 18, 1986, and I was packing up the last items in my dorm room. In a few minutes two student workers from campus would be arriving with a truck to help me move across town to a $375-a-month bachelor apartment, which Pamela had found for me very close to where she lived. It was small, even compared with my dorm room, but it was on a quiet street, and right outside the front window was a garden with a hedge and an infant birch tree.

I lifted the box containing the survey responses. An entire vocation in exchange for the responses to four questions. *Was it worth it?* I wondered. I still did not understand why the General wanted this data suppressed. Identical questions had been asked in other surveys, and two of the four questions had even been asked of the U.S. bishops sixteen years earlier. But there was no time to worry about this right now. The Provincial and the Rector wanted me out of the university as soon as possible. I had to focus on the packing, not the emotions that came rushing in with every item I packed.

I packed up the golf-ball Snoopy the handicapped children at Saint Martin's had made for me, then the photographs of European artworks that Richard Chamberlain had taken and given me as a gift. Then the drafts of *The Thorn Birds* miniseries, the paintings that Michael Tang had given me, and the lithograph that Edith Vonnegut had given me in New York of her Crucified Christa. I gathered up the large photographic reproduction of Michelangelo's Sistine Chapel, which Mary had brought back from Rome. On my desk was the Saint Patrick's Day card that she and the children had signed and sent. An image flashed through my mind of the children running up to me during the Greeting of Peace and embracing me. The card, printed with green and white colors, was a prayer from Saint Patrick's Breastplate. It said:

CHRIST BE WITH ME
CHRIST WITHIN ME
CHRIST BEHIND ME
CHRIST BEFORE ME
CHRIST BESIDE ME
CHRIST TO WIN ME
CHRIST TO COMFORT AND RESTORE ME
CHRIST BENEATH ME
CHRIST ABOVE ME
CHRIST IN QUIET
CHRIST IN DANGER
CHRIST IN HEARTS OF ALL THAT LOVE ME
CHRIST IN MOUTH AND FRIEND OF STRANGER

For a long time I stood holding the card. Finally a screech of brakes brought me out of my reverie. I looked out my window to the service area four stories below. The student workers were getting out of the truck. I called to them out my window, "Up here!"

I walked over to my desk and picked up my vow crucifix, which had been given to me twenty-two years earlier, on September 8th, at Our Lady Queen of Peace Novitiate in Montecito. On that day I had vowed perpetual poverty, chastity, and obedience in the Society of Jesus. I held the crucifix in my hand, trying to decide whether to take it with me or to set it on the desk and walk away from it forever.

In my heart a prayer was forming. *They don't want me. They don't want who I am. You know that feeling, don't you? The crucifixion doesn't stop—it's just a matter of what cross you're going to be nailed to. How could you continue to pray for them, even when they despised you? How could you possibly find the strength to say, "Father, forgive them for they know not what they do"?*

The elevator door on the fourth floor rolled back. I heard the students rounding the corner and quickly dried my tears. I took the crucifix with me.

22

PAMELA

"Too heavy?" Terry asked as I scooped up another box of books and headed down to the truck.

"I'm too numb to notice," I smiled.

It wasn't until the elevator doors closed behind me that I would choke back the tears, as load by load I helped carry twelve years' worth of Terry's life on the Loyola University campus out of the dorm. He'd had to borrow the student truck another day in order to get everything moved across town.

In the end the worst pain wasn't the sadness of leaving the lovely campus, the sorrow of leaving behind students and friends, or even the physical and emotional separation from his Jesuit brothers with whom he had shared many precious years. These were difficult, yes, but they could not compare with the disillusionment and betrayal that were carving out a piece of Terry's heart. The Provincial's order to destroy his research had hit him with such force that he was still shaken. The directive had been explicit. Destroy! Of what were they so frightened that it had to be destroyed? Terry had even been willing to abandon his love for me, so strong was his love for the Jesuits. Yes, he was disillusioned. Yes, he hurt.

And I hurt for him, with every boxload I carried. Yet I was also grateful that it had taken only three weeks for Terry to learn the truth. It could have been a discovery made long after we had drifted apart. I was ashamed that I had lost my faith so quickly. But even though I hadn't been able to see it, God had been with me all along. And I was grateful—oh, so grateful—that Terry had made the decision he had that cold Thanksgiving weekend. Now he knew for sure. Now he would never have to wonder if he'd been wrong about obedience. There would be no doubts, no unanswered questions. There would only be the pain of knowing the truth.

"Well, that's the last of it. Pam, would you wait for me outside? I'd like to call my mom. This has been very hard for her. She's been terrific about it, but I know she feels like a source of great joy has been wiped away."

As I stood on the bluff looking back up at the dorm, I could see Terry's silhouette in the window as he placed the phone back in its cradle for the last time.

The apartment was ever, ever so tiny. Only one room. For hours Terry organized: computer on this wall, books on this wall, desk over against the wall with Michael Tang's painting over it. That just leaves the table and chairs in front of the window. But what a window!

"Just think of all the hours you can spend writing here at this table looking out at all the trees."

"Pam, that's why I put the desk over there facing the wall, so I wouldn't be distracted! And you'd better not distract me either," he chided.

"Okay, okay. Terry . . . did you notice that you're missing anything?"

He was standing on top of a chair with nails in his mouth to hang a curtain rod.

"Nope, not really. What do you think I need?"

"Well . . . this is a great room, and you've organized it really well, but . . . well, you know it is only one room. Terry . . . to put this bluntly—do you have a bed?"

His face turned white, then red, and he began to laugh. "Oops!"

"Don't worry, I'll get you a futon. They're really comfortable. You just put it out on the floor at night and store it in the closet during the day."

"Good idea. What would I do without you?"

"That's what I keep asking myself."

Over the next few weeks it became abundantly clear that Terry did need me. Years of seminary life had not prepared him for bachelor life. Basically it was little things, such as those cellophane bags at the market. I stood chuckling as he pulled one down and the entire roll unraveled to the floor. After he had finally managed to get them all rolled up again as neatly as he could, he stood turning one of the bags over and over again in his hands trying to figure out how to open it. Perplexed, he turned it every which way. I hid behind the produce counter in stitches until some benevolent soul came to his rescue.

And rent. When the first of the month rolled around, Terry asked incredulously, "You mean you can't pay your rent with a credit card?"

As strange as the transition was for Terry to move to Beverly Hills, it was a bit strange for his neighbors as well. Every morning Terry would walk very slowly in prayer from his apartment to Sierra Drive, up to Sunset Boulevard, and back home again. Sierra is a quiet residential street. It was the same routine everyday, and it was unusual to those looking out their windows along his way. They were much more used to the fast pace of joggers and cyclists. One morning two little children were on the sidewalk playing with their nanny. The little boy was pointing at him. "Here he comes, here he comes! . . . Why do you walk so slow?" he demanded of Terry.

"Because I'm praying," Terry replied.

"Can't you pray any faster?" he asked innocently.

Next came an elderly couple. "Oh, hello," the woman said in greeting. "It's good to see you."

Terry smiled, never having seen them before.

"Everyday . . . rain or shine," she whispered to her husband as Terry continued on his way.

One morning a woman walking up her driveway commented, "Boy, you sure walk slow! You're not going to get any exercise that way!"

"I don't walk for exercise," Terry replied. "I walk to think."

"Oh," mused the woman, trying to understand. "Are you a lawyer?" she finally asked.

"No," Terry said as his face turned Irish red.

Terry would recount these experiences to me with glee.

One afternoon he was sitting at his table by the window working on his research when a black BMW pulled up in front. A man in his late twenties got out and dumped a pile of trash on the front lawn. The man then proceeded to walk over to Terry's neighbor's Volkswagen convertible and get in! This seemed extremely suspicious to Terry, who decided to see what was up. So he walked out and approached the young man.

"There's a garbage can out back. Would you mind throwing your trash there instead of on the lawn?"

"Oh, sure," said the guy.

"Are you looking for something?" Terry inquired.

"I was just waiting for my friend."

Terry definitely sensed something was wrong and went to check with his neighbor.

"Geoff, do you have a friend who's supposed to be meeting you outside, a guy in his late twenties who drives a BMW?"

"No," Geoff replied.

"Well, he was just sitting in your car."

Both men ran downstairs, but the guy was gone, so they called the police. Ten minutes later the man was apprehended, and it turned out that not only did they find a gun in the backseat, but the BMW was stolen too!

Though Terry was used to the street gangs of East L.A., Beverly Hills was proving to be interesting as well. I still chuckle when I think of the comment his friend, Mike Mitchell, made when he heard that Terry had moved from the Jesuit Community across town to Beverly Hills. Not realizing how tiny Terry's apartment really was, he wrote, "That sure doesn't sound like 'biting the bullet' to me . . . it's more like gumming the marshmallow!"

And cooking: Terry's apartment didn't have any kind of kitchen at all; however, he did have a small microwave. But most of the time he would walk over to my apartment for a home-cooked meal. Now, the kitchen and I were not on the greatest of terms. Up until that point in my life it was "that room around the corner where you make coffee in the morning." Suddenly I was faced with creating meals such as Terry was used to in the Jesuit Community Residence. The food there was always varied and delicious, so I tried desperately to learn how to create a different dish every night.

Whether or not my meals were healthy or nutritional, I don't know. But eventually Terry began to put back on the weight he had lost over the last few months. Color returned to his cheeks, and the dark circles disappeared. Even his stomach cramps vanished. And it was fun for me.

I found him to be grateful for even the smallest things. He didn't take anything for granted or expect anything. Consequently, even the most trivial kindnesses brought him great joy.

I loved having Terry so close and looked forward to our dinners in the evening at my little dining-room table by the window. For the first time since I'd known him, it was as if we had the beginnings of a normal relationship. Everything seemed to be pointing toward a future together. And although we hadn't talked about it, in my heart I believed that we would be married very, very soon.

The only person in whom I had been able to confide about my relationship with Terry was Ginger. She had been my sounding board, my conscience, my emotional punching bag. She'd been my friend, and she'd stuck by me. Over time I'd lost touch with the other two girlfriends who knew of my friendship with Terry. They had come to believe that I was living in a dream world that would never come true. The prince would never leave his ivory tower, and I was wasting precious time in a situation that would never have a happy ending. My close friends didn't understand—all except for Ginger. She had cautioned me to take care of my heart and to be aware of how a loving relationship could harm Terry. She'd warned me to protect his heart from the pain our love could cause. She, too, had been skeptical—but she'd grown to understand. "You've found your knight in Terry," she'd say. "After a love like this, you'll never be the same."

My arm was tired of holding the phone, my ear ached, my voice was hoarse, and I was exhausted from this conversation which was now in its second hour. Ginger was definitely curious.

"I think it's time I met this man." Ginger paused. "What do you think?"

The thought was strange to me. My entire relationship with Terry had been so private. Just the thought of going out to dinner with a friend made me nervous. Here were my best friend and the man I loved, and I hadn't even been able to introduce them.

"Okay, but let's go somewhere 'normal,' like El Coyote, so that we'll all be more relaxed, okay?"

"Sure. I won't bite him, Shoop."

Terry took the whole thing in stride. He had heard me talk about Ginger and he was aware that she had played a major part in helping me through the emotions of the past months.

He looked out the window through the lace curtains of my apartment. "Does she drive a green Pontiac?"

"I'm not sure if it's a Pontiac, but it's definitely green. Her cars are always green."

"Well, then, here she comes!"

We both took a deep breath. I was visibly shaking as I opened the door to my crazy blond buddy. There she stood, dressed to the nines in a low-cut sweater with her diamond oak-tree necklace shining around her throat. It is an exact replica of the tunnel tree at the entrance to her property. In one hand she held a magnifying glass and in the other a bag of crushed ice.

"Well, well, well," she mumbled in her best Sherlock Holmes voice, "let's see what we have here!"

She proceeded to march right up until she came nose to nose with an astonished Terry, placing the glass against his face. This was not how priests were usually treated!

"Aha! I seeeeeee! Yes . . . yes . . . So this is the one, eh?"

With that she shoved the bag into his hand. "Here! This is to help break the ice!"

Well, that was enough. We burst into laughter. Ginger was hilarious and had accomplished exactly what she had set out to do: She had put all three of us at ease. We drove to the restaurant giggling all the way.

The evening turned out to be more relaxed than we'd expected as Ginger asked Terry question after question about the laws of celibacy and his own particular situation with the Church. At last she leaned back in the booth and grinned at us.

"It's obvious how you two feel about each other."

Terry winked at me. "It's one thing, Ginger, to know that the laws of celibacy are really hurting the Church. But it's another thing to feel it because you love someone. When I began all my research, I had no idea that God would bring such a wonderful grace into my life."

Though he was still speaking to Ginger, he turned and looked directly into my eyes. "You really have an extraordinary friend . . . and I love her very much."

We sat there for a silent moment, and all three of us had tears in our. eyes.

23

TERRY

Having traveled as a Jesuit to ten countries in Latin America, to Portugal, Spain, France, Italy, Greece, Jerusalem, North Africa, India, and China, I tried to reassure myself that moving into an apartment less than twenty miles from Loyola Marymount University would be easy. It wasn't. Even though Pamela had been extremely helpful, and even though I enjoyed spending time with her, living in the apartment reminded me that I was an outcast.

The stress of being cut off from everything I had known was compounded by the frustration of not knowing why Rome wanted the bishops' opinions suppressed.

On February 15th I wrote to the Superior-General explaining that nearly fifty percent of the American bishops had responded to my survey and that I needed to know, for my own peace of soul, why he felt it would bring "harm to the Society and the Church."

Because the Provincial and Archbishop Mahony had expressed doubt about the scientific quality of the survey, I decided to consult with the chairman of the Sociology Department at UCLA, the head of the Sociology Department at Mount Saint Mary's, and a highly respected sociologist at Loyola Marymount University. All of them said the survey was unquestionably valid both in method and in content. They thought that a less than ten-percent response rate from the cardinals was not a large enough sampling to formulate accurate sociological conclusions, but that a forty-six percent response rate from the U.S. bishops was indeed substantial enough to use in formulating conclusions. Moreover, the sociologists found the survey to be "extremely timely, fascinating, and important."

The General's directive, enforced by the Provincial's ultimatum to suppress the survey or leave the Jesuits, had come as a shock to me. I had heard of theologians like Kung and Boff and Curran being reprimanded for points of view the Vatican claimed were at odds with official teaching, but I had not heard of a priest being ostracized before he had written a single word or publicly said anything to challenge Church policy. Was asking questions so terrible? How could we devote ourselves to truth if we weren't permitted to ask questions?

It felt as though the Society was trying to censure not only whatever conclusions I might write down, but also the very process of my thinking. Even more disturbing, the General and "some cardinals in the Vatican" felt they had the authority to suppress the written responses I had received. What kind of authority is this that destroys the thinking of bishops on issues of vital importance to the whole Church? What kind of institution is this where a few cardinals and other officials in the Vatican can dictate to the rest of the hierarchy which opinions they are allowed to express?

There is a book by Richard Hughes called *In Hazard.* It's the story of a freighter struggling for survival in the midst of a hurricane. Many times images from that book would flash across my mind, warning me in some kind of intuitive way that the Catholic Church was on the brink of disaster.

One passage in particular comes closest to describing this danger. Hughes portrays the eye of the storm, where the "air was gaspingly thin, as on a mountain: but not enlivening: on the contrary, it was damp and depressing; and almost unbearably hot, even to engineers. Big drops of sweat, unable in that humid air to evaporate, ran warm and salt across their lips. The tormented black sky was one incessant flicker of lightning." And the whole surface of the deck and its upper structures were covered with "living things. Living, but not moving. Birds, and even butterflies and big flying grasshoppers." As the officers made their way on deck, they kept stepping on live birds. "I don't want to dwell on this, but I must tell you what things were like, and be done with it. You would feel the delicate skeleton scrunch under your feet: but you could not help it, and the gummed feathers hardly even fluttered. No bird, even crushed, or half-crushed, cried."

I felt like a bird struggling for survival in the fury of ecclesial hurricane winds, finally settling for breath and life on the "bark of Peter." And even as an officer of the Church crushed my head, I could see thousands upon thousands more being trampled.

Against the evening twilight a sailboat glided peacefully along the harbor. I had driven across town to Shanghai Reds restaurant in the Marina to dine with two Jesuit friends. Ernie and Herb both raised their drinks and clinked them to mine. "Cheers. Good to see you, Terry," Ernie said.

"Yes, how are you doing?" Herb asked.

"Surviving."

Ernie set his drink down and looked at me with concern. "How's your family taking it?"

"It's been pretty hard on my mother and my oldest brother, Dudley. Dudley has a lot of questions, and my mother had been very proud of having a son who was a Jesuit priest."

"Where do things stand now with the Society?" Herb asked.

The waitress came by, took our orders, then left.

"The Provincial told me I could appeal his decision. I asked him what good that would do, since my appeal would go to the General, and the General is the one who told him to tell me to destroy my research. So, I've written a letter of resignation to Clark, but I've also written to the General, asking him why he wanted my research suppressed. Do you know how long this process of resignation takes, Herb?"

"Not too long," he replied.

"Can the Society dismiss me before a bishop accepts me into his diocese?" I asked.

"Yes," Herb answered. "The Society has a special privilege in that regard. It can dismiss a priest from the order before that priest has been incardinated into a diocese."

"If I'm not a Jesuit and if a bishop has not accepted me, will I be able to minister as a priest?"

"No, Terry, I'm afraid not," Herb answered empathetically.

I felt a sharp pain in the center of my heart, as though I were falling into a black, frightening chasm. I felt like screaming or crying. Instead I stared at him in silent shock.

"Sorry, Terry," Herb said. "You'd be a *vagus*, a priest without a bishop or religious superior, a priest without delegation or authority."

The Latin word said it all: wandering, uncertain—a vagrant priest unable to minister, a useless priest living in limbo, neither heaven nor hell. The fluids in my stomach turned bitter.

The waitress set our food on the table.

"Are you going forward with your research?" Ernie asked.

"Yes."

"How are the bishops answering?"

"I'm still tabulating their answers. It's too soon to talk about results."

"You know your efforts are futile, don't you, Terry?" Herb asked.

"I've been told that, but I prefer not to believe it."

"Rome won't allow priests to marry, no matter what the bishops say," Herb commented.

"Why does the Vatican presume to know better than Jesus what's best for the Church? Most of His apostles were married."

"This pope has made it very clear," Herb said. "Churches are already shutting down in Europe, people are going without the Sacraments. He'd rather have that than abolish the celibacy discipline."

"But celibacy isn't a matter of dogma or faith. How can the Pope demand it when Jesus did not? If the Pope passed a law tonight that all priests must marry, I'd have the same objection! Who is he to decide whether or not a priest will marry? God gives that right to individuals, not papacies!"

Herb looked at me patiently. "By speaking out, Terry, you're going to be driven out of the priesthood as well as the Jesuits. And no one will listen to you then."

"Over one hundred thousand priests have resigned in the last twenty years," I replied. "Someone has to speak out."

"Why don't you give your research to someone else?" Ernie asked.

"Because the Provincial has explicitly forbidden that. He said that I could not use it in any manner, nor could I give it to anyone else for use in any manner whatsoever. Besides, why should someone else take the fall for something I started?"

"But, Terry," Herb interrupted, "Rome won't change. Many before you have tried and failed."

"They may not change, but I have to speak out anyway."

"You're just going to bang your head against a brick wall and destroy yourself and your priesthood in the process."

"But, Herb," I protested, "if I destroyed my research as the General and Rome have asked me to do just so that I could stay a priest and practice my priesthood, then I would have sold out not only myself but the priesthood. How could I get up in the pulpit knowing that I had sold out the priesthood just so that I could continue my ministry?"

Herb's voice grew louder, "You are not God's prophet, Terry! You should not start a battle you know you are going to lose."

The dinner had started out warm and friendly, now it was turning sour. I felt blood rushing to my face. "There are some battles where you don't ask that question. If your house is burning down and your family is inside, you don't ask yourself if you're going to come out alive. You go in. You don't wait for the 'authorities,' the fire department, to get there and put out the fire. By then your family is dead."

Herb looked straight at me and quoted, " 'God, grant me the serenity to accept the things I cannot change, the courage to change the things I can, and the wisdom to know the difference.' You cannot change the priesthood policy, no matter what you say or do. It is foolish to try. You will fail, Terry, and in the end you will have nothing."

"So," I replied, "because I will lose, because I will have nothing, you're saying I should follow the order to suppress the research. Is that right?"

"Yes," Herb answered.

"I can't do that, Herb. I feel like that scene in Scripture where a man was beaten, robbed, and thrown in a ditch. And there I am standing on the rim looking down at this poor man, and a Pharisee is standing next to me telling me it is the Sabbath and that I should not go down into the ditch. And I say, 'But the man will die if he isn't helped.' And the Pharisee answers that such a grave matter as working on the Sabbath should be taken before the Sanhedrin, and besides the ditch is very deep. You know who that man in the ditch is, Herb? He's the priesthood, and I can't leave the priesthood in the ditch dying, even if it means breaking the Sabbath, offending authorities. Even if it means that I'll never make it out of the ditch!"

There was a long silence at the table. Herb looked away from me to Ernie. "What do you think?"

Ernie stopped eating. He paused for several moments collecting his thoughts. "I think he's right, Terry. I think you're going to lose. But I also admire you for following your convictions. I don't think many people would be willing to give up as much. I wish I could be like you. Maybe I'd have the courage . . . if I were ten years younger."

On March 17th three letters arrived in the mail. One was stamped *Poste Vaticane,* another was from the Provincial, the third was from the Rector of Loyola Marymount University. With considerable apprehension I opened the Vatican letter first. It was from Peter Hans-Kolvenbach, the Superior-General of the Jesuits.

I read the six-sentence letter several times. Father General did not explain why he thought the survey harmful, nor did he explain by what authority he was presuming to suppress the hierarchy's opinions on optional celibacy and women priests. Instead, he commented that reflections on my "actions in light of Jesuit obedience," Jesuit adherence to Church teaching and discipline, and the scientific quality of my survey had prompted him to conclude that he could not "add anything to what Father John Clark has already said to you."

Church teaching and discipline regarding the exclusion of marriage and women from the priesthood were rife with conflict, contradiction, and error. Did the General honestly believe Jesuits should unquestioningly support this policy? And what did he mean by "scientific quality"? Professional sociologists considered the survey not only valid, but timely and important. Besides, the Provincial had refused my offer to submit the survey for evaluation to any sociologist of his choice. It did not seem to matter to the General or to the Provincial that many of the bishops, plus the majority of Catholic priests and laity, felt the priesthood policy needed reform. All that mattered was that Jesuits obey their superiors and uphold Church teaching.

I got up from the desk and paced restlessly around the room. If the Provincial always does what the General asks, but without knowing why, and the General always does what the Vatican asks, where does truth or Christ's teaching enter the process? How does new thinking or inspiration revitalize the Church? How can needed change ever take place?

After several minutes I opened the certified letter from the Provincial. My eyes froze on one sentence in the letter: "But you remain a priest bound by celibacy who may not exercise priesthood until a bishop receives you."

Tell me not to eat, tell me not to sleep or to breathe—don't tell me not to be a priest. It's my life. It's what I am.

What kind of Church is this, where you can be barred from the privileges and duties of ministry and at the same time be bound by its celibacy obligations? Barred from the life and love of priesthood and cut off from love's intimacy by the law of celibacy? Trapped, bound, powerless, loveless. Oh, God.

My body started to tremble.

After a long time I forced myself to open the third letter. A brief note from the Rector was attached to a Decree of Dismissal from the Society of Jesus. The Rector wanted me to contact him and set up a time when I could meet with him and sign this last document severing me totally from the Jesuit order.

My hands were still shaking as I put down the Decree. Outside the window a hummingbird skirted into the garden, hovered over the branches of a birch tree, then, in a sudden, sweeping motion, perched on top of a limb. The round left eye of the bird stared through the window at me. The eye was light green. I wondered if the bird had ever been in a hurricane or landed on the deck of a freighter.

Suddenly the trembling stopped. So did the tears. But the pain in my heart grew sharper, more intense. It began dragging me down into a dark, bottomless chasm.

24

PAMELA

The early months of 1986 passed in a blur and a flurry of emotions. I had realized that this period of transition would be a difficult one for Terry, but I was not prepared for the effect it would have on me.

It is with a great deal of sorrow that I reflect upon this chapter of our relationship. I am reminded of the painful isolation I felt, my lack of identity, my conflicting desires. I think today of the thousands of women who have been in love with priests and left alone to sit in the shadows, waiting for a day, a life, that might never come. My heart goes out to those women, with a deep sense of compassion for and understanding of that period of loneliness and self-doubt.

My situation was very unclear. My idealistic view of my relationship with Terry, coupled with the passage of time and the constant uncertainty of Terry's struggle within the Church, led to a restlessness and loss of identity that eventually pervaded all my thoughts and feelings. I watched my dreams, little by little, crack with uncertainty, then crumble beneath the weight of time. What was I waiting for?

Though he had moved from the Community, Terry was still in deep conflict with the Jesuit order and the vow of "Holy Obedience." In trying to make some sense of Jack Clark's directive, he began to wonder whether, indeed, the Vatican's Sacred Congregation for Religious would stand behind the Provincial's behavior, which he perceived as radical in both its effects and its implications. He was debating whether or not to appeal the directive to Rome. Privately I wondered what that would mean to me. If his superiors were to reverse their decision, would that mean that Terry would reenter the Jesuit order and move back to the campus? I was afraid to ask. One afternoon, after a long hike up the Franklin Canyon path, Terry said, "Let's pray on the way down. Then I want to know what you think I should do."

I didn't want to answer. The future of which I dreamed was very clear. I knew what I wanted: for us to be married and to begin a family. But that wasn't a subject I could even bring up. Terry would have to come to that conclusion by himself—if he ever did. At the moment, he felt the need to exhaust every possibility with the Jesuits in order to truly understand the inner workings of obedience. He needed time, and I had to let him have it.

I realized that I had been frightened like this once before. I had doubted my own heart, my own reason, even God. But God had answered the questions Terry had been asking in a very short period of time. He needed answers now, and if I'd learned anything, it was to trust that the right ones would be given to him.

As we walked in silence down the path, a saying I had once heard kept running through my mind. *If you love with an open hand . . . If you let something go three times and it comes back to you, it is yours for life.*

When we reached the road, I gave my answer. "I think you should appeal. The more answers you have, the better it will be, the more peaceful it will make your own decisions."

I kissed him on the cheek. And so he did appeal—and it took a long time for an answer to be given.

Terry's days were spent tabulating the results of his survey and continuing his research on the priesthood and authority in the formulation of his conclusions. He spent late nights pouring over countless books he had brought with him from the university library. On my nightly walks around the block with Devon, I could see him through his window hunched over a book or pounding away at his computer. And I, wanting to learn more about what had taken place years ago between the Church and priests and their wives, began to read each book as he finished it. Over dinner and on weekend walks we discussed the gradual formation of ideas that was taking place. The more I read, the more involved I became. I began to understand the pain of the wives of priests whose lives had been destroyed. I was horrified at the names they were called and at the way in which they were perceived to be evil and dirty. Little did I know that in just over a year, some of those names would be hurled my way. I read about the bloody history of the Church. I read Kung and Schillebeecx, Lea, Boff, Anne Barstow, and Rosemary Ruether. The more I read, the more real our own situation was becoming. I began to feel a cause welling up within me too.

During this time Terry was continuing to say Mass at Good Shepherd. But, realizing that once he signed his resignation papers he would be without a parish in which to practice his ministry, he began to seek incardination.

"What does that mean?"

"It means that if a bishop somewhere in the country will accept me, I can continue to function as a priest."

My heart asked privately, *Without a wife?*

Again the instability of my situation presented itself. Terry longed to continue the practice of his priesthood—it was part of his soul. But what if one of the bishops agreed to welcome him into his diocese, where would that leave me? Would I then be abandoned and left behind, no longer needed? Just where exactly did I stand? I became increasingly confused and insecure. Every day when the mail would arrive, I expected Terry to rush over to my apartment with the news that he would be moving to some other part of the country. Where did I fit into the equation? I was too afraid to ask all the questions that were pounding at the doors of my heart. I continued to make frequent visits to the Church of the Good Shepherd, where I would sit in the silence in an effort to calm the quiet terrors. Somehow, though I was living a compromise of heart and identity, I must continue to be patient and loving for Terry's sake. And all the while I tried to assure myself that the love in his eyes should allay my fears.

———

Sally's face was ashen. My half sister was visiting from New Jersey, where she lives with her husband, Bill, and her daughter, Sissi. She is my father's daughter by a previous marriage. When we were children, Sally would come to spend each summer with us. Though distance had separated us over the years, we had remained close. It had been a blessing to have Sally so nearby when I had moved to New York, and I had spent many weekends with her family on their farm. Though we had always kept in touch by letters and seen each other fairly often, during this time we had really been able to develop our relationship as adults—and, more than half-sisters, we were friends.

Sally had been my houseguest for a few days. We'd had lunch at the Farmer's Market, tea at Trump's, and the inevitable dinner at El Coyote, where she had met Terry for the first time. I had decided not to mention to her that he was a priest. At the time it seemed too complicated to explain.

She sat on the edge of the couch and looked at me with wide eyes.

"Why didn't you tell me?"

"Tell you what?"

"This."

She handed me a book out of my bookcase she had been perusing.

The book was entitled *God &*. It was a collection of thirty people's experiences of God, including those of Richard Chamberlain, William Peter Blatty, Kurt Vonnegut, Jr., Gene Roddenberry, Martin Sheen, Ray Bradbury, and others. It was written by Terrance A. Sweeney, S.J.

"Sally, I wanted to tell you, but I couldn't. I wasn't sure what you'd think. I love him, Sally."

"Pamie, be careful." She sighed. "I wondered why you didn't come back to New York. I knew there must be a reason. I just don't want you to get hurt."

"That makes two of us."

She gave me a big hug, and we talked until the wee hours of the morning.

Sally's concern for Terry and me over the ensuing months was evident. Through countless letters and hours of phone calls I could feel her support, her love. She clipped articles from East Coast papers about Terry when they began to appear and watched whenever he was interviewed on TV. Gradually she came to understand the ethics of his position and, more importantly to her, the presence of her sister in his life.

I had not been prepared for Terry's social life. As a priest he was frequently asked to dinner parties, black-tie fund-raisers, and evenings with friends, parishioners, and fellow priests. Since he was still a practicing priest, these engagements took up much of his spare time. On the other hand, I, as a single woman, was not asked out often by couples unless they wanted to fix me up with someone, and I did not want to date for fear of compromising my relationship with Terry. Eventually people stopped asking, and with the exception of a few friends, my social life dropped down to next to nothing.

Although intellectually I could appreciate the situation, emotionally it was a very painful one. Many a night I would sit on my couch alone while Terry dutifully attended some function or other. My growing lack of identity gave way to anger and jealousy. My life was completely on hold. I was in a state of suspension which could conceivably last a long time. The waiting became a long and lonely process. It would have been less painful if I'd felt there were a promise of something in the future, if there had been some deadline in sight. But there was no such deadline. There was only that private inner belief that things would work out.

When Terry and I were together, one of the greatest sources of tension between us revolved around the constant restraints and limitations placed on our physical relationship. Here he was, living so close by. We were in love and tremendously attracted to one another. Now what?

Sexual frustration began to increase as night after night Terry would give me a kiss and then leave me. I am sure that many people will find it difficult to believe that two adults in this situation, as close as we were, refrained from entering into a sexual relationship throughout this whole time. Looking back, it is hard for me to believe it myself. It would have been very easy for us to fall into an affair. And there is a measure of sadness that in the bloom of our love we were not able to express to one another the depth of our passion. However, it was important on many levels that we did not.

Terry felt his research was important to the future of the priesthood, whether we were to see a change in policy in our lifetime or not. His findings, his conclusions, and all that they represent to the issue of married clergy were a responsibility to the Church, to the public, and to God. His personal integrity and character were at the very heart of this responsibility. I, too, had respect for Terry's promise of celibacy. If people were to believe in us and what we stood for, then it would be crucial that they believe in us as individuals.

From my own perspective, there was another reason why I chose to remain celibate in our relationship. The love I felt for Terry was so much bigger than a simple affair. And with my growing need for identity in his life, I realized that if I were to become his mistress, I would compromise my own integrity. I needed to know that our love was right. And if it was necessary, as it was at present, for me to remain in the background, then it would not be right for me to have a full sexual relationship under those circumstances. I would not allow myself to compromise Terry, his vow, or myself.

These feelings are so difficult to express, but after all the soul-searching and doubting I had done regarding my place in the life of a priest, holding onto this one area of my own self-esteem became vital. My reputation, my pride, my body—they seemed the only areas over which I had any control left. I could not make decisions for Terry regarding incardination or the Jesuit order or the priesthood. The only thing I could control was my own behavior, and I desperately needed to respect myself. Then, too, Terry continually expressed his love for me as "loving with a divided heart." Part of his heart still wasn't free to love me. Until that love was whole, it was appropriate to wait. But as the attraction grew, so, too, did the frustration.

Terry had moved close by—yet it was a very lonely time.

25

TERRY

Standing at the sink in the coffee room of the chancery, Bishop Juan Arzube opened a can of fruit cocktail, poured out two portions onto the plastic plates in front of him, and asked, "You like fruit cocktail?"

It was March 29th, Holy Saturday, and Bishop Arzube had wanted to talk. He handed me the two plates, grabbed some glasses of orange juice, and motioned me to a table nearby. His manner, as always, was friendly, warm, comfortable.

He said a short blessing over the food, then looked up. "I asked you to come down here as a friend, Terry. Since I ordained you, I feel a special closeness to you and want to help you if I can. So, why did you do the survey?"

"Because the priesthood is going under. In 1970 there were thirty-seven thousand diocesan priests, but in the year 2000 there will be only fifteen thousand left to minister to a Catholic population of more than sixty million. A priest has an average life span five years less than the rest of the male population. Priests are burning out, growing old, and dying before their time. The four questions on my survey were the most frequently proposed solutions to this crisis."

"The Pope will not change his mind on those issues, even if the majority of bishops want a change," Arzube said. "The Church is not structured that way. It is not a democracy. It is not ruled by majority opinion."

"It may not be a democracy. But I thought the Church was the people of God—a community in which the Spirit of God can be found in the hearts of all those who live lives of faith and love. A significant majority of Catholics want the policy to change. And if so many goodwilled people want it to change and the Pope still refuses, it seems to me that it is not the Spirit of God guiding the Church, but one man's opinion."

"You're wasting your time. *Roma locuta est, causa finita est.* Rome has spoken, the matter is closed. This pope will never allow married clergy or women priests."

"Why?"

"People see in a celibate priest someone who has made a special sacrifice in order to help them. And certainly a priest's availability would be greatly reduced by a wife and children."

"I know doctors, lawyers, and migrant workers who work longer hours than most priests. That hasn't stopped them from marrying. Aren't we carrying this availability thing a little far?"

"I don't know the Pope's reason. Maybe he's afraid of the scandal that would happen if a married priest wanted to divorce his wife." He got up, brought his empty plate to the trash can, and began washing the silverware in the sink.

I followed him, still trying to make some sense of what he had just said. Priests might get a divorce, therefore, they shouldn't be allowed to marry. What kind of reasoning is that? People might divorce, therefore, they shouldn't be allowed to marry. Marriage might end in divorce, therefore, marriage should be banned! Is this the kind of thinking that rules the Church?

Arzube turned to me. "Let's continue this up in my office." He led me up the stairs and down the long marbled-floor hallway of the chancery.

"Do you have the authority to incardinate me?"

"No," Arzube answered. "Only an Ordinary does."

"Do you think Archbishop Mahony would accept me?" I asked.

"No. If you're asking to pursue your research under the wing of a bishop, I don't think you'd have a chance with any bishop in the country."

I couldn't believe my ears.

Arzube continued. "But if you drop your research right now, there might be a couple of bishops who would take you."

"Who?" I asked.

Arzube opened his desk drawer, pulled out a book listing the Ordinaries throughout the United States. He flipped through all the pages, giving me a total of six names. After each of the names given, he would make comments like, "He might take a chance; he's not interested in climbing the ladder. . . . This one's not looking for a red hat. . . . This one has a small diocese and is close to retirement. . . . This one doesn't have much to lose, he's dying of cancer."

I walked out of the chancery in a state of shock, hoping that Bishop Arzube was wrong, praying that he had exaggerated the bishops' fear of the Pope.

Five days after meeting with Arzube I telephoned Bishop Howze of Mississippi, a progressive, eminently respected leader. I explained my situation to him and asked if he would consider incardinating me. He said he would not. I then asked if he could think of any other bishop who might be receptive. In a gentle tone he replied, "No, I think most bishops would be cautious. They wouldn't want the Vatican looking over their shoulders."

I wrote letters to Ordinaries in different parts of the United States, including Los Angeles, and petitioned each of them to incardinate me. All of them refused.

With each rejection it became clearer to me that Bishop Arzube had been right. The bishops were afraid of Rome's power. This blind obedience, based not on love or commitment to truth but on power and fear, could only harm the Church.

Considering the possibility that I might be exaggerating the Pope's influence over every aspect of Church authority, I had decided to appeal again to Rome. Surely there must be someone in the Vatican who would agree that "obedience" did not mean that a Provincial could order the hierarchy's attitudes on the priesthood suppressed. Surely there was some official arm within the Church that realized that "authority" was not a carte blanche to destroy vocations and research under the unexplained rubrics of "unity" and "good of the Church." I decided to delay the signing of the Jesuit Decree of Dismissal until the Sacred Congregation for Religious in Rome had answered my appeal.

Three weeks after sending the formal appeal, I telephoned the prefect of the congregation, Cardinal Hamer, and offered to fly to Rome to answer any questions the congregation might have. He answered rather brusquely that this would not be helpful and that my case would be decided according to the "classical terms of religious obedience."

In the first days of June the Congregation's formal reply arrived, judging that I owed obedience to the Provincial's command to suppress the research, " 'just as if it were coming from Christ our Savior' since Jesuit obedience is 'to one in his place.' " The letter stated further that "the Provincial was justified in asking you to 'cease and desist' from a public process of taking a poll on four issues on which the Holy See's position is very clear."

Reading this one-page judgment left me profoundly disillusioned with the Vatican's judicial process. It proved to me that the "classical terms of religious obedience" was yet another virtuous-sounding rubric by which one of the most powerful congregations in Rome, rather than looking to the pastoral needs of the Church, the Gospel, or God's will, blindly protected the "mind of the Holy See." The Vatican congregation's "judgment" demonstrated that the Pope's opinions were being protected as absolutes in themselves and not because they reflected God's will. My awakening to this ecclesial totalitarianism filled me with despair because I realized this authority was crippling the Church and destroying my vocation. This was not an authority based on the truth of Christ's teachings, but on sheer power. The enormity of this power was overwhelming: It stretched into every country in the world, unaccountable to any government; it alone had supreme jurisdiction over all the churches and all the bishops and all the formal definitions of faith and morals affecting the lives of nearly one billion people. And this papal power was not even accountable to God.

I finally understood why the bishops were afraid of the Vatican.

They, too, could be removed from their dioceses; they, too, could be suspended, neutralized. And their actions were much more carefully scrutinized by the Pope than those of a Jesuit priest.

A burning feeling churned inside my stomach as I tried to calm the bitterness welling inside me: The Vatican doesn't burn you at the stake anymore, they don't even throw you in prison anymore—all they ask is that you confess that your mind and heart are in their authority, their unerring, infallible, all-controlling authority. Not Christ's, not God's, theirs.

My heart was filling up with anger and cynicism. All this time I had held out the hope that, even though I was being forced out of the Jesuits, I would still be able to serve as a priest. Now I was realizing, from a series of rejections throughout the country and from this latest reproof from Rome, that bishops were afraid to accept me as a priest. The instant I signed the documents severing me from the Jesuits, I would become a kind of black-listed priest—one no bishop would accept. This prospect filled me with dread. To be a priest yet to have to say to those who came to me for the Sacraments, "Sorry, I cannot help you." To have the soul of my ministry taken from me, yet still be bound by the celibate discipline of that ministry. I would have to keep my mouth shut, think the correct thoughts, obey the powers of Rome, and refuse to fall in love with Pamela. I would have to abandon truth, pretend I did not know what I knew, and pretend I didn't feel what I felt. Was this the kind of priest the Vatican wanted? When did silence and duplicity become holy virtues?

The Church, the "people of God" who had come to me with their struggles and sins and hopes, had taught me the importance of God's forgiveness and grace. And now the institutional Church, the Vatican, was severing me from the people and telling me it was the Pope's mind, not Christ's or the faithful's, that mattered.

I saw my Jesuit and priestly identity crumbling before my eyes, and I knew that the power which was destroying me had already ruined the lives of countless thousands. But the Vatican had two thousand years and enormous resources to define and protect its power. In less than three hours of telephone conversations twenty-three years of my life had been wiped out, and my future would never be the same. What could one scorned priest possibly do against such power?

As the months wore on, I found myself being dragged down into a dark and nearly paralyzing depression. Hanging over me was the threat that as soon as I signed the final release papers from the Jesuits, I would be suspended as a priest, unable to say Mass, baptize, forgive sins, marry, or anoint—anywhere in the world. And staring me in the face were policies and forms of authority that were threatening the very heart of the Church—but who would ever listen to an ex-Jesuit, a suspended priest? The burden of this realization plunged me into a feeling of total helplessness. There were days when I would find myself unable to read, to write, or to think. Sometimes I would sit for hours at my desk, unwilling and unable to move. Over me I felt a blanket of heaviness; inside I felt fragmented, useless.

Something deep inside of me wanted to be free of the pain, the conflict, the knowledge, the burden of seeing evil but feeling powerless to stop it. There was something inside of me that wanted to be forever free of this.

And even as the words tumbled unwillingly from my heart, I knew they were not a prayer, but a cry of despair: *Lord, I am broken. Take my life.*

The following day, during morning prayer, while I was feeling raw and vulnerable from the inner struggle the night before, a scene from Christ's life presented itself with unusual clarity in my consciousness. It was that moment in Jesus' life when Satan led Him up to a high mountain and showed Him all the kingdoms of the world and their glory and said to Jesus, "All this will I give you if you but fall down and worship me." I sensed the exhaustion Jesus felt, His weakness from prolonged fasting, the abyss of looking into His own nature as a man—His need for food, for warmth, identity, acceptance, His fear of death, of abandonment, betrayal, and the constant temptations to take the easier path, the one with food, accolades, power, glory.

I felt Jesus' answer to the Tempter: "You must worship the Lord your God and serve Him alone." Jesus' words, the inner feelings that uttered this truth that His heart had learned through great anguish, brought me peace and understanding.

Those words of Jesus made me realize that the priesthood, first, last, and always, was the servant of Christ's truth, of God's will—these were not to be sacrificed even to save my own priesthood.

These and similar thoughts began to dispel the anguish I felt in the stripping away of my Jesuit and priestly identities and in my awful awakening to the evil in the Church I am part of and love. Finally realizing that Jesus, even in His darkest hour, cried out His despair to the God He loved, and that not for one second would the risen Lord leave someone alone who so needed Him—for the briefest of moments I felt enveloped and warmed by His love.

I felt His grace lifting me free of the eye of the storm—not that His mercy would spare me from the breaking or the crushing. No, indeed, that was to continue. Rather, it was the awakening to His presence, that He was right there on the deck of the ship with me, and that whatever death I was still to experience, His love was there. He would not abandon me.

26

PAMELA

It seemed incredible to me that it was already summer again. The six months since Terry had left Loyola had passed quietly as he worked day after day at his computer. Not only was he completing his work on the results of the survey, but he had also begun writing a book. His conflicts with the Jesuit Provincial, Archbishop Mahony, the Sacred Congregation, the Apostolic Delegate, and his own conscience were as fascinating as any mystery novel. Events seemed to unravel so quickly and unexpectedly, and though we discussed every aspect along the way, what toll they would eventually take on Terry I could not be sure.

As time passed, I grew more and more frustrated. In my näiveté I had imagined that shortly after his departure from Loyola, Terry might ask me to marry him. But that had not been the case. The focus of Terry's life was his current struggle. I began to grow edgy and argumentative. Where was the partnership I had longed for, the bliss, the union? Terry was a priest in limbo: no bishop, no Jesuits. I was a woman in limbo: no husband, no identity. Yet within the little world behind the courtyard wall, our existence was one of nurturing, privacy, and peace. It felt secure and safe. Lulled by the pleasure of discovery and serenity, we continued to grow. I was not about to abandon Terry in his darkest hour, and I could not walk away from him as long as there was even a tiny spark of hope for our future together.

The Fourth of July was spent in Dudley's backyard with the aroma of hamburgers and hot dogs, guacamole and potato salad, Dr Pepper and Key lime pie. A rousing game of volleyball with the entire family eventually led to the long-awaited darkness. Rosemarie walked up to us, her hands thrust deeply in her pockets. Shyly she touched Terry's arm.

"You know, Pat always used to help Michael with his fireworks, and he's still pretty young to do it himself. Do you think maybe you could help him this year? Would you mind, Terry?" A knowing look passed between them.

"Sure, I can. Hey, Michael . . . why don't you show me how to do that, okay? What do you have there?"

Rosemarie pulled up a chair beside me and threw on a sweatshirt.

I wondered how she must feel watching her son, missing her husband.

"How about a glass of wine?"

"Great idea."

"How are you doing?" I asked. "About Pat, I mean?"

"It's hard, Pam. I miss him so much. Sometimes I just get so angry! And then there's Michael. It's so hard for him without a father. I'm constantly afraid of making a mistake. I just have a feeling I'm going to make all the wrong decisions. I keep thinking to myself, 'Pat would know what to do. Why isn't he here?' But it hurts too much to think about it, so I just keep myself so busy that I don't have time to think."

"Someday, when you're ready, you need time to just go off alone someplace without Michael and allow yourself some time to heal. It'll be hard, and you'll cry a lot, but I really think you'll feel better. But don't let anyone make you feel you have to let go of Pat. He's yours. His memory is yours to keep for as long as you need— maybe forever. And if not, then you'll know when to let go."

"You know, Pam, I really worry about you and Terry. It's obvious to me how you feel about each other, and I just know how hard this all must be on you."

Now it was my turn to cry. She understood. I could see it in her eyes—and she cared about me. Rosemarie wasn't worried that I was stealing her relative from the priesthood. She was worried about two people who loved each other and wanted to be together and hurt badly because they could not be. Perhaps it was because she had so recently lost her own love that her compassion touched levels of understanding so deep. I grew to love Rosemarie that night, and she will always be as close and as dear to me as a sister.

Across the yard in the darkness Terry and Michael crouched over some newfangled fireworks with great glee. The Fourth of July was a difficult day for a boy who had lost his dad. Yet I wondered which one of them benefited the most tonight. Terry was like a boy himself as he and Michael set off their fireworks in turn. Father-Son-Priest-Father. As he stood with his arm around Michael, I knew that a corner of Terry's heart was still unfilled. A beautiful burst of color showered over our heads.

It was sunrise, six A.M., out at the Disney Ranch in the Antelope Valley where countless movies and TV shows are filmed. Across the way three elephants were having their morning bath, and lions strolled by.

I gingerly placed my right foot on the wire. Though I was only a few feet off the ground, it was scary. I desperately needed another cup of coffee. The trainer, Bob Yerkes, called out, "Okay, Pam, balance with your torso. It will be a lot easier when you get the pole in your hands, but you have to learn to balance without it first. Ease it out . . . that's it . . . grip with your toes . . . No! . . . don't look down . . . keep your eyes on the horizon."

I was only a third of the way out on the wire when I fell. Thank heaven for the pads protecting my knees and elbows. It was early morning on the set of "Murder, She Wrote," and we were shooting a two-hour circus show. When I had been offered the role with Jackie Cooper, Martin Balsam, and Greg Evigan, I knew it was to play a high-wire performer. But nobody had ever asked me if I was afraid of heights! In fact it had never occurred to me that I would actually have to perform on a wire. They would have a stunt girl for the really high shots, but I would be about twelve feet up for the close shots. I would even have to do a fall into an air bag! Not only that, but I would only have a few rehearsals in which to master this new craft.

"Up you go. Try it again. Try to be graceful! Eyes front . . . okay . . . you made it to the center—now, hold on one foot and try a tiny arabesque with your left leg. Chest up . . . that's it!"

This was going to be fun. I landed with a thud and a giggle as a tiger wandered by with his trainer.

Maybe it was the tranquil setting or maybe it was the particular crew on "Murder, She Wrote," but working on the show was such a pleasure. There was no yelling, no pushing for time. It was terribly civilized by comparison with other sets, due in great part, I'm sure, to its star, Angela Lansbury. I'd loved every minute of the last few weeks. I'd adored the feeling of the circus, the animals everywhere, and learning the wire.

I'd already shot a number of sequences sliding down the pole from the top of the tent, falling into the net, and somersaulting to the floor. But today would be my "performance" on the high wire. I stood looking into the mirror at my reflection. A knock came at my trailer door.

"We're ready for you, Pam."

I closed my eyes, *Dear God, please don't let me get hurt. And please don't let me make a fool of myself!*

I slipped on a robe and walked over to the main tent. A pole and wire had been set up for me off to the side, with an air bag placed underneath. The makeup man adjusted my makeup as the stunt coordinator gave me some last-minute instructions.

"Camera's ready."

"Okay, Pam, can we see you up top?"

I slipped off my robe and climbed the ladder. It was cold—or was it just my nerves? I took a couple of deep breaths and tested the wire. The tricky part would be concentrating with some sort of confident, attractive expression on my face—not the panic that

I really felt. I stepped out to the edge of the platform.

"Camera's rolling. We have speed."

"All right, Pam. Take your own cue."

It was silent below; even some of the cast had come to watch. I took another deep breath and flashed a smile to a make-believe audience. Then, taking the pole in my hands, I started across the wire. Hitting the center, I knelt down on one knee, holding the pole in my right hand and gesturing to the "crowd" with my left. Rising slowly, I went into an arabesque. After another maneuver or two I was to pretend that there was a problem with the pole and fall off the wire into the net. Even though there was an air bag beneath me, it was quite a fall. I tossed the pole, falling directly into camera . . . and completely missing all but a little corner of the air bag! I didn't even feel it!

"How'd it look, guys?" I yelled as the crew burst into applause. What a great feeling!

Long after "Murder, She Wrote" and the circus tents had been left behind, I wondered why that world had been so important to me. It always feels good to be acknowledged, but it was more than that. My world with Terry had become so serious. Our futures were at stake, the future of the Catholic priesthood was at stake, and our lives were filled with questions. The set had been an escape to a fantasy place where, for a time, reality had been suspended and I'd felt transported to a magical land.

I could sense in Terry a growing anger. The more he learned, the stronger was his desire to speak out and to inform others. The anger was growing in me as well. As night after night I sat in my apartment reading book after book on the atrocities that had befallen the wives of priests, I began to feel strongly that their pain was already a part of my heart. There are no words to describe the loneliness of loving someone and being told that your love is a sin. I could feel the chill of humiliation that must have shivered through the wives of priests when, shocked and surprised, they were suddenly told they could no longer live with their husbands, could no longer carry their children, could no longer express their love intimately. Abandoned and humiliated as they were, what had become of their faith, I wondered? Were they able to hold on to their beliefs, their God? Did they recognize the source of such malevolent edicts of certain popes for the human frailty it was, clinging still to the God they loved? I wondered.

Sunday, July 6th, was a perfectly gorgeous day, sunny and bright. Terry had been saying Mass at Good Shepherd every Sunday for the last number of months because Father de Souza, with whom he usually alternated, was away. It had been good for Terry, as it had kept him in contact with his parishioners and his fellow priests. This Sunday was vocation Sunday, and the priest was supposed to speak about vocations to the priesthood and religious life.

As usual I dressed for the twelve-fifteen Mass. I strolled through the courtyard, now in full blossom, and got into my car. Terry would have finished the eleven-o'clock Mass and would be greeting parishioners about now. When I arrived, I was surprised to see Terry's youngest brother, Dan, and his girlfriend, Tracy.

The whole family had planned to gather at Terry's mom's after Mass for brunch, but I hadn't expected them to be at church—especially Dan, whom I had seen there only on rare occasions. The three of us took seats in the center of the church, and as the procession began, we looked back to see Terry's whole family sitting a few rows behind. At that moment none of us realized how important this Mass would be, nor how treasured the coincidence would become that all of us were there together. Looking back, I have to wonder if coincidence isn't frequently the hand of God.

The congregation sat down as Terry finished reading the Gospel.

" 'The harvest is rich, but the laborers are few.' This saying of Jesus has often been the basis for sermons throughout the Church on the need for vocations, and in particular on the importance of our praying for vocations to the priesthood. I want to spend a few minutes talking about this vitally important saying of Jesus, because the future of the priesthood affects all of us, our families, our children, our grandchildren.

"Some of what I'm about to say may sound harsh, but please recognize that what I say comes out of my love for the priesthood and the Church.

"There are some four hundred thousand priests worldwide. In the last twenty years over one hundred thousand priests have resigned the priesthood. In a U.S. survey of resigned priests conducted in 1969 and 1970, the two foremost reasons mentioned for resignation were, first, conflict with authority, and second, problems with celibacy."

Suddenly my throat went completely dry, and I began to perspire heavily. Not once in the seven months since he had moved out of the Jesuit Community had Terry spoken publicly about any aspect of his research. And he had said nothing to me about this. Could it possibly be his intention to share his knowledge with the congregation on this morning in July?

"What does this mean? This means we will have priests burning out, priests overworked, priests having heart attacks—this means the community of the faithful will have less opportunity to receive the Eucharist, to celebrate Mass, to receive the Sacrament of Reconciliation and other Sacraments.

"What are some of the solutions proposed to address this crisis? The most frequently proposed solutions concern themselves with two areas: married clergy and women priests."

I glanced sideways at Tracy, who was sitting on my right. I felt self-conscious, as though the entire church full of people must be looking at me. But they weren't; their attention was riveted on the pulpit.

"The first rulings regarding the sexual continence of married priests were heavily imbued with a notion of cultic purity. Because the Sacrament of Christ's body is holy, a priest offering Mass must be holy. And because elements of Gnosticism and Manicheanism had affected some of the most prominent popes and Church Fathers, all desires of the flesh, including marital intercourse were considered impure. Married priests, therefore, were forbidden to make love to their wives. Bishops, priests, and deacons who made love to their wives were dismissed from the clerical state.

"At the very core of these rulings was the notion that sexual intercourse between a priest and his wife was at best tainted, and at worst sinful. How do you feel about that?"

A stunned silence filled the church. Terry's voice was filled with sorrow and pain.

"What do you think these kinds of rulings did to priests and their wives? You can imagine. For over seven hundred years there was a long, bitter, and sometimes bloody struggle between the popes and bishops favoring the law of continence and the married clergy. At times the wives of priests were forced to live outside the townships, their children were called bastards. Sometimes the wives were imprisoned and even turned into slaves.

"Finally, due to the strong efforts of popes favoring the monastic tradition and the law of continence, especially due to Pope Gregory the Seventh, the Second Lateran Council in 1139 declared priests' marriages, already contracted or to be contracted, invalid—'So that the law of continence and that purity which is pleasing to God may spread among ecclesiastical persons.'

"Today, as we look forward to the year 2000, as we recognize the dark possibility that the priesthood as we know it will be disappearing or vanishing—or that our children or grandchildren may find it difficult to receive the Sacraments—let us be informed of how serious is the debate concerning the priesthood. Let us pray that future decisions of the Church regarding the priesthood are based on wisdom, on an almost brutal honesty with mistakes of the past, on respect, and on love."

Tracy gripped my hand and whispered, "Wow!" into my ear. I was completely stunned, unable to believe that I had heard Terry saying those words aloud in such a context. I knew the courage it must have taken to stand before these people and give those facts. It was unorthodox, unusual—but, appropriately, it was vocation Sunday! Had he been terrified or confident? He must have said much the same thing at the earlier Mass. Had the reaction then made it difficult to take the podium once again? It was easy to sense the unrest among the assembly. It wasn't a peaceful conclusion to the Mass—or was that just my imagination? And how would Terry's family react to what he had just done?

We left the parking lot and drove in our separate cars over to Terry's mother's house. For the rest of the afternoon I experienced my first Sweeney family "discussion." For hours they debated church history, the shortage of priests, the possibility of a married priesthood and its ramifications. And all the while I sat quietly cross-legged on the floor in the corner and never uttered a word. It wasn't my place; I wasn't the expert. There was so much I longed to say, but in the context of this emotional family gathering, all I wanted to do was disappear.

Does the Church have the right to tell a person not to marry? Does the Church have the right to stand in the way of love? Ethics were bantered back and forth until the family finally began to understand what Terry meant when he said that the laws were unethical. They had a terrible time trying to comprehend that. If the Church were wrong about that, what else might she be wrong about?

After a period of silence Terry's sister, Therese, a wonderfully strong-willed, modern-day child of the sixties, jumped in.

"Well, now, wait a minute. What about Pam?"

Everyone looked at me. I blushed. It would have been physically impossible for me to scrunch any closer to the wall. She gestured over to me from her place on the piano bench.

"I see a girl sitting over there who looks like she's in a lot of pain. What about her? The Church is an institution, but she's a real person. What about her feelings, Terry? You can't just disregard them."

222

Terry's eyes filled with tears, and his voice broke into a harsh whisper. He looked at his sister.

"I don't, Therese. I think about them every single day of my life."

Therese had brought things into a perspective that had not been broached before. Terry had never hidden me from his family. But until then, it had all been unspoken.

Suddenly I found myself in the middle of a dispute that had been going on for over eight hundred years. It was a new discussion for the Sweeney family in 1986—but, as for me, I was suspended in time, floating through the suffering, heartache, and blood-shed . . . through the tears, the courage and despair of couples through time, clinging to the desperate hope that somehow, some way, history could be altered, that everything would turn out all right. I felt surrounded by eyes and a thousand silent dreams that depended on me to come true.

On July 12th Terry got a phone call from Father de Souza, who informed him that he would no longer be needed at Good Shepherd. Yes, there had been a number of complaints about his sermon on vocation Sunday, but basically they had enough priests for the summer. After six years—a phone call. Terry went over to the rectory to meet in person with Monsignor Healy, the pastor of Good Shepherd. When he pressed for a more straightforward explanation, Monsignor Healy admitted that there had been some complaints, that the Church does things in her own time, and that Terry was no longer welcome. Two weeks later another priest from Loyola took his place.

For Terry it was the beginning of the end. He now had no parish in which he could function until another bishop would incardinate him, and all the ones he had asked had said no.

Looking back, how grateful we all were that his whole family had been present on that sunny Sunday in July when Terry said his final Mass within the walls of the parish he loved so well.

27

TERRY

In late spring the Provincial had called and asked why I still had not signed the resignation papers. I explained that I was trying first to find a bishop who would grant me priestly faculties. Father Clark said he didn't want my resignation process to drag out any longer.

In a certified letter dated July 7th the Provincial warned me that if I did not assure him within three weeks that I would follow his command to suppress my research, I would be dismissed from the Society.

Two weeks after my last Mass at Good Shepherd I sent a four-page reply to the Provincial explaining why I thought it would be right for him to rescind his "command."

On August 5th the Provincial wrote back saying he had read my letter very carefully and that he had no intention of rescinding his order that was issued in his letter of July 7, 1986.

That was it, then. Since Father Clark had first issued his ultimatum seven months earlier, I had exhausted all forms of ecclesial appeal. Because bishops were afraid of Rome, whether I resigned from the Jesuits or was expelled made little difference—my priesthood would be suspended. But it pained me deeply to consider the prospect that the Jesuit order would have in its history the dismissal of a Jesuit for refusing to suppress the hierarchy's discernment on the priesthood. Rather than allow this blight on the Society of Jesus, I chose to resign. I called the Rector of the university and set August 15th as the day.

The last seven months had revealed several important facts. I had finalized the survey responses and now knew that twenty-four percent of the U.S. bishops responding to my poll would approve optional celibacy for priests and that twenty-eight percent would approve ordaining women to the diaconate. I was now certain that, because the "mind of the Holy See" on the issues of married priests and women priests had been clearly expressed, the Vatican judged it consonant with obedience to suppress what the college of cardinals and the U.S. bishops thought about these issues. This proved that the Vatican, even in matters not infallibly defined, looked upon the cardinals and the bishops as servants of the Pope's mind. Finally I had learned from their reluctance to incardinate me that bishops were afraid of the Vatican.

Given these facts, I felt it would have been irresponsible for me to resign quietly. Vatican authority on these issues was based neither on Christ's teachings, nor on the needs of the faithful, nor on the discernment of the hierarchy. Rather, it was based on one man's opinion, the Pope's. Such "authority" supported the chilling notion that the Pope was accountable to God alone and not to the Church; and that the entire rest of the Church was not accountable to God, but only to the Pope. According to this model of Vatican authority, only the Pope was truly capable of knowing the mind of God.

Such authority is inimical to the Spirit of Christ and to human dignity and therefore can only harm the Church. I resolved to do whatever I could to challenge this authority. I realized my next task would be to complement the survey results with a thorough biblical and historical analysis of the Church's policy on the priesthood, and on its authority. The years of research I had done on these issues would finally have to be clarified and written down. This would take many more months. Meanwhile I had to decide exactly what to do about my resignation.

For seven months reporters and journalists had been asking me to explain why Rome wanted my survey suppressed. But I had refused to comment because it had taken all these months to discover why and because I had hoped to resolve this conflict privately within the Church.

It was now clear that it was impossible to resolve my dilemma through canonical appeal. The only choices left to me were to say nothing, which would have been wrong, or to attempt to hold this "authority" accountable to the goodness of people's hearts. Let the faithful really see the kind of authority governing their lives. Let them decide if this was what they wanted. Through a very good friend and publicist, Rupert Allan, I contacted Russell Chandler of the *Los Angeles Times* and Bob Garon of the *National Catholic Reporter.* They were invited to attend my resignation.

Since I had celebrated my first Mass of Thanksgiving on the Loyola campus thirteen years earlier, and since most of my life as a Jesuit priest had been at the university, it seemed fitting that the last Mass I would celebrate as a Jesuit priest would take place there. I set about inviting my family and some fifty friends to share this final Mass with me. I invited Father Bud Kieser, Father Tom Fitzpatrick, and six Jesuit priests to concelebrate the liturgy. Bud and Tom said yes, as did two of the six Jesuits. The other four said they were busy. After the Mass there was to be a reception at the Bird's Nest, which Pamela offered to hostess. The Bird's Nest had been the place of Pat's reception eighteen months earlier, and the place of my ordination reception in June 1973.

Driving onto campus the night of August 14th was a strange experience. It was the first time I had returned to campus since moving out on January 18th. It felt as if a blanket of mistrust and pain was now shrouding all memories of life there.

Entering the patio adjacent to Leavy, I asked God to help me make it through the Mass without breaking down. Since my ordination I had celebrated Mass thousands of times. After this evening all that was to stop. No more Communions, no more Confessions, no more baptisms, weddings, funerals—my ministry as a priest was coming to an abrupt halt.

Inside, Leavey Chapel was already filled. I hugged my mom and said hello to Dudley and to the rest of the family, then walked back into the sacristy to vest. In a few minutes Bud and Tom joined me. Bud and I had worked together for six years at Paulist Productions; Tom and I both worked in the East Los Angeles area for several years with street gangs. As friends and priests they understood how hard it would be to face suspension. The two Jesuits were already ten minutes late, so we decided to start without them. As it turned out, only one of them made it to the Mass. The other never showed up and never explained why he didn't.

After the Gospel reading, everyone sat down. I could see Pamela in the back of the chapel looking up at me. In her eyes there was compassion, support, and love. More than anyone else there, she knew my struggle. While the Jesuits, the bishops, and the Vatican had turned me away in order to protect their honored places in the "mind of the Holy See," Pamela had encouraged me to follow my conscience and my heart—even if it meant she would lose me. While they had acted out of fear, she had acted out of love.

As I took the bread and wine in my hands for the last time as a Jesuit priest, God whispered in my heart the painful and life-giving meaning of His words: "Take, eat. This is my body, which will be broken for you. Take and drink, this is my blood, which will be shed for you." His body, broken on the cross, His blood, shed on the cross, are the Second Passover. Communion with Him through this bread and wine, blessed by God's love, is communion with His Passover. But this Second Passover is not a freedom from physical death, it is a freedom from death of the soul.

Because of our communion with Him we, too, will be broken. We, too, will suffer and die. His anguish and pain and death will become ours, and ours will become His. And it is precisely in this Communion with Him that we are saved, that we will rise again, that his Passing Over will become ours. It is in this Communion that Life is ours, for in this Communion death does not exist.

As I distributed Communion for the last time that night of August 14, 1986, and as I saw the faces of family and friends as they said "Amen" to Him, I felt a fire burning in my heart.

The next morning, August 15th, I drove into the faculty parking lot behind the Foley Theatre Arts Building. I could see Mona, Rosemarie, Michael, Dudley, my mom, and several others standing near the campus post office. I had asked Pamela if she wanted to be there, but she had said no. She preferred to spend those moments alone, quietly praying in the university chapel.

After introducing those who did not know one another, I read a brief statement about why I was resigning. I tried to point out that a command given "in the name of our Lord Jesus Christ" to destroy the attitudes of the American bishops on the priesthood violated the very purpose of authority. In a sealed envelope addressed to His Holiness Pope John Paul II, I had placed a copy of my survey conclusions. Up until that moment no other eyes but mine had seen them. According to Jesuit "obedience" and to the "mind of the Holy See," under threat of dismissal and priestly suspension, no other eyes but mine ever should see them.

I pulled back the iron slot of the mailbox, dropped in the envelope. My last action as a Jesuit was to send this research to the Pope. It struck me as absurd that this very act was a disobedient act, contrary to the mind of the Holy See. As the metal slot clanged shut, I knew in my soul that the "obedience" the Jesuit order and the Vatican demanded was undermining the Church.

After this we walked over to the Jesuit Community. I asked the Rector if my family, Russell Chandler, and a photographer could witness the resignation. Father Caro said yes and asked me to sit at his desk and sign the dismissal papers.

My eyes were tearing so much that I could not read the words. For a long moment I thought I might break down right then and there. If my mother and brother hadn't been standing at my side, I probably would have. I begged God for the strength to be able to sign my name. To this day I don't know how writing so few letters could have been so difficult. For a while I lost track of time and space, as though my mind were floating in some dark void.

The sound of whispering in the room brought me back, and I forced my signature across the line.

While we were leaving, Father Caro was very gracious to my family and to me.

———

After several embraces I again thanked everyone for coming, and then started walking alone toward the parking lot.

In the distance Pamela walked out of the chapel and started toward me.

Suddenly I felt as though a tender breeze was sweeping through my entire being and was lifting away the heavy shackles of blind obedience that had been crushing my spirit. I felt free. Free in body, free in mind, free in heart.

28

PAMELA

I was awakened, as usual, by Devon's ferocious bark as the paperboy hurled the *L.A. Times* against my front door. But on this particular morning I was glad to be awakened. I switched on the light and ran out to pick up the paper. Hurriedly I turned to the front page of the Metro section, and there it was. The headline ran, PRIEST WON'T BOW TO VATICAN, QUITS OVER CELIBACY SURVEY. A picture of Terry signing his resignation papers from the Jesuit order was accompanied by a lengthy article. I was stunned! I'd had no idea that the story would be so extensive. As I spread the newspaper out on my living-room floor and began to read, the article renewed in me a horror and fury that the Church would place such censorship on its own bishops.

But the article was only the beginning. Within hours Terry's phone began to ring off the hook. There were calls from friends and acquaintances who had read the article, from TV stations requesting interviews, from journalists, radio stations—everything you can think of. Terry was being besieged. His good friend, Rupert Allan, had offered to field the calls and set up the appointments. Terry did *"The Today Show"* with Bryant Gumble, *"World News Tonight"* with Peter Jennings, *"Larry King Live,"* and many more.

As I sat in the middle of my bed glued to each TV report, I was relieved that others felt as appalled as I at the sanctions the Jesuit Provincial had placed upon Terry, and I was so very proud of him for not backing down and vanishing into the woodwork.

The Associated Press carried variations of the *L.A. Times'* article in newspapers all over the country, and within days it became a story of national magnitude. A follow-up article by Russell Chandler in the *L.A. Times* quoted the results of Terry's survey in a piece entitled, 24% OF BISHOPS WOULD LET PRIESTS WED, POLL FINDS. The *Times* also printed an article, written by Terry himself, headlined, ROME'S COMMAND SILENCES THE HIERARCHY. Several weeks later *The New York Times* carried a major article. There was an aura of shock, horror, and dismay among those who heard the story.

Because of the current climate in the United States regarding religious and academic freedom, Terry's story had taken on giant proportions. It followed closely on the heels of the stripping of theological faculties of Father Charles Curran of Catholic University at the request of the Vatican. There had been major student protests, as well as appeals on the part of Father Curran. All had been of great interest to the press. In Seattle Archbishop Hunthausen had had restrictions placed upon him in five different areas of his authority. He was greatly loved, and the people of his diocese as well as his fellow bishops had come to his defense, causing the Vatican eventually to retract its position. Little did we realize that in just over three months the December 27th headline of the Religion section of the *Los Angeles Times* would read,

VATICAN CRACKDOWNS LISTED AS YEAR'S TOP RELIGION STORY
HUNTHAUSEN, CURRAN, SWEENEY AMONG TARGETS

Russell Chandler would write, "Vatican crackdowns on U.S. Roman Catholicism were seen by the nation's religion news specialists as the top religion story of 1986, according to year-end reports and a poll of members of the Religion Newswriters Association."

In attempting to suppress Terry's research and forcing him from the Jesuit order, Rome had hoped to silence Terry. Rome had failed. Priest friends had warned Terry that were he no longer in good standing, he would have no platform from which to speak.

In reality it was just the opposite. Having resigned, he now had the freedom from obedience to follow his conscience in doing and saying what he thought was best for the Church.

Father Herb had once said to Terry, "You are not God's prophet." How could he make such a statement, I wondered? Who are we to judge whom God might choose? I knew Terry's emotional struggle. I knew that he at last was willing to accept ridicule and embarrassment if need be to do what he believed was being asked of him. And from somewhere within, God was giving him the strength. How proud God must be, I thought.

I would watch Terry's interviews in awe. One of the things that most impressed me was the way in which he dealt with the occasional personal attacks against him. He had been prepared for personal ridicule and insults, but meeting them face-to-face was quite another matter. What would usually happen is that after debating the situation with Terry for a while, his opponent would resort to personal attack and insult to Terry's character. Suspicion is a natural emotion when an institution that one loves is brought into question, and it is far easier to place blame on one "misguided" priest. It was in these moments that Terry shined the most. Never did he succumb to personal attacks of his own; he simply continued to direct the conversation back to the issues they had been called upon to discuss. Whatever personal, private pain took place inside of him, he never let it show. But, sitting watching, I felt it all too well.

It had been a long summer, I thought, as I sat among the guests at the Harvard Club of New York City waiting for the wedding to begin. I marveled at the elegance and sophistication around me. Ellen and John were finally getting married, and since both were originally from the East, they'd decided to hold the wedding there. I had flown in to make sure that John definitely said, "I do."

Sitting there that night, everyone looked so beautiful, smiling cheerfully at one another in their black-tie attire. It felt strange to be in such surroundings, with the constant pressure of life with Terry on hold for a day or two.

Not all of my stay in New York had been pleasant, however. It had been my intention to retrieve the rest of my clothing from my New York apartment while I was here. Over the phone I had sublet the apartment to a "friend" of a friend of mine, when I realized that I was going to remain in L.A. for a while. Since our mutual friend had arranged things, I'd assumed the person was trustworthy. At the time it had seemed a godsend. But it had turned out to be an enormous mistake. This tenant had promised to have my clothes boxed and delivered to my hotel upon my arrival, but he had not done so. Over the past few days I had tried repeatedly to get into my apartment to pack up my belongings, but he had refused to open the door. I could not possibly understand why, except for the fact that he owed me back rent. In desperation I finally went to his brother's business address and pleaded my case. The brother offered to help. Eventually I received a small portion of my belongings, but when this "friend" finally moved out of the apartment some time later, the rest of all my things had vanished.

As I'd walked away empty-handed from my beautiful little apartment, I had felt irresponsible for not having returned for my things earlier and foolish for trusting someone I didn't even know. I also felt as if I had once again betrayed my childhood dreams. Walking back to my hotel, I looked around me at all I had given up. Time was moving so fast. It had been twenty months since I had left for a Christmas holiday, and I was beginning to realize that a lot more time would have to pass before I could return to New York. Terry was in the thick of things now. As long as people would listen, he would speak. I realized how important it all was, but everything seemed to take so much time. I loved Terry, but was I right to have given up a life that was moving forward for one that might never even begin?

The wedding march began. John smiled radiantly as Ellen gracefully started down the aisle. Her gown was so lovely, with a magnificent train. Tears started to fall. It didn't matter that my makeup would be ruined. I was happy for them—but my heart ached. Would I ever, ever have my own wedding day?

29

TERRY

The telephone receiver clicked into a dial tone as I set it back in its cradle. The conversation with Archbishop Mahony's personal secretary had been brief, cordial, and unexpected. The Archbishop wanted to meet with me on Monday, September 29th. I wondered why. Ten months earlier he had complained about my research. In May he had refused to incardinate me. And when I later wrote him asking for his reasons for refusing to incardinate me—in light of the fact that he had never met me in person, nor had he spoken to the Provincial about me—he wrote back saying that my letter requesting incardination was "very open and complete" and that he really did not feel "it was appropriate to speak with you or the Provincial in person." He had gone on to say that there was no such thing as a canonical "right" to incardination and that he was not required to give any further information. "I am only required to review your petition, take whatever counsel I feel adequate, and then so advise you." Even the letters of support that had poured in from Good Shepherd parishioners in July and August complaining that I had been suddenly and inexplicably absent from the parish hadn't seemed to sway him. But after the attempted suppression of the survey had become a topic of both national and international press, he wanted to meet with me. Why? Was it to incardinate me? Or to reprimand me further?

In the weeks following my resignation the intense public outcry against Rome's efforts to suppress the bishops' opinions proved that many others shared my concern about Church authority and the priesthood. This reassured me of the importance of continuing my research. Further, it prompted me to begin a series of informal consultations with various experts in the fields of canon law, Constitutional law, and human rights. My hope was to learn their opinions on whether requiring priests by law to be celibate violated Church law, fundamental human rights, or the U.S. Constitution. I wondered if the Archbishop intended to curtail the freedom I needed to pursue these discussions.

The Archbishop walked briskly into the reception area inside the second floor of the chancery. He extended his hand to me with a cheerful smile on his face. "Well, it's good to finally meet you. I feel like we've already met in the press. Come on down to my office where we can talk."

His manner was so friendly and relaxed that I found it hard to believe this was the same person who had so abruptly denied my petition for incardination. Which was the real Archbishop—the man who refused me then or the person smiling at me now?

He led me down the hallway to the last office on the southeast corner of the building.

"I thought it would be useful for us to have a conversation about all that is going on. I don't know, and I'm not interested in, all the dynamics of what's gone on between you and the Jesuits. I am really concerned about where you are now, where you go in the future, and what's happening to you. Because I don't think it's good just to leave you out in the middle of nowhere."

It was puzzling to hear him express such concern more than four months after his own decision to exclude me from priestly ministry in Los Angeles. I told the Archbishop that I was in a state of "nonpenal" suspension and that I was trying to find a bishop who would accept me.

"I really think you should understand why I didn't, just so that you'll know that it's not as dark and sinister as you might think."

He went on to explain that there is a general policy between bishops and major superiors of religious orders. "If a man leaves or is dismissed from an area where he spent a significant amount of time or ministry, normally the bishop of that place doesn't accept him into his diocese. We all feel there's advantage in a fresh start in a new place without the baggage of the past. It also creates some bit of tension between the bishop and religious superiors.

"At the same time we normally have kind of an understanding that if there's a situation that reaches a certain level of publicity, it really does create some problems in our relationship with the archdiocese and the community. It doesn't give the man the freedom to enter fully into whatever ministry again, because there's a history there."

That seemed an odd thing to say in light of what he had done. "I'm glad you brought that up because apparently one of my friends at Good Shepherd parish had written to you about me. And you wrote back saying pretty much what you just said now concerning a matter that has been publicized. But in fact the publicity happened August sixteenth, and you refused to incardinate me three months before that time."

There was a moment of silence as the Archbishop considered what I had just said.

"Well, I entered the thing of publicity only as an addendum."

Addendum? I thought, *that's not how your letter read and that's not how it was interpreted.* I then brought up the matter of the survey, his criticism of it, and his assertion to a parishioner that he had absolutely nothing to do with my leaving the Jesuit order. I mentioned to him that the heads of the Sociology Department at UCLA and at Mount Saint Mary's had considered my survey unquestionably valid both in method and in content. I said further that his and the Apostolic Nuncio's criticism of the survey were explicitly mentioned by the Jesuit Provincial as one of the reasons why the survey had to stop.

"I just want you to know I've never had a thing against you doing this or anything else. I just felt it was inadequate treatment of the very serious nature of the four issues. That's all. The

Nuncio's never contacted me about that. I never heard from Rome."

"Oh . . . ?" I asked.

His comment about the Nuncio confused me. During our phone conversation the previous November he had said the Nuncio had called him and written him a letter asking about the survey. Archbishop Mahony had even asked me to explain in writing why I was doing the survey and to send copies of that explanatory letter to him and to the Nuncio.

"Are you saying the Nuncio did not contact you with a complaint about the survey?" I asked.

"No. No. Uh—he did, excuse me. I should say he contacted me because he was in Los Angeles. And I had already, though, written you a letter."

No, he didn't; yes, he did. What kind of answer was this? When the Archbishop first contacted me, which was by phone, he had said he had already received both a letter and a phone call from the Nuncio. The ambiguities and discrepancies in this conversation were making it increasingly difficult to follow. But even more disquieting was the still-unanswered question: Exactly who pressured the Jesuit General to have the survey suppressed? Who would presume to have the authority to silence the attitudes on priestly ministry of all the cardinals in the Church and all the bishops in the United States? Would the Apostolic Nuncio presume that authority? Cardinal Ratzinger? The Cardinal Secretary of State? Or would it only be the one whose authority they represented? Was it the Pope himself who had initiated the suppression? But Archbishop Mahony was evidently not the one to be asked these questions.

I asked him if he knew of any Ordinaries in the United States who would consider incardinating me. He replied that he couldn't guarantee anything, but he thought, given my background in media, that I should think of applying to a diocese that had a significant commitment to media, adding "I'd be very happy to talk to these bishops personally—I mean, by letter, in your favor."

"Thank you. I would appreciate that very much."

"As a matter of parenthesis I've been toying with the idea of asking you to do something for us, for Los Angeles, in the future. I'm going to have to talk with John Clark and see what he says—kind of a special assignment for which we could give you faculties and have you stay for a year or something—but I'm not sure whether they'd buy it."

"Buy what?" I asked.

"We're having the Pope here next year. And the main theme we've been assigned is communications. We're doing two things with the Pope with communications: one, he's going to address top national leadership in the five areas of radio, television, film, recording, and print. And we're doing this at the Sheraton Universal. But in the Universal Amphitheatre we're doing a nationally televised thing with the Pope and youth, space-bridging three other cities in the country.

"Well, anyway it's this that I was thinking of. And when all this came up, I said, Terry Sweeney would be a great person to help."

The purpose of the meeting was now becoming clear. He was offering to lift me out of "priestly limbo" by helping to place me in another diocese; he wanted me to assist him in preparing the media coverage of the papal visit, and he was willing to grant me priestly faculties during those preparations.

Both suggestions at that moment seemed a godsend, and I welcomed them gratefully. But the last comments he made as I was leaving turned my elation into uneasiness.

"Give the papal visit some thought just in case we're able to pull that off too."

"I will."

"Maybe we can do it without a whole lot of fanfare that involves your picture and name. That may be a condition we would have to go with."

The meeting with the Archbishop left me in a quandary. On the one hand, I longed to regain priestly ministry. On the other, I found it difficult really to trust the Archbishop and was afraid that the conflict I had been in with the Jesuits over the issues of authority and the priesthood would be repeated with him. Furthermore there was Pamela. Though I had not made up my mind whether to ask her to marry me, I knew that she would have to be part of any decision I would make regarding incardination. Finally I knew that Archbishop Mahony would feel compromised if I had accepted priestly faculties and then began speaking out on the controversial issues of authority, married priests, and women priests. He should know up front that I felt a moral obligation to address the crisis facing the Church.

On October 21st I wrote to the Archbishop, thanking him for offering to help. I suggested that before he contacted the three dioceses in question it might be helpful first to work out whether he would grant me faculties as a priest in Los Angeles, where, except for the first eleven years of Jesuit training, I had lived all my life.

A week later the Archbishop wrote me a letter stamped "Confidential" in which he strongly urged me to refrain from further press and media interviews. Regarding my research, he advised that it not continue to be a primary part of my current or future ministry.

After prayer and reflection I wrote to the Archbishop declining his offer.

On November 13th Russell Chandler called me from Washington, D.C., where he was attending a national meeting of the bishops. To my surprise he said that Archbishop Mahony had told him that he had granted me priestly faculties. I said that I had not been informed of this action, and I asked if the Archbishop had mentioned the conditions he'd placed on the granting of the faculties. He said the Archbishop had not. When, later, Mr. Chandler asked the Archbishop if he had put conditions on the granting of priestly faculties, Archbishop Mahony replied that he had not.

On November 21st the Archbishop wrote again explaining why he was granting me faculties and why the matter showed up in the press. He did not explain why he was not incardinating me, nor why he was granting me faculties for six months rather than a year, nor did he explain why he informed the press before me that he was granting me faculties, nor why he had contravened his own counsel in "keeping my name and face out of the press."

Instead he suggested that we meet again in person, this time with

Father Bud Kieser. Bud had already told me that the Archbishop had asked his help with the media preparations for the papal visit and had asked him whether I might be a good person to produce the media event surrounding the Pope's visit with youth at the Universal Amphitheatre.

It was all starting to fall into place. The next "in person" meeting would end up being a planning session for the papal visit.

But in accepting the faculties and in assisting with the papal visit, I would be swept up into another ecclesiastical storm. Before the media coverage of my resignation Archbishop Mahony had refused to incardinate me and did not offer any help whatsoever in finding diocesan placement. After the media coverage he offered to help me find a diocese and he offered priestly faculties—but conditioned on helping him promote the Pope's visit and on setting aside my research on the priesthood crisis that the Vatican wanted suppressed.

I couldn't help thinking again of that infamous temptation in Scripture: "All these things will I give you if you but fall down and worship me."

On December 1, 1986, I wrote to the Archbishop declining his "offer" of priestly faculties and said there was no reason for us to meet.

30

PAMELA

Rage: Violent anger or passion; fury. I felt, most of the time, as though an intense fire blazed away in my chest. Frustration, isolation, desperation, longing, and desire had finally snapped something vital inside me. I slammed the kettle onto the stove. These were not good times.

Do you know what the name Pamela stands for? It means "all sweetness and honey." That's who I had always been; that's who I was supposed to be. What had happened to her? What had happened to that solicitous person whose understanding had comforted Terry over the loss of his brother so very long ago? She had vanished. In her place was an angry, bitter woman with a constant furrow between her brows.

As the holidays approached, things grew worse. Everything seemed to upset me. It had been months since Terry had resigned from the Jesuit order, but still he continued to seek incardination.

Time was passing, and I felt that I had been patient for a very long time. For two years Terry had been the focus of my life: his problems, his life decisions, his quest. I longed to be the center of his universe, as he was mine. As it was, though, I began to feel that every detail of his life must fall into place before I would—if I ever did—become a consideration. I saw failure in every aspect of my life, and certainly in this relationship. The patience with which I had approached our situation was bit by bit being replaced by an instinct for self-preservation. I became impatient and harsh with Terry, and frequently we argued for hours. It would start over some small, seemingly insignificant misunderstanding and then escalate to intense proportions. Terry's course of action seemed to be to deal first with his situation with the Church, his book, his survey, the dwindling priesthood, and then his love for me. The silent implication was that I "could wait." Well, I was beginning to get tired of waiting. Time passing with the promise of a future is one thing, but time simply passing you by is quite another.

Outwardly my actions appeared to be born of frustration and anger, but underneath it all I was in tremendous pain. With all this waiting and hoping I had compromised my own identity. This fact, coupled with the lack of any assurances of a future with Terry, was beginning to take a heavy toll on my heart. With every day I grew more frightened, more threatened, more alone, and more jealous. Where once I had been secure and nurtured by our love, I now felt threatened by every phone call, every social request. Occasionally women would call to invite Terry to some function or other. And I, as a woman with no identity in his life, felt threatened by these friendships.

As my confidence in any future with Terry waned, so did my self-confidence. At last I sought help from a psychotherapist whom I had seen for a period of time prior to making my decision to move to New York. She had been very helpful to me at that time. As I poured forth my fears and concerns, I could hear the petty ring of jealousy and insecurity in my voice. The fringes of my stability were raw and frayed, and I felt that I was clinging to sanity by a thread. In shame and despair, I blamed myself for my emotional roller coaster. I wasn't fit to love! I had lost my self-respect. My self-worth was gone.

As I look back on it now, it is far easier for me to recognize the desperation which lay at the heart of my behavior. I felt rejected and unimportant and insignificant. I was angry that I came last in Terry's life. I resented having this wonderful love that couldn't be shared with anyone. And I was sexually frustrated. I wanted desperately to express my physical desire and love for Terry, but was in a constant state of having to suppress those desires. It seemed that I had been holding all those tremendous passions inside for so long, and now the steam was beginning to escape. And often the lid blew completely off the pot! Eventually my therapist helped me to see that it was easier to fly into a rage than to cope with the disappointment I felt at having to hide our love, suppress my sexual feelings, or to allow to surface from the darkest corners of my heart the deep, deep terror that I would eventually lose this love.

From Terry's point of view, which was less emotional and far more accurate, things were moving very, very fast. In the last year, the previous twenty-four years of his life had been altered drastically. He didn't understand my behavior at all. The more I tried to explain, the less he understood—and the more skeptical he became, not only of our relationship, but also of my stability. There are dark places—private, desolate pits each one of us goes to in our personal pain—the pain no one else could ever share. Those places scare me still. Terry had felt that despairing place once, and in it he had longed for death. As for me, I felt as though I was in a living death.

This period of time was difficult not only for me, but also for my family. My mother had sensed very early on that I had strong feelings for Terry. Even before she had met him, she had sensed something different in the way I spoke about him. When I confided in her, she respected my confidence and tried to help me work through my confusion. She had stood by me all my life . . . and this time, it was the same. I valued my mother's advice now, as I had from the time I was very young. I had always looked up to her and wanted to be just like her. When I was a little girl, I used to love to sit on her dressing room floor and watch her get ready to go out for the evening. We'd talk and talk. I learned a lot from my mother: about acting, about life, and about becoming a lady. Along with her deep spirituality, she has a clarity and wisdom about her which I greatly admire.

After they had met Terry, it became clear to everyone in my family how he and I felt about each other. Needless-to-say, they were deeply concerned. To them it seemed an impossible situation.

Terry was a priest, and there was no way that the two of us could ever be together. My family had seen me in love before, but they knew that this relationship was different from any other I had experienced. And what they saw frightened them. Feelings this deep for a Roman Catholic priest could only lead to a broken heart and an empty future.

However, after having spent time getting to know Terry and learning about everything he had gone through with the Jesuit order, my family grew to understand and appreciate his integrity. They saw clearly that the feelings on both sides were mutual . . . but what could be done? In concern for my parents' feelings, Terry had written them a letter in which he had explained the complexity of his situation. Although the letter was helpful, their daughter was still left in a state of limbo.

During this time, my parents and Steve were extremely patient and supportive. As my desperation grew, I began to share it more and more with my family rather than to burden Terry. I remember one day sitting up at Steve's house and crying for the better part of the day. They all listened to me and offered their advice when it was needed. My mother frequently spent long conversations with me on the phone, and one day when I was feeling particularly despondent, she and Ginger parked themselves on the couch in my apartment and flatly refused to leave until I felt better. Bill, too, understood my emotional roller coaster and spoke privately to Terry about it on my behalf. It was a difficult situation for all of us, and I am so grateful for my family's support. They shouldered a burden that none of us could ever have expected to experience.

"Okay, Devo, up you go!"

My brother, Steve, loaded Devon up onto the wing of the twin engine airplane he had rented to fly us to Mendocino for Christmas.

"Atta girl."

She trotted up the rubber matting and slithered between the seats. Devon is pretty used to flying by now. I pulled her up onto my lap for takeoff. Terry was up front, acting as Steve's copilot for the flight. He read the preflight checklist as Steve tested each of the instruments.

"All strapped in back there?"

"Yep," I called back.

"Okay, we're off."

The flight was smooth until just beyond San Francisco, where we began to hit some pretty bad weather. I have never felt comfortable flying commercially, but when I fly with my brother, I always feel completely safe. The plane began to bounce, and Devon, who usually sleeps the whole way, roused herself enough to look up at me with questioning eyes. I held her tightly next to me and put on the extra set of headphones Steve had brought along so that I could hear him talking with the tower.

A thick bank of fog was beginning to cover the entire coastline. They call it the marine layer, and it can last for a number of days or longer. This layer of fog is one of the problems with flying into northern California. Like a lot of the smaller airports in the area, the Little River Airport does not have provisions for an instrument-landing situation, meaning that the pilot flies a visual approach. He has to be able to see the airport and runway in order to land. Occasionally we have had to land at an alternate airfield farther inland when Little River was socked in.

The clouds were rolling in steadily, and I knew it was a race for time. I could see Steve and Terry in the cockpit immersed in total concentration. Steve would occasionally say something, and Terry would nod his head.

"Pam, we're coming into Mendocino, but it's pretty thick. I'm going to make a pass and see if we can find a break in the clouds. Keep your eyes peeled. Still strapped in?"

"You betcha!"

Down we weaved through the fog. I couldn't see a thing out the window. Devon sensed something was up, probably due to the change in cabin pressure. The sound of the engines changed noticeably as we descended.

"Do you see it, Terry?"

"Nothing, Steve."

We climbed up out of the marine layer and circled what should be the field below.

"Well, let's take one more pass, okay?"

"Shoot."

Again we swooped down through the clouds in an effort to catch a glimpse of the runway.

"There it is," Steve pointed. "If we hurry, I think we can make it. Pam, there's a little patch down there. I can get through, but it'll be a tight turn. We'll be on the ground in a minute."

"Okay, Steve."

A word about my brother. Steve is an inspirational human being. He inspires confidence in everything he does. There is a calm assurance about him that enables others to feel at ease. He has a strong ethical and moral conscience, and his abilities as a surgeon and as a pilot are greatly respected by his peers. Everything he does, he does with kindness. He is capable, sure, calm, and poised—even in the thickest clouds you ever saw!

I couldn't even see the hole he was heading for. Suddenly the plane banked into a tight left turn, and by the time I could finally see the ground, we were seconds away from touching the runway. It was the smoothest landing you can imagine—and I burst into applause. Terry looked back at me from the cockpit with "Isn't he amazing?" written all over his face. Devon yawned.

Our Christmas stay with my parents was wonderful. I was anxious for Terry to spend some time with my folks and to see the beautiful area where they live. I slept in my favorite little bedroom with the tiny blue rosebuds on the wall and the hand-painted beams on the ceiling. Steve stayed in the guest quarters downstairs, and Terry got the large guest bedroom overlooking the meadow. The guest shower in that room has a wall-to-ceiling window so that while you are lathering up, you can look out at the deer grazing on the bluff. Mom's Christmas tree was as magnificent as it could be, and though it would only be a four-day holiday for us this year, every moment was special.

My parents welcomed Terry warmly into their home. We showed him the ten-mile beach, took walks on the bluff, showed him Heritage House, where they filmed *Same Time Next Year*, and wandered through the little village of Mendocino. And, of course, there was the flying.

As a surprise for his birthday a few years before, Mom had given Bill a beautifully wrapped package. Inside was an envelope filled with cherry pits. Bill looked at them, perplexed. "Cherry . . . cherries . . . oh, Julie . . . pits!" She had given him an aerobatic airplane called a Pitts Special. Steve, who had gone through U.S. Air Force Pilot Training before entering medical school, also loves to fly aerobatics, and when he and Bill get together, they always spend a good deal of time out at the airport. And this vacation was no different. An hour or so after leaving for the airport, we'd hear the familiar sound of their engine as the plane buzzed the house. Mom, Terry and I would run out onto the bluff and watch as each, in turn, would put on a private airshow for us out over the water. Snap rolls, aileron rolls, Cuban eights, outside loops, Immelmanns, Lomcevaks, torque rolls and six-point rolls, hammer-heads, inverted spins. It was really a thrill!

The next day, it was Terry's turn as Bill gave him his first ride in the open cockpit biplane. As Steve strapped him into the parachute harness and briefed him about how to pull the rip-cord in case he had to bail out, I asked, "Are you sure about this?"

"Sure, I am . . . I couldn't be in better hands!"

Terry climbed into the front cockpit with that trusting Irish smile on his face, and they were off. Bill always explains each maneuver to a passenger over the intercom before he executes it just to make sure his passenger knows what to expect. From the ground we watched as the plane took off in a steep climb and then headed off into the distance upside down! A little while later, they came in for a landing. As the Pitts taxied up to the hanger, we could hear Terry exclaim "What a blast!"

On the afternoon of Christmas Eve I popped into the kitchen to find Terry mulling over a cookbook. My mom's glasses were perched on the tip of her nose, and her hands were covered with flour.

"Hi, honey. Terry's helping me make a pumpkin pie. I couldn't have done it without him!"

247

This was a sight to behold. The man who didn't know how to open those little baggies at the market a few months before now was baking pies! I tiptoed out of the kitchen, leaving them to it.

Christmas Eve is my favorite night of the year and has been ever since I was a little girl. Eggnog, turkey, stuffing, cranberries, mashed potatoes, biscuits, Christmas carols, candlelight—and a million dishes to wash up afterward. After the festivities were finally at an end, Terry and I drove into the little town of Mendocino to attend midnight Mass. The night was pitch-black, with only the tiny Catholic church alight on this Christmas Eve. Christmas carols floated on the wind. The serenity of the Mass, of the night, of the darkness, and thoughts of the manger filled me with a peace that had been missing for many months. I left the church with a prayer that I would once again find within myself that gentle person I used to know.

I awoke Christmas morning to music: Christmas carols, the signal that the day had begun. Ramos Fizzes and presents would be waiting. I showered and dressed, and wandered out onto the balcony.

"Morning, honey," Mom called. "Terry's down on the bluff." In the distance I could see his green flannel shirt as he stood overlooking the sea. Devon romped through the tall grass. I started down the winding path just as Terry turned. As he saw me, he opened his arms wide and ran to meet me, just like Heathcliff and Cathy in a scene out of *Wuthering Heights*.

"Merry Christmas," he called as we ran into each other's arms. As we hugged and laughed, I could see Bill watching from the terrace of the house.

The day was spent opening presents and playing games downstairs in the game room. Leftovers were on the dinner menu, and they couldn't have been more scrumptious. As we finally pushed our chairs back from the table, Bill raised his glass in a toast. It had been a wonderful holiday.

"Terry, you know how delighted we are to have you here with us. But, as I'm sure you can imagine, we've been pretty worried about the kid here. Naturally we're concerned about her and the situation the two of you are in. The letter you sent to us a number of months ago was very helpful, and we appreciate it—but what are your plans now?"

"I share your concerns, Bill. Our situation is delicate. As I mentioned in my letter, we've really needed this time to get to know each other—without all the stress and upheaval accompanying my brother's death and my resignation from the Jesuits. There's a very old and I think very wise Ignatian counsel about making life decisions: Make them during times of emotional stability, not during times of emotional extremes. Also, as I mentioned to Pamela many times, I feel a serious responsibility toward the priesthood and to finishing research on several key areas vitally affecting the Church."

"How much longer do you think that will take?"

"Well . . ." Terry paused. He knew what Bill was asking. We all did. He was asking for a deadline, some sort of a timetable, without which Bill sensed that I couldn't go on.

From the very first time I had met Terry, I had decided that if we were to have a future together, that decision must be his to make. I had made every effort not to coerce him in any way, believing that if I were to do so, our possible future might be ruined. If, later on, he were to feel that he had been pressured or manipulated by me, it would undermine the very foundations of our relationship, which most probably would never last. I had wanted to tell Terry all these things, but I knew I couldn't. Instead, my family had shouldered the burden of my fears. They could well appreciate the dilemma, the pain, the frustration. They had been patient and supportive for many months, but they were worried about me.

Now Bill was asking for an answer. Bill knew I needed some help, and without my having to ask, he had come to my rescue. I sat holding my breath.

"A couple of months, Bill."

"Good. We wish you well with your research, and once again, we're so happy to have you here with us."

I crawled into bed Christmas night elated. Just two more months and the waiting would be over! I closed my eyes and slept the soundest sleep I had slept in months.

31

TERRY

Even before my vows of chastity, obedience, and poverty were nullified by Rome, I knew that I loved Pamela. I loved her as the best of friends and as a treasured companion. Sometimes, even, there were flashes of intuition prompting me to feel that one day we would marry. But my vow of celibacy and my conscience made me very wary of those intuitions. Just the idea of "falling in love" while professing celibacy would fill me with feelings of guilt and hypocrisy. From our earliest days in the seminary we were constantly reminded in exhortations and in readings of the nobleness and virtue of celibacy and of the wickedness of "temptations of the flesh." And marriage, even though praised in Church teachings, was, for priests, denounced as a sacrilegious concession to materialism and selfishness. We were taught to love Christ and His Church, but warned never to "fall in love" with anyone. Priests falling in love were "unfaithful" to their "spouse, the Church."

I had been so conditioned in my training regarding celibacy to automatically think of all the reasons why "falling in love" was wrong that it took an entire spiritual awakening of mind, heart, and body to begin to realize that falling in love might well be a grace. Before I had entered the seminary, I'd told the Jesuit counselor that it was hard for me to give up the possibility of marriage. He'd said that if I wanted to be a priest, it was a sacrifice I'd have to accept. Until Pamela it never occurred to me that I'd made the wrong sacrifice and that being a married priest might be the "sacrifice" God was asking.

Years of pastoral experience and research had led to a more profound understanding of what priestly life really meant. But habits and attitudes formed since teenage years by seminary training, and constantly reinforced by the way the Church exercised its authority, would minimize and ridicule this new understanding.

Ironically, in the very act of Rome's nullifying my vows, my heart was led into the radical freedom it needed to finally experience their true meaning. In time I came to realize that authority is born "from above"—not "above" in the institutional or hierarchical sense, but "above" in the divine sense. God, who is wisdom, life, and love, creates in each person a unique dynamic toward life, wisdom, and love. The more a person realizes this dynamic, the closer that person draws to the fullness of identity, both human and divine. Authority is born from and creates the fulfilling of life, wisdom, and love.

In time I came to realize the proper connection between vow, law, and individual choice for celibacy or marriage. Each person is created to enjoy life, wisdom, and love. These are the most fundamental of all human rights. For some their love will best be expressed in living celibately; for others love will best be expressed in marriage. The right to vow either celibacy or marriage is an inalienable, God-given right. Law should protect that right to choose, not coerce someone into vowing either marriage or celibacy. Unfortunately Church laws requiring celibacy for priests coerce all those priests who would not spontaneously choose celibacy as the best way for them to love. Thus, mandated celibacy compromises law, vow, and priesthood because it dictates that the only way for a priest to love is celibately.

When I met Pamela I had so much to learn about love, about listening to the movements of the heart, about treasuring rather than resisting or feeling guilty about any personal thought or desire for emotional and physical intimacy. Intimacy became one of the most difficult, yet most important discoveries in our relationship. We realized that our love was deeper than the frustrations that resulted from abstaining from sexual intercourse, and we both began to appreciate our love as a gift from God.

Pamela was much quicker to realize this than I. Gradually, through her more integrated understanding and expression of love, I began to see the passion for intimacy not as a form of lust, but as a gift of love. I began to feel not guilty about sexual desire, but glad. I began to realize that love has a body as well as a soul and that the intense longings for physical and emotional closeness are incontestable proof that the human spirit is made for union, and will not rest until it has finally united with the one loved.

As this awakening led me to deeper discoveries about love, I became convinced, as Jesus himself was, that both celibacy and marriage are wholly compatible with discipleship, that both celibacy and marriage are wholly consonant with the priesthood—and that neither the vow of celibacy nor the vow of marriage best furthers the kingdom of God, but rather the love in which those vows are lived.

It was one of those rare, soothingly peaceful evenings. Pamela was happy that I had asked for a second helping of the peach upside-down cake she had baked. It had been Pat's favorite dessert, and Pamela had asked Rosemarie for her recipe. Strange, I thought, how people die, but recipes live on, resurrecting memories, feelings, fragrances.

Immediately next to the dining-room table were two lace-curtained windows that faced out to the apartment courtyard. Pamela raised her window a little higher, breathed in the night air, and gazed at the courtyard garden. Moonlight had transformed blackness into blue-white, flower silhouettes. The sweet smell of roses and gardenia hovered over the table as she looked away from the garden and back toward me. The warm glow of candlelight shimmered against her flushed cheeks as she lifted the chilled wineglass to her lips and sipped leisurely.

Her hazel eyes were stunningly beautiful and revealing. When she was happy and excited, they would be wide and childlike; when she was serious and concentrating, they would focus intently; when she was angry, they would be sharp and piercing; when she was feeling vulnerable and exposed, they would be shy and averting. That night as she placed her wineglass back on the table and smiled across at me, her eyes were filled with wonder, with shyness, and with longing.

Earlier conversation about my research and the day's events had trailed off into unfinished thoughts as the hauntingly spiritual voice of Jane Olivor in her *Chasing Rainbows* album quieted our minds and urged us to listen to other voices within.

Pamela's face reflected the lovely sadness of the lyrics. Candlelight danced in her eyes as they glistened on the verge of tears. I raised my wineglass, toasted her: "To you, and to your eyes, your incredibly beautiful eyes. The most beautiful eyes I've ever seen."

Her whole face flushed with color. She smiled briefly, then got up quickly to change the album. She took out *Chasing Rainbows* and replaced it with William Ackerman's *Passages*. As "Remedios" began playing, I sensed that the compliment had made her thoughts even more painful. I had hoped that the toast would reassure her, would cheer her up—but it made her even sadder. It seemed as though in changing the music she wanted to change her feelings, to blanket her fears with other melodies.

In the few seconds she was gone, it felt as though I could read her thoughts: loving, but not having that love fulfilled; wanting a future, but never certain whether there would be one; longing, but always frustrating that longing with patience, with respect and propriety. What was that she had said about love? It has its own timing, its own desire. If you always carefully guard its expression, if you suppress it long enough, you lose it. I suddenly realized that love could in fact be destroyed, that even a true and resounding love could wither from neglect.

I stood up from the table, blew out the candle, and walked into the living room. Moonlight filtered through the lace curtains and left a warm glow over the coffee table. Pamela looked up from the stereo, surprised to see me standing next to her. Even in the muted light there were tiny but brilliant stars in her eyes. I reached down, pulled her close to me, and began kissing her eyes, her cheeks, her lips. She responded with wonder and delight.

I kissed her neck, her shoulders, and every exposed part above her V-neck sweater. Inside me a voice was screaming to stop, but the warmth of her chest and the desire in her lips as she kissed my cheek, my neck, and my ears drowned out the voice.

Hugging her tightly, I lifted her from the floor and carried her to the front door, kissing her deeply. I yearned to feel every inch of her body. I held her up against the door, smothering her body with mine. She cried softly, "Terry, oh, Terry." Finally I lowered her feet to the ground and kissed her cheeks, her hair, her neck, her breasts.

Inside, the voice was shouting out again, *Thou art a priest and thou shalt not love!* But I knew now that the voice forbidding love was a lie, a temptation, an insult against God and everything human. Her love, her body, her passion—this was grace, this was virtue, this was life.

I guided her over to the center of the living room, undressed her. For what seemed like seconds, but were really hours, we caressed and kissed and reveled in the cool discovering fire of touching and being touched.

Suddenly I felt a wonderful, tingling sensation dancing on the surface of my body, as though heaven and total pleasure were about to permeate my entire being. I reached up to her black lace panties, grabbed them at the hip, and ripped them in half. She moaned with wild anticipation as I pulled them free of her body and tossed them away.

Totally naked, we embraced. As I raised my body up, longing to make love to her, I heard her voice inside my memory, calling to me: *"I don't want to be your mistress. I don't want to be a woman in the shadows."* Immediately she sensed the change and opened her eyes to look at me. "What's wrong?"

I looked down at her, "I want to and I will, but not this way. If I make love to you, I want it to be as my wife, not as a woman of the shadows."

She looked at me, a whole range of emotions racing through her eyes. From the many long and difficult conversations we had shared about why each of us felt it was better not to have sex until we were married, she understood exactly what I meant.

"I've changed my mind!" she cried. But I knew from the frustrated smile in her eyes that she hadn't changed it completely and that in a less passionate moment she would see things differently.

There was an awkward silence until she laughed, reached over, grabbed her torn black lace panties, and held them up for incredulous inspection. "The price of desire," she retorted.

"Sorry," I said, embarrassed.

"Don't you dare apologize," she threatened. "Feel free to do it anytime!"

We laughed and kissed and hugged some more. When I awoke at five in the morning, my lips were still kissing hers and we were still lying on the living-room floor.

32

PAMELA

I stared at the dishes in the sink and the remainder of the pot roast I had made for New Year's Eve dinner. My first pot roast. It hadn't been too bad, actually. Terry had come over at seven-thirty and we'd had a quiet, reflective meal. There was a lot to think about and a lot to be grateful for. But even though the New Year was only hours away, Terry had headed back to his computer as soon as we'd finished eating. Close to finishing the first draft of his book, he was pushing at a frantic pace. I stood facing the mountain of dishes, feeling very much alone.

Terry had promised to come back over before midnight for a toast, but it was already eleven-thirty. I felt terribly sorry for myself as I paced back and forth in my living room. I replaced the ice in the champagne bucket for a second time. Perhaps he had forgotten. At four minutes to midnight his knock came at the door, and the smile on his face told me he never suspected for a minute how long and lonely the last few hours had seemed for a single girl in love with a celibate priest on New Year's Eve.

"Happy New Year, Shoopy!"

"Happy New Year!" I cheered.

The ball dropped in Times Square, we toasted with champagne, and off he went again. Thoughts of standing in the moonlit street New Year's Eve 1985, the night before I had first laid eyes on Terry at Good Shepherd, filled my mind. "New Year's Eve is an extraordinarily odd night," I muttered, as I turned out the light of a brand-new year.

It had been two years since my spiritual quest had led me up those steps of Good Shepherd Church. In my search for fulfillment, for understanding, for God, I had found many things—some I had expected to find, and some I hadn't. The hours I had spent in solitude and prayer had given birth to a deep longing to become a part of the Catholic Church. I had attended all of the adult catechism classes in the adjacent rectory given by the two nuns in residence there. Week after week I had listened, questioned, tried very hard to learn all that I must to become a good Catholic. I longed to kneel at the Communion rail and receive the Body of Christ. I wanted to belong, not only because I was drawn to the Sacraments, but also because I was drawn to Terry's world. I had come with an open heart and an open mind.

But gradually I began to realize that there were a number of things that were difficult for me to accept. I couldn't reconcile myself to the pronouncement that it would be difficult to see in a woman at the altar the person of Christ. I had been brought up to believe that we were all created in the image and likeness of God. How could it be that women didn't image Christ? It was so far afield from the God I knew—the God of Love, the God of Compassion. In sharing Terry's struggles, I had seen far too much. I had seen the workings of authority, the strict hierarchical side of the Church. I'd read too much of the sins of past popes who, in despising women, had cast them from grace. And I'd seen the cold, calculated way in which his superiors had treated Terry.

Where was their compassion? In the present Church it seemed to me, women did not hold an equal place with men. I did not believe that God ever intended such inequality. Nor did I believe that because I was in love with Terry, God would turn His back on me. But in reality, I knew that if Terry and I were ever to marry, the Church would turn its back on me. Simply because I loved a priest, the Church itself would accuse me of committing a mortal sin. I would be excommunicated.

In this Church, this haven I thought I had found, I would be unwelcome and unwanted. The spirit I longed for, the God of Peace and Mercy, would have to be found somewhere else.

D*estiny* is such a wonderful word. It is comforting and powerful, and it kept creeping into my mind.

Was it destiny that I had never married? Was it destiny that for two years Terry Sweeney and I came and went through the doors of Good Shepherd Church, our paths never crossing? Was it destiny that I had moved to New York, only to find Terry in my own backyard?

I believed in destiny. And I believed that Terry and I had met at exactly that moment in time when we were meant to. Had it been any earlier, neither he nor I would have been ready. But now we were, and I was beginning truly to believe that our love had been in the hands of God all along. So many things could have come between us, yet here we were. Somehow that seed of love which began so long ago . . . those prophetic words, "There's the answer, now what's the question?," that had rung in my heart the very moment I first looked at Terry . . . the tears in his eyes as he confided in me at our first lunch . . . the seed had been planted deeply, and we had nourished it and believed that it was planted by God.

Terry's retreat was approaching, and I was anxious for him to go. I knew that he was ready to make a decision about our future, and I was finally ready to live with the answer. I had no idea what course he would choose, but the inner conviction that had given me strength to hold on this long, the sense that Terry was my destiny, was growing ever stronger. Through all the months of doubt and fear there had remained a part of me that was positive that we would be together, that we belonged together, and that God wanted us together. And now that voice in my heart was

TERRANCE A. SWEENEY & PAMELA SHOOP SWEENEY

speaking louder and louder until I couldn't deny it—I had to listen.

As a little girl in Christian Science I used to say, "Nothing can keep me from my Good, from that which is right for my life." That didn't mean that nothing could keep me from what I thought was good for myself, but rather, that nothing could keep me from God's vision of what was good for me. I had trusted in that as a child, and now I trusted again. We had come a long, long way, my priest and I—and I dared to hope that nothing could keep us from the love God had placed in our hearts. I began to dream dreams of bridal dresses and bouquets and of the long walk to the end of the aisle where the most precious person I had ever known would be waiting. I longed for union with the other half of my being, my soul, my self. But marriage takes two people to share a dream, to share a love.

No, I didn't consciously know for certain what Terry's choice would be, but I began to ask myself, *Could it be possible this dream may really come true?*

Soon I would know.

33

TERRY

The floor-to-ceiling chapel window framed a lush meadow that trailed off to a grove of giant redwoods. Early-morning mist drifted up from the meadow and disappeared through the massive branches. As I sat in a Zen posture on a meditation pillow at Our Lady of the Redwoods Monastery in Whitethorn, California, I was comforted by the knowledge that some of the trees in the grove were on earth before Christ was born. Continuity, growth, majesty—all found in earth, water, and living wood. What happened when that Holy Man walked the earth—did the trees nearly halfway around the world feel His presence? What would Jesus say, sitting in that grove, peering up through those giant branches to the blue sky far above? Would He, too, feel the silence, the mystery, the grandeur? Wouldn't His heart fill with wonder and praise? Yes, of course it would.

It had been over six and a half months since I had celebrated Mass as a priest. I felt a deep sorrow for the pain the priesthood was suffering and an intense longing to pray once again, "This is my body, which will be broken for you."

The chapel lights suddenly went on, signaling the start of community prayer. I stood, picked up a psalmody from the bench in front of me, and joined in the community's singing of the morning's psalms.

After morning prayer, breakfast was taken in silence in the community dining room. Lunch and dinner, for retreatants, was served in the guest dining room, a small building located some fifteen yards from the main house. The daily routine was very simple—morning prayer, breakfast, noon prayer, lunch, late-afternoon Mass, dinner, night prayer, sleep. During the intervening hours of the day the sisters would work at the bakery, in the garden, or in the house. The chaplain, Father Roger, whose quarters were in one of the two retreatant lodges located some two hundred yards away from the main house, would work on his book. The retreatants would spend those extra hours in the chapel, in their rooms, or walking around.

The crisp air and beauty of the forest were a perfect setting for reflection, and I would spend hours each day walking through the redwood groves and along the streams.

I knew exactly why I had come here this early March of 1987. I needed finally to decide whether to ask Pamela to marry me.

Two months earlier I had finished the first draft of my book on the issues of authority and the priesthood. A biblical and historical analysis had proven the mandatory celibacy laws to be in violation of the Ninth Commandment, the Church's own teachings on the indissolubility of the marriage bond, and the inalienable right to marry.

From our many conversations Pamela knew that I considered the celibacy laws unethical and that for me to seek "laicization with freedom to marry" would have been pointless. The Vatican was granting such dispensations rarely, if at all. Further, to have sought laicization would imply that I no longer wanted to be a priest. That would have been a lie. To have asked the Pope for permission to marry would have implied that he had the power to decide whether I was going to marry. Asking this permission would have given credence to the very policy that was crippling the priesthood, namely that the Vatican had the right to prohibit ordination until celibacy was promised.

Even with the conviction that the celibacy laws were unchristian and invalid, and even though I knew that Pamela and I should marry soon if we ever hoped to have children, I still had not asked her to marry me. Why?

This question became my prayer. The long walks in the redwoods, chapel meditations, the Mass, even my dreams were absorbed in this discernment.

The suppression of our desire for intimacy, and Pamela's uncertainty about our future, had cast a shroud of tension over our love. Sometimes, in our arguments, love turned into spite. This concerned me a great deal because we would be under even more pressure if we were to marry. In light of the international media attention given to Rome's directive to suppress my research, the press undoubtedly would do follow-up coverage were we to marry. This would expose Pamela to what might quickly become serious criticism and accusation. Could she sustain it? And why would she want to? Celibate priesthood was my cross, not hers. After being anonymous for so long, why should she now have to suffer public humiliation for a Church and a set of laws that weren't even her own?

I had already told her that my conflict over authority and the priesthood might destroy my health, but that I had a responsibility to see this struggle through to the end. But wasn't it harsh and cruel to expose the person I love to such stress? Was this asking too much of her?

Further, our marrying might easily undermine the credibility of my research, giving an excuse for Church officials to disparage my conclusions as coming from a married priest trying to justify his own actions.

Gradually I was able to see through the clouds of fear and hurt feelings that had surrounded our love. Reflecting on the twenty-six months of our relationship, it became clear that Pamela had put her life and heart on hold while I had struggled with the Jesuits and the Church to discover who I was and what the priesthood should be. I was the one who had loved with a divided heart, not Pamela. It shamed me to realize how much of my love depended on the ways she reacted to pressure. Who was I to decide how she should respond to stress, or how much she was willing to suffer for our love? Those should be her choices, not mine.

My love for Pamela had been guarded, divided, and demanding. Without being conscious of it, I had held Pamela to an idealized notion of love, that goodness creates beauty, and that beauty inspires love. I had acted as though my love for her should be measured according to this beauty in her. When Pamela and I would argue, this would create an emotional ugliness, and rather than letting love heal this ugliness, I would instinctively hold back love for fear it would cause more pain.

On this retreat I realized that love doesn't work that way. Love is not dependent upon goodness or upon beauty. Love is the grace that creates both. Love is the energy that moves chaos toward harmony, ignorance and falsity toward truth, evil toward goodness. Love does not rest. It inspires, forgives, unites, generates, and flows out through human hearts and the universe to create anew. Trying to control love is as foolish as trying to control God.

From the very first lunch conversation with Pamela, my heart was filled with joy and discovery, grateful that she was on this earth the same time as I. Within minutes after that lunch my heart was asking, *Is she the one my heart was created to love?* But my mind had put this off as a passing emotional exuberance inappropriate for a Jesuit priest. And when my heart longed to be with her and to know everything about her, I had wrongly tried to define this as friendship. She had come into my life precisely at that time when I had been afraid to challenge the Vatican's policy on authority and the priesthood. My mind knew that I should do this, but my heart had lacked the courage, until Pat's death and Pamela's love.

Pamela had supported me through Pat's death, encouraged me to continue the research and to follow my conscience. It was as though God was trying to make it totally clear to me that priesthood, first and last, is only known through love and should ever be at the service of love, and that any priesthood that excludes love, whether celibate or conjugal, will die.

Through biblical and historical analysis I had searched for the meaning of priesthood, but through Pamela's love I had learned far more, risked far more, and in the end experienced far more of what priesthood truly means. Because of Pamela my whole being longed to restore the discipleship inspired by Jesus, where women and men, married and celibate, served others out of love.

The eight days, though difficult and intense, passed all too quickly. The night before the retreat ended, I stood in the back of the darkened chapel, long after everyone else had left, and gazed at the stone altar. On the altar was a candle and a burning incense stick. The flame from the candle cast a soft, white glow over the thin trail of incense smoke. The smoke rose higher and higher up from the altar until its trail became a gentle wave, and the gentle wave became a white mist, and the white mist was embraced by the night.

Pamela's face broadened into a smile when I said, "Let's go for a drive."

"Where are we going?" she asked as she grabbed her purse.

"You'll see."

"Is what I'm wearing okay?"

"It's fine."

We piled into my car and headed east. It had been a week since my retreat. Pamela and I had spent many hours sharing our concerns and reservations regarding marriage. I reminded her again of the stress she would immediately be exposed to if we married. She was wonderful. She said she loved me and that being with me was the most important thing in the world. She could take the accusations and the humiliations, as long as we went through it together.

So, on that March 17th, Saint Patrick's Day, as we drove over Coldwater Canyon into the valley, we both sensed a kind of happy anticipation.

She leaned over and hugged me as we drove into Forest Lawn. Sitting together by her father's gravestone, we thanked God for our parents and the gift of life they had given us. We prayed that they would see our love as a gift from God. And we asked that our love would "give wings"—courage and faith—to others.

Then we drove across town to Holy Cross Cemetery to pay our respects to my brother Pat and to my father. I felt profoundly grateful for my brother's courage in the face of death and for the love he and Rosemarie had shared.

Then we drove to Franklin Canyon for a long walk. On the lawn in front of the ranger's station I told Pamela I was sorry for the hurt I had caused her, for the long, anxiety-ridden delay my uncertainty and the responsibilities of my priesthood had caused her. I was sorry that our spontaneity and trust, so essential to intimacy, had suffered significantly. I felt that God was asking us to love not only one another, but all those priests and women who have been and would be blessed by love and then crucified because of the laws forbidding it. Both loves, not just ours, required time and attention.

I took her hand, held it in mine, caressed it gently.

"I know it hasn't been easy to love me," I said. "I know that whenever we've argued, I've never been the first one to say, 'I'm sorry.' "

She squeezed my hand tightly, as though the truth of what I'd just admitted released painful memories locked away in her body.

"As the months and years have passed, I've seen something beautiful and spontaneous and precious in your love clouded over by my uncertainty and ignorance."

Tears were forming in her eyes. I could see her pain, and it made me turn away and look down again at her hand.

"I'm sorry," I said.

I looked again into her eyes. With her free hand she brushed away the tears from her cheeks.

"Will you forgive me?" I pleaded.

"Yes."

Several minutes passed as we quietly held each other's hands. I knew her forgiveness was full and generous, but that it would take a long time for the pain to heal.

I walked her over to the bandstand where, nearly two years earlier, we had clowned around with old dance steps such as the Charleston and the cha-cha-cha. Then our dancing had been filled with laughter and joyful discovery. Now, as I took her into my arms and began dancing slowly, the only sounds were that of our feet brushing over the wood and of the wind rustling through the pine branches above.

I don't know how to describe it, but after several silent minutes as we began to move in unison over the dance floor, we seemed to be dancing to a soundless music that was composed by the feelings of our hearts—happiness and sorrow, peace and conflict, trust and caution, uncertainty and conviction, denial and desire, forgiveness, hope.

I guided her head back from my shoulders so that I could look into her eyes. They were tearful, curious, humbling.

"I love you."

"I love you," she said.

"When I ask you to marry me on Easter Sunday, will you say yes?"

Her whole face lit up with a radiant smile. "Yes!"

34

PAMELA

We sat in the passenger seats of the Cessna 340 holding hands and looking into each other's eyes. Occasionally my parents would smile back at us from the cockpit.

Terry had called them a few days before and asked if we might fly up to Mendocino in order to discuss some "important and confidential matters." If my parents guessed, they never uttered a word. They picked us up from Oakland Airport, and we had clear skies all the way to Little River.

"Are you nervous?" I asked Terry as we headed for dinner that evening.

"Not yet, but if you keep asking me that, I will be!" Over dinner, in an effort to give my parents some background, Terry spoke of his longing to become a priest. He described what the priesthood meant to him and how he had felt when he had first heard the call from God. He had been in the fifth grade when he'd first felt the stirrings of God in his heart. By the time he was a senior in high school, he knew he wanted to be a priest. He spoke of his love for the people whom he served and how much it meant to him to stand at the altar as a servant of Christ.

I found myself listening from someplace far away. My parents seemed to be listening with their entire beings—alert, expectant, hopeful. At last, long after dessert, Terry produced the material on which he had been working for so many years.

"Bill, Julie . . . if it isn't too much of an imposition, I would like you to read this. It may take quite a bit of time, but it is extremely important and sensitive material, and I need for you to understand it."

"Of course we will. We'll start tonight."

Later, as we finished up the dinner dishes, I saw Bill remove from the ice bucket an unopened bottle of champagne that he had been chilling in anticipation of a celebration. Silently, he placed the unused chilled champagne glasses near the sink. There was sadness in his posture and confusion in his eyes as he smiled good night.

The next day my parents read . . . and read. I can't remember it ever being so quiet around the house. My mom perched on her bed or in the living room, while Bill sat in the library with the smoke from his pipe swirling over his head. They exchanged chapters all day. At last we assembled in front of the fireplace, and the questions began.

The statistics were surprising to my parents, but they were far more interested in the history of married clergy and Terry's ethical stance regarding authority. They were receptive and probing. My mother, especially, felt the sting of the stigma applied to the wives of priests in the past. The discussion continued for many hours until it was time to change for dinner.

I opened the door to my armoire. Mendocino is a fairly casual place, but Heritage House is a little bit dressier, and besides, I wanted to look especially pretty tonight if I could. I chose my ivory-satin turtleneck blouse and the skirt I had worn to Terry's last Mass at Loyola. Somehow the connection was a comfortable one.

Terry and Bill both stood as I entered the living room, and we all piled into the car and drove the few miles to the exquisite hotel-restaurant nestled in the cliff overlooking a violent sea. It was pouring outside. The fireplace in the lounge was ablaze. Built in 1877, the walls seemed to whisper the secrets of famous artists and writers, lovers and dreamers. Conversation was joyful, and if my parents were expecting something, they were once again let down. A howling wind carried us back to our car, and we crept through the rain and fog over the winding roads back to the house.

Bill lighted a fire, and as soon as we were comfortably seated, Terry began.

"I would have brought this up at the restaurant, but there were so many people there, it wasn't private enough for what I wanted to say. Thank you for taking all the time to read my material. I realize there's a lot to assimilate. I asked you to read it not only to help you to see how important this issue is for the survival of the priesthood, but also so that you would understand that this whole issue of married clergy is an extremely emotional one. I wanted you to know what has happened to the wives of priests— the insults and humiliations they have suffered. It's quite possible that, because of our love, your daughter and you will be called names and subjected to public scorn. I felt I had an obligation to tell you exactly what you might be up against."

"They're only words, Terry. I think we can rise above all of that." My mother's face was serious as she regarded Terry closely.

"I'm really sorry that there is this kind of emotionalism and fanaticism associated with this issue. It is possible that either Pam or myself may be physically harmed, and I want you to consider this carefully.

"Pam has been so helpful and loving. She has respected the priestly vow of celibacy and all the implications there are to that. Even when there has been tension or disagreement that has reached a serious level of conflict, she has always been the first to try to reconcile. My brother, Pat, instinctively knew how much she meant to me. Even she and my family get along. She has helped me in so many ways with her advice and just by being there. She is perceptive and intuitive, and there is a wholeness to her love that has been a source of great wonder to me.

"All this is a pretty clumsy way of saying that I love your daughter very much and I would consider it a great blessing and a gift from God if you would do me the honor of granting me your daughter's hand in marriage."

There was silence as my mother, Bill, and I looked at Terry with tears in our eyes. My mother was the first to speak.

"What a beautiful way to say it. We would be honored."

"Did you think we would say otherwise?" Bill smiled as he rose to get the long-awaited champagne from the fridge.

The next week Terry's mother had an opportunity to read the material from his book, after which he said he wanted to take her and her husband, Owen, out for a meal. We picked them up at six o'clock and drove to Giovanni's Italian restaurant in Playa del Rey. As we were walking across the parking lot, Angie squealed, "Well, do you two have something to tell us?" Did she already know? Had she guessed?

"Wait till we get inside, Mom," Terry answered.

As soon as the waiter departed, Terry could hold back no longer. "Mom, Owen . . ."

"Yes, yes?"

They knew what was coming.

"You know that I love Pamela very much. And now you've had a chance to read my material. And I wanted to tell you that on Easter Sunday I'm going to ask Pamela to marry me, and I would love for you to be there."

Before the words had passed his lips, Terry's mom was on her feet.

"Hooray!" she cheered. "I just knew it! I'm so happy!"

Owen clapped his hands.

"This is just wonderful. There is nothing more important in the world than love, absolutely nothing. Oh, this is a happy day!"

I marveled at their response. It could so very easily have been one of scorn, anger, or disappointment. I particularly admired Terry's mother. How proud she'd always been of her son, the Jesuit priest. Terry's accomplishments meant a great deal to her, and her joy was always evident on her beaming face. She loved to show up unexpectedly at church on Sunday to hear Terry say Mass. And it was especially moving to have him officiate at family weddings, baptisms, and funerals. It had always been a blessing for her to be able to turn to him at those times.

It would have been understandable had Angie been disappointed at our plans to marry. Her response might just as easily have been anger or rejection. Having a priest in the family was important to her, and she might have rebelled against Terry's choice or tried to influence his decision. But she did not. Angie never tried to impose her will in any way. When he had decided to leave the Jesuits, Angie had cautioned Terry to look at the realities in the outside world, but she had stood by her son. And now, again, she embraced his decision. As a mother, she wanted, more than anything else, her son's happiness. Whatever hurt she may have experienced, she kept it to herself. She radiated pure excitement and glee. I knew I was in the presence of a very strong and remarkable woman.

Two days later, during a lengthy dinner, Terry explained the situation to Steve, giving him as much background as he could. Then he told him of our plans to marry. My brother realized at once the implications in regard to Terry's future with the Church and to the two of us in general from society's point of view. More than anyone else, he seemed to understand how serious our situation really was.

"This is a huge sacrifice for you especially, Terry—but I believe you two can handle it. I really admire your courage. I'm really happy for you both!"

We dropped Steve off at his car, which was parked outside my apartment. I stepped back onto the sidewalk while he and Terry stood quietly beneath the stars.

"Steve, we haven't really made any preparations yet, but I'd like to ask you if you would stand up with me at the wedding."

"I'd be honored to. I look forward to having a brother. I've always wanted one."

The two men embraced in the moonlight.

"Thank you, Steve."

I watched from the sidewalk until my wonderful brother had disappeared out of sight.

Easter Sunday, 1987, Terry would propose to me in the presence of both our families. Until now he had been under "nonpenal suspension" from the Church for having refused to suppress his research. But the moment he would ask me to become his wife, his suspension would become far more severe. Canon law stipulates that a "cleric who attempts marriage, even if only civilly, incurs a *latae sententiae* suspension." Though he had already been ostracized from Good Shepherd, when he became engaged to me, he would no longer be able to practice his priesthood. When that moment came, he wanted those he loved around him. Since his dismissal from Good Shepherd, it had been nine months since Terry had said Mass. But in the months to come, in the eyes of those who admired him, it was I who would take the blame for his departure from the altar.

Rupert Allan, Terry's close friend who had helped him with the flood of media calls at the time of his resignation, offered his home to us for the occasion. His spontaneous generosity and warmth were a special grace. He became a shining light of hope and a haven of safety to me in all the deprecation that was to come. Some people assumed that because Terry intended to marry, overnight he had become another human being altogether. They simply assumed that he had "changed." But Rupert saw with his heart. He saw from instinctively deeper levels that Terry would continue to be the man of love, of faith, of courage that he had always been, and his love for his friend remained the same.

Easter Sunday dawned cheerful and bright. This was the day that Christ had rolled away the stone, the day He had risen from the dead, giving life and hope to the rest of a troubled, desperate world. It was a day of thanks, of peace, of promise. It was also the day Terry Sweeney would ask me to become his wife.

Saint Paul's was once again filled, so Terry and I had to stand in the back along with many others. I prayed for the priests who had gone before us in marriage and those still living the pain of hidden love. I prayed for the women in love with those priests, and for the strength and courage in the coming weeks to serve them by shedding what light I could on their private hell. I prayed for wisdom, a clear mind, and a pure heart. But, most of all, I gave thanks—thanks for a dream come true.

Around five o'clock I slipped into my pale-pink dress. I was nervous! At about six-thirty I opened my front door to the most handsome man I have ever seen. Terry stood there in his dark suit and his Roman collar with a file folder tucked under his arm.

"Well, Shoop, are you ready? You look beautiful."

"I'm terrified," I cried.

"Aw, come on. This is what you've been waiting for! Let's go!"

He escorted me to his freshly washed VW Rabbit and opened the door.

"Aren't you ever nervous?" I demanded as we drove to Rupert's house overlooking the city.

"No, Shoop . . . not when I'm prepared. Not when I've had so much time to think everything through."

"Can you believe we're doing this?"

"Yes." He reached over and patted my knee.

Rupert Allan is one of the most elegant and gracious men I have ever met. There is grace and dignity in everything about him. He greeted us downstairs and led us up into his exquisite home. The walls were covered with artwork any connoisseur would treasure, and the tables held artifacts and special pieces Rupert had collected from all over the world.

My folks and the Sweeney clan arrived shortly after we did. The gathering was small and intimate. Neither of our families had met one another before, and we hoped that this would be a special night for them as well as for us. During the cocktail hour I was overcome with emotion. I felt that my face must be terribly flushed, and my eyes kept welling up with tears while Terry's joyful spirit was the center of the room. On his face I read wonder. He was experiencing feelings that only men apart from the priesthood feel, precious moments he had only witnessed before.

When the hors d'oeuvres had been passed for the third time and people had relaxed into easy conversation, Terry asked for everyone's attention. All breath left my body as I retreated to a corner in the back of the room next to a bookcase. I looked at the faces: Angie and Owen, Dudley and Dori with their four children, Rosemarie, Michael, Therese, Mom, Bill, Steve, Rupert's friend, Stephen. Terry began to speak, and from that moment I couldn't think of anything but my husband-to-be. He thanked our host for his hospitality and our loved ones for their support in a time when only their comfort and that of the Spirit could sustain us.

"There are a lot of emotions that have brought us together tonight. There are a lot of feelings that might be too deep for words. But for a minute I want to direct my comments to the children: to you, Michelle, Aileen, Lisa, the two Michaels. You may find in the coming weeks that some of your friends or teachers at school may get upset because your uncle, a priest, is now engaged to be married. And some people may tell you that this is wrong. I want to explain to you why it's not wrong and why my love for Pamela is a gift from God.

"Many centuries ago most of the priests were married, and many popes were also married. Peter, the very first pope, was married. But for reasons not all of which were spiritual, some of the popes decided that they wanted priests no longer to have children or to be able to pass on their property and income to their sons, who usually became priests in their place. So these popes passed laws forbidding priests to get married and to have children. These laws broke up many existing marriages and caused a great deal of suffering. Unfortunately, the laws of today are directly related to those passed many centuries ago.

"As I was going through my priest training, I wasn't told how these celibacy laws came to be, nor was I told how much pain and bloodshed they caused. It took me ten years of research to find out these things, and I feel that God is asking me to speak out against these laws that divide priestly love and married love. The laws are wrong, and they have to be changed. I have a duty to do everything I can to change them.

"I love Pamela, I love the priesthood, and I love God. There is nothing wrong about this. There shouldn't be any reason why I can't be married and also be a priest. I'm convinced that celibacy freely chosen and lovingly lived is a great virtue—just as marriage is—but that to require priests by law to be celibate is wrong. If I didn't truly believe in my heart that what I say is right and that God is leading me to say these things, I wouldn't be here right now."

The children watched and listened, and so did each person throughout the room. Private thoughts, private dreams, private tears. Terry looked over to me.

"Not all of you may know how much Pamela means to me—and I'm not sure I can put it into words—so I'd like to quote a poem by Elizabeth Barrett Browning that expresses only a shadow of the way I feel. I hope I don't forget the words! Pam, could you come over here?"

I felt surely that I would fall as my trembling legs carried me across the room. Terry reached for my hand. Looking into my eyes, he began,

> *"How do I love thee? Let me count the ways.*
> *I love thee to the depth and breadth and height*
> *My soul can reach, when feeling out of sight*
> *For the ends of Being and ideal Grace.*
> *I love thee to the level of everyday's*
> *Most quiet need, by sun and candle-light.*
> *I love thee freely, as men strive for Right;*
> *I love thee purely, as they turn from Praise.*
> *I love thee with the passion put to use*
> *In my old griefs, and with my childhood's faith.*
> *I love thee with a love I seemed to lose*
> *With my lost saints—I love thee with the breath,*
> *Smiles, tears, of all my life!—and, if God choose,*
> *I shall but love thee better after death."*

"Pamela, I love you very, very much. And I would consider it a great blessing if you would do me the honor of becoming my wife."

Tears streamed down my cheeks. Terry's voice choked with emotion. "Will you marry me?"

"Yes," I murmured almost inaudibly, "Oh, yes, Terry, I will." I melted into his arms and buried my face in his neck.

There was a long moment of silence.

The clarity of Terry's conscience and heart, the wholeness of his love, were not to be mistaken. Quietly, I tried to speak.

"Mom, Bill, I know I haven't always been the kind of daughter you may have wanted me to be, or accomplished all the things you wished I would have, and I'm sorry for that. But I just want you to know how much I appreciate all the love and support you've given me through all of this. And I want to thank all you Sweeneys for always having been so kind to me and for having accepted me so graciously into your lives."

Bill's hands were shaking as he raised his glass in a toast. He began to speak, then had to stop himself as emotions gripped his throat. "No one can tell me this love isn't from God—no one. It is right, and I want you to know that we love you both. And Terry . . . I am so proud to have you as a son-in-law."

His embrace to each of us was full and strong, and he held Terry for a long moment.

Steve rose to his feet and addressed the room. "Pam and Terry had what seemed to be an impossible love. Most people would have seen the barriers and just given up. But they didn't. They had a dream—and they stuck by it and fought for it." Steve turned to us. "I've learned a lot from you—about what the word *sacrifice* means."

All the while Terry stood with his arm around my waist, holding me tightly. Being more than a centimeter apart was unthinkable. We were a couple, a unit, one being of two.

Angie smiled an angelic smile as she, too, raised her glass in our direction. "Pamela, I would like to drink a toast to you. I know how hard all this has been on you—everything that Terry has gone through. You've shown a great deal of inner strength. I don't know how you did it. But I just want to tell you how grateful I am for all the support you've given Terry. And I am very proud and grateful that you are going to marry my son."

Sitting across from Terry at Rupert's beautiful dinner table, listening to the joyful conversations all about us, I looked at my fiancé's eyes. He looked back at me, sharing the same thoughts. Surrounded by the laughter of our loved ones, we were enveloped, sheltered, and caressed by God's protective arms. We felt at last the presence—the absolute certainty of God's love, the warmth of

"Home" in our own love, and the peace that honesty and being true to your heart and conscience can bring. On Easter Sunday Christ changed the world forever. And today, another Easter, His unfathomable Love had changed our lives forever.

35

TERRY

Responses to our engagement announcement ran the gamut from strong and enthusiastic support through silence to severe criticism, insult, and warning.

America, a Jesuit national publication, accused me in an editorial of depreciating priestly celibacy rather than admitting that "he has in any sense retreated from a moral or ascetical position previously staked out." A Jesuit priest from a well-known Catholic University wrote, "Your continuing preoccupation, amounting to an obsession, with the celibacy question suggests, contrary to what you say, that you do not have a clear conscience about what you have done." Others called my actions embarrassing, shameful, self-justifying, scandalous, destructive, lustful, sinful, demonic.

Letters from different parts of the country came pouring in. Most were congratulatory, some were not. One person said that I was trying to make a martyr of myself when in fact I was just a "bloody fool."

> "You have given up everything—being a Jesuit, being a priest, and now your religion. And for what? I can't understand your throwing away your life and your soul. Nor can I understand what sort of woman would allow you to do this."

Another person wrote,

"The blood of Christ Jesus cleanses us from all sin. Whoso-
ever is not found written in the book of life will be cast in
the sea of fire. The wages of sin is death, but the gift of God
is life eternal through Jesus Christ our Lord. Ask the Lord
Jesus Christ to save you now!"

Still others, by letter or by phone, said they were offering up
prayers and novenas for my salvation. Some of my Jesuit friends,
whom I had known for decades, did not acknowledge my letters
or phone calls.

Pamela was subjected to angry glares and gossiping by members
of the Church. In conversations she would frequently be ignored,
or merely tolerated because she was "the woman Terry loved." In
letters to me some called Pamela a "seductress," "temptress,"
"agent of the devil," "bitch." Some snidely commented that "she
must be pregnant."

As much as possible I shielded Pamela from the letters and
phone calls coming to my apartment in which vehement criticisms
and curses were directed toward either of us. I felt she had enough
to contend with, as, day after day, I would tell her of yet another
priest who had refused to witness our marriage.

But some weird things happened that finally prompted me to
inform her that we might be in some danger. Not only were some
letters particularly vituperative and condemnatory, but I would get
phone calls during which the caller would say nothing when I
answered the phone. Other times, whispered and inaudible messages would be left on my answering machine. While listening to
thousands of confessions over the years, on several occasions I had
heard in a penitent's voice a fanatical and destructive obsession
with purging sin from the world. Sometimes I sensed this evil, not
in the penitent's words but in his silence, his breathing, the spirit
of his voice. Such intuitions were reactivated when I received
phone calls from this silent caller whose only communication was
heavy breathing.

One Sunday after Mass, while we were having lunch at a nearby restaurant, I told Pamela that I had been receiving some very strange calls.

"Do you have any idea who might be making them?" she asked.

"No."

Her eyes expressed deep concern. "Are we in any physical danger?"

"I don't know. Religious fanatics are unpredictable. The calls are coming to my place, not yours. I suspect whatever negative feelings this person feels are directed toward me—but you might be at risk because of me."

"How much of a risk?"

"I wish I could answer that. And I wish I could say that there is no physical threat. I haven't received any direct verbal threats, but when I get letters screaming, 'Repent!' and phone calls with no voice on the other end, it makes me wonder."

She was worried and frightened.

"You don't have to go through with this, you know." I wanted to set Pamela free, if that was what she wanted. "Getting married should be a joy, not a threat. Starting all this, I knew it might cost me a great deal—but it's not my place to decide whether to risk your life. Only you can make that choice."

"Is it that serious?"

"I don't think so, but it might be. And it's unfair not to warn you."

"Should we hire security for the wedding?"

"We can discuss it with Bill, but there's a much larger issue here. Your safety. You have a right to love without fear. Loving me shouldn't jeopardize your life. If you think our love is asking too much, I'll understand."

She reached across the table and took my hand in hers. "I want to be with you—in this life and the next. You're my soul mate, my life."

As the weeks passed, the rejections mounted. Thirty-one priest friends I had asked refused to officiate at our wedding. They didn't want to go against Church canons that forbade priests from marrying. Two priests said a tentative yes, but only on the condition that the wedding be done in secret.

I remembered the distasteful experience that one married-priest friend had related to me. He had finally received a dispensation to marry, and he and his fiancée were asked down to the chancery office. On a weekday afternoon, after work hours, the Judicial Vicar told two priests to come into his office along with the engaged couple. He bound the priests to absolute secrecy and then, while standing behind his desk, separated from the engaged couple, proceeded to witness their vows. The ritual lasted less than five minutes. As the couple left the chancery, the "bride" turned to her "groom" and asked incredulously, "Are we really married?"

I would not subject Pamela, her family, or mine to this kind of affront to the dignity of marriage. Our love was a gift from God, one to be celebrated and shared, not hidden. Since 1965 over 100,000 priests had married. But this startling fact had had little impact on Church policy because most of these marriages were done quietly, to avoid "scandalizing the faithful." I was convinced that the real scandal was not that priests fall in love; it was that Church laws for over a thousand years had preempted the God-given right to marry.

A bishop from the East, who was personally in favor of a married clergy, also declined to witness our marriage. Archbishop Mahony said that he would not witness our marriage, nor would he permit any other priest to witness it.

After six weeks of no's it was clear that the doors to marrying in the Roman Catholic Church were firmly closed. From those priests who had said no, I experienced no rancor, no vehement objection, just concern that their priesthood might be suspended if they witnessed our marriage. Many agreed that the laws of celibacy should be changed, but that until they were, they would not jeopardize their priesthood to challenge them.

I must admit that even though I understood their reasoning, I could not respect it. Wasn't the priesthood meant to serve the Truth? What I kept on seeing were actions that subordinated Truth to the priesthood. Needless to say, I felt deep sadness for the Church, with all this mounting evidence that love is subordinated to invalid laws, priesthood is subordinated to celibacy, right is subordinated to fear.

For the next few weeks Pamela and I began to attend church services throughout Los Angeles, particularly in Episcopalian churches. We tried to meet with Father Gregory Richards, rector of All Saints Church in Beverly Hills, but he was away on vacation. We went to Saint Augustine's in Santa Monica, and to the rustic Church of Saint Matthew in Pacific Palisades.

One Sunday in late June, after attending Eucharist at Saint Matthew's, Pamela and I were standing in church, commenting on the happy spirit of the congregation and the beauty of the church's architecture. Father Peter Kreitler, who had just finished saying Mass, walked up and introduced himself. He asked what brought us to his parish. We told him that we were looking for a church in which to get married. He looked at me with a kind of intuitive expression and suddenly asked, "Are you a priest?"

"Yes, I am."

"So, you're the one—I've been reading about you. You were a Jesuit, weren't you, and you used to work at Paulist? And you're the one who was asked to suppress your research?"

"Yes."

We told him briefly about our engagement and that we were hoping to marry, but all the Roman Catholic priests we had asked to witness our marriage had refused.

He looked at us and very naturally and spontaneously said, "Well, if you'd like to get married here, you're welcome."

It was a simple sentence, but even as he uttered it, I understood how even the simplest gesture, offered in kindness and understanding, can reveal God. Tears immediately began to stream down Pamela's face. His compassion released a floodgate of pent-up emotions. All the waiting, all the rejections and insults, all the fears and uncertainties were suddenly healed by an Episcopal priest reaching out and trying to help two people fulfill their love.

Father Kreitler was surprised by Pamela's tears. He had no way of knowing how much she had suffered, nor how much joy his priestly kindness had brought to our hearts.

36

PAMELA

With all the decisions of the last two years behind us, we thought we were finally at the end. But there was still one more that needed to be faced. The crucial choices Terry had made up until now had changed his life forever. By my marrying a priest, my life and reputation in some circles would be altered severely as well. We had chosen to take this step, but the question now was whether or not to do so privately or publicly. The question became, Do we hide our love?

It would have been much, much easier for us to marry quietly, with only family and friends knowing of our marriage. We would have been able to explore our love privately and enjoy the special bliss that comes with an engagement period. No one would have been watching us, or judging us. We could have moved quietly into our new life together.

It is the Church's preference that any priest who makes the "unfortunate decision" to marry do so quietly and, whenever possible, move with his new wife to another parish or town. Terry and I had no wish to cause the Church any scandal, nor to offend any of the people in the diocese of Los Angeles, or anywhere else for that matter. However, Terry had already been extremely visible with his resignation from the Jesuit order, and the questions from reporters would most likely continue. From the hundreds of years that this quiet battle had been going on, we also knew that no change in church policy would come until people realized the serious problems facing the priesthood. So many had walked away silently to marry. Someone eventually would have to take a serious stand. Terry had felt called by God long before he'd met me to address this issue. All his study and preparation were now complete. Part of his call as a priest was to speak the truth as he knew in his heart God was asking of him. For him, the choice was clear.

During the time that I lived through the experience of loving a priest, I felt totally alone. I knew that there were 100,000 married priests in the world, which also meant that there were 100,000 women with whom they were in love. But I most certainly had never met one. I was also aware that there must be many more women living the isolation of a "forbidden love," still grieving quietly alone in the shadows. Their desperate, anguished prayers resounded in my heart. Though I had known the bitterness of that isolation, I was now moving into the light. I reflected upon those less fortunate—those who, in despair, had taken their own lives. And finally, I thought of Father Franco Trombotto, the forty-five-year-old priest who had hanged himself just outside his bedroom door in the corridor of his parish house in Vilaretto, Italy. Having been in love with a woman for twenty years, he could no longer live with either the loneliness or the duplicity. His last letter had said, "I have carried my cross a long way: now I fall under the cross." Father Trombotto had taken his life on January 26, 1985. The date stared back at me from the page where I read it, and suddenly it was all very, very clear. This lonely priest in the Italian Alps had committed suicide on Terry's fortieth birthday—the year we'd met, one day before our lunch at the Magic Pan, the day it all began. All this time I'd known nothing of Father Trombotto. I hadn't known his pain. But I had lived it—and I wondered whether Father Trombotto's anguished spirit had passed that cross to us as we sat, unknowingly, in the restaurant that day.

"This issue is much bigger than just our love."

So often Terry had said that to me. And I knew, now, how right he was. I was grateful to God for this love I had found, and now I could not turn my back and walk away any more than Terry could. If he was willing to face whatever personal attacks might come, then neither could I shrink from the responsibility God had placed on my shoulders. If we must fight for the right to love each other and defend our right to marry, then I must fight not only for myself, but to give a voice to all those women still loving in secret and in silence. It was more than a responsibility; it was a privilege. And I welcomed it. When I walked down the aisle on November 15th, it would be not only for myself, but for all those women who were unable to walk down the aisle to marry the men they loved.

Terry and I both knew there would be ridicule and disbelief, hurt and scorn—but our love was the blessed gift that gave us strength. In the end, realizing full well that we might be ostracized, we knew that we could not turn from the One who had given us life, who had given us love. We could not deny God's call.

The ensuing weeks were both celebratory and chaotic. Along with all the joys of a normal wedding preparation, there were added tensions of varying kinds.

The greatest source of tension over the next few months came from Terry's oldest brother, Dudley. Of all the difficulties we were to face, this was one of the most painful. Dudley and Dori had four children in Catholic school. Needless to say, it was awkward for them to have their children face the questions and difficulties that presented themselves. Terry desperately wanted his brother to understand why he was taking the position he was, and why, deep in his heart, he knew there was simply no other choice he could in conscience make. But Dudley had not had the benefit of ten years of study on the origins of the laws of celibacy, as had Terry. Hours and hours of discussion led to an impasse. It was impossible to explain in the course of normal conversation what had taken Terry years to process. And it was equally impossible for Dudley to comprehend so quickly. In a letter to Terry he explained his position:

. . . although I am convinced you are acting with a sincere heart and according to your conscience, and even though I am in agreement with your goal (though not your method)—I cannot support you in an action in which you are both disregarding a vow made to God and disobeying a valid imperative from the Pope.

Several times Terry tried to explain that Rome had abolished his vows for refusing to suppress his research and that the laws binding priests to celibacy were unethical. But Dudley didn't agree. "You made a vow, you have to stick by it."

How often we were to hear that argument in the days to come, not only from Dudley, but others. It was, and still is, extremely difficult for people to accept the idea that the celibacy laws are wrong. Understandably, a psychological and emotional transition such as this can take a long time to make. If one is told over and over that it is a mortal sin to eat meat on Friday, and then suddenly one day the rules change and it is no longer a sin at all, it can shake the foundations of one's beliefs. One might ask, If the Church was wrong about that, what else is she wrong about? When you've been taught that the Mass is always said in Latin, and then one day there is someone speaking to you from the altar in English, it can cause great confusion. After a thousand years, when the Church changes a tradition, it can be very upsetting to some people. But change is how growth takes place. Unfortunately people assume that celibate priesthood is biblical tradition, when in fact it is a man-made discipline, and it can be changed. It saddens me greatly to think of the suffering that will be endured by hundreds of thousands of men and women until these laws are reversed. I have known that suffering, and I can only say that, though difficult, change is far less cruel than injustice.

In the end, Dudley refused to be Terry's best man at the wedding—not because he didn't love his brother, but because he couldn't support Terry's action. The sorrow and disappointment this caused my fiancé became a cloud over our engagement and marriage. And though Dudley always treated us with kindness throughout the discussions and his final decision, I was never sure whether he ever completely understood or appreciated the sacrifice Terry had chosen to make—or how very much, at that moment in his life, he needed his brother's support.

I had known all along that there would be criticism of our marriage. It had occurred to me that people would assume that I had "seduced" Terry away from the priesthood, and I was prepared for accusations such as this. But I was not prepared for how jealous the women friends in Terry's life would be. I could see it in their eyes and hear it in the snide remarks they occasionally let slip. The insults were there, often under the guise of a "polite joke." It sometimes seemed that they thought I was just too dumb to notice. I decided that the best way, for the moment, would be to let the insults pass. I hoped that these women would get used to me as they came to know me. Perhaps they might even come to like me. But whatever the outcome, the problem lay in their hearts, not in mine. I had no wish to take Terry from them. He was still in their lives as counselor, as friend. I existed in his life in a very different way.

It saddens me to think that my presence threatened some people, and I wondered why no one had the courage to speak to me directly about it. Rather than get to know me, many ignored me completely. Terry had always cared deeply about the peace and happiness of his friends and parishioners. But it now seemed that, with some people, Terry's own personal fulfillment became a threat—and I was the cause. Terry had chosen me to love, and if they never accepted me, at least I would attempt to remain a lady through it all. That is what I told myself.

But at night, alone in my bed, I would cry. It hurt. It hurt me deeply—more deeply than any of them will ever know. I had expected it, but I wasn't prepared when it finally came. I can understand jealousy. I can understand people grappling with our unusual situation and the fact that women would be more likely to scorn me than Terry, the object of their jealousy. But it hurt me that our personal happiness meant so little to them. And it made me feel that whoever Pam Shoop was, whatever integrity regarding her sexual relationship with Terry she had maintained, whoever she was in her whimsical moods and her moments of serious contemplation, was of no importance to them at all.

For those who looked and saw, for those who were kind, I am forever grateful.

The innocence of the days when I had walked the streets of New York with a deep yearning to find my heart's home had long since passed. The tiny spiritual awakening I had felt long ago had led me on a journey I could never have imagined. I had asked many things of God, and He had answered me. At last I knew where my future lay and the man with whom I would share the rest of my life. Much of my heart was at peace.

Yet, with all the stress of the past months, I began to long for a cleansing of my spirit. The weight of many new experiences had burdened me more than I'd realized and in the last weeks had left me craving to be refreshed, renewed, uplifted. My spiritual quest had never quite been fulfilled, and now I wasn't exactly sure where to turn. I still longed for a church I could call my own.

My situation became all the more distressing one evening at a dinner with Terry and a visiting priest from the East. He had been happy and supportive of our engagement. For at least half an hour he'd sat there telling me how wonderful Catholicism was and how important it would be for me to be baptized in the Church. I listened as politely as I could, but finally I could restrain myself no longer. "Father John, I've always wanted to become a Catholic. That's not the problem." I paused and then said quietly, "When Terry and I get married, they would just excommunicate me."

Father John sat back in his chair. Tears filled his eyes. He was embarrassed and very sad—it hadn't even occurred to him. There was nothing left to say.

But the experience had awakened in me a renewed desire for baptism, for healing, for forgiveness of my sins. I wanted to wash away the doubts, the fears, the mistakes and the pain of the past. I longed to be able to kneel at the altar next to my husband on our wedding day and at last receive the sacraments. But the way things stood, this would be impossible. Finally I approached Peter Kreitler, the Episcopal priest who was to marry us at Saint

Matthew's. Two weeks prior to our wedding, on November 1st, they would be holding a Baptismal Mass and I would be welcome since I had already attended all the classes at Good Shepherd. The only problem now would be to find a sponsor.

A member of Terry's family, being Catholic, would be an inappropriate choice, and my family had their own reservations. At last I asked Father Kreitler if he would be my godfather. Once again, he responded with a spontaneous yes.

As I stood amid crying babies, one of only two adults, I felt my innocence return. The water tricked slowly over my face. *Purify me, dear Lord, wash away my sins,* I begged. Father Kreitler's face smiled down at me as he made the sign of the cross on my forehead.

"Pamela, you are sealed by the Holy Spirit in Baptism and marked as Christ's own forever. Amen. We receive you into the household of God. Confess the faith of Christ crucified, proclaim his resurrection, and share with us in his eternal priesthood."

This simple prayer welcomed me with words I would never have heard in a Catholic church.

I had needed to know that Oneness with Christ, needed to feel His healing love. I had longed for my soul to be filled with grace. And now, as I knelt for the first time at the altar to receive Communion, I knew at last that I belonged. For the first time since my childhood, my heart had found a spiritual peace.

37

TERRY

A crack in the curtains cast a stream of moonlight over my futon lying in the middle of my floor. I knelt down, pulled back the covers, and crawled into bed for the last time as a single man. Bill's words from his toast during our wedding-rehearsal dinner resonated again in my heart: "These two haven't had a courtship, they've had a trial." In the dark and quiet of my tiny apartment, it seemed fitting to listen respectfully to the images flooding through my mind and to the feelings of both happiness and sorrow they evoked.

From the moment of our engagement something new in Pamela had come alive—a spirit that was deeply joyful, enthusiastic, confident, and filled with a peace that I had not sensed in her before. There must be truth to that expression *soul mate*, because in Pamela, after I asked her to marry me, something very precious suddenly came alive in her. It was as if treasures of her identity, long held secretly in her heart, were now flowing through every cell of her being.

She had suffered the shadows, the uncertainty, the pain, the insults, and though these had left their scars, they had not killed her love. Now she was experiencing the light, the certainty, the joy and praise love brings, and she was radiant.

It was fun to watch her throw herself so totally into all the numerous details of the wedding preparation—the church, the liturgy, wedding rings, her bridal dress specially designed for her by Kioko, the guest list, reception, dinner menu, and other details. It was humbling to experience her parents' generosity in happily bearing the expense of an elegant reception for 250 guests at the Beverly Hills Hotel. They had taken great pains to make sure that all of their friends and ours knew that they believed this love was cause for celebration, not shame.

Although Dudley's refusal to be my best man left an emptiness in my heart, I was delighted that Jim Brown had accepted this role. As Jesuits we had shared many years of friendship; as ex-Jesuits our friendship would continue. I felt very privileged to have Jim and Pamela's brother, Steve, and my actor-and-producer friend, Jimmy Hawkins, standing on the altar with us. Hawkins had been such a good and loyal friend, I wanted him to have a special place in the wedding.

As an image of Pamela's beautiful face danced before my mind, I felt a tremendous sorrow in realizing that in the very moment of expressing my love for Pamela before God, family, and friends, our marriage would be "invalidated" by Church law.

There was sorrow in knowing that countless thousands of priests before me, and the women they loved, had suffered far worse sanctions.

I felt a deep sadness for all those who had gone before us, unable to love both their priesthood and their wives—forced to abandon one for the other. I felt a quiet, burning pain when I reflected on the probability that the bridge between a celibate and a married priesthood might not be completed before I died and that I might never again, with the full approval of the Church, offer up His prayer: "This is my body, which will be broken for you."

Engagement. Happiness. Sorrow. Pamela's radiant loveliness. These were my thoughts and feelings as I finally drifted off to sleep the night of November 14, 1987.

38

PAMELA AND TERRY

I awoke to rays of sunlight cascading through the branches of the trees outside my bedroom window. The delicate prism in the shape of a cross which Steve had given me for Christmas cast brilliant shafts of color all over the walls. As the crystal swayed gently, the rainbows swung back and forth, urging me to awaken. I stretched and pulled Devon up close next to my side. She rested her nose on my chest. I could feel her soft fur under my chin.

"I'm getting married today, Woofie—today."

I imagined Terry lying on his futon, probably still fast asleep. I wondered whether he had come to a decision about what to wear to the service: his collar or his tuxedo. Even today the decision forced a note of discord into the harmony of the occasion. No matter, today was ours. I huddled close to Devon for another brief, safe moment beneath the covers. Prayers formed in my heart, and I whispered them up through the rainbows, the branches and the trees, through the sunlight and the clouds to God's listening ear.

At eight forty-five Steve picked me up at my apartment and drove me up to the Beverly Hills Hotel, where our reception would be held. I felt especially close to my brother this morning. I wondered if my marriage would alter our relationship. For so many years it had been "Pam and Steve." I hoped that nothing would change between us. Steve's love had been supportive and patient, and I wondered if he realized how grateful I was to him. I hoped that he knew. He deposited me at the hotel, where Mom and Bill were waiting for me in the lobby with my wedding dress. I had also asked Sylvia, the hairdresser from "Murder, She Wrote," to do my hair and help with my veil. She arrived a few minutes later, and all four of us went up in the elevator to the suite where we would all get ready.

"Well," Bill said, "I'm going to leave you ladies to it. I'll see you back here at one o'clock. Have fun!"

One by one the bridesmaids arrived. Deciding on the bridesmaids had been easy for me. There had only been three women whose loyalty and everyday support had not wavered. They had taken time out of their own busy lives to call me, to listen when I'd needed to talk, to cry with me when I'd needed to share my tears. They were Rosemarie, Sally, and Ginger, who would be my maid of honor.

I sat in Sylvia's chair a bundle of nerves. My hair wasn't going right. Whenever I want it to, it never does. This was obviously going to take longer than I thought, so Mom and the girls decided to go downstairs to check on things.

"Okay, Mom, but please be back here by twelve forty-five, okay? We have to be ready to leave at one o'clock—the press conference starts at one-thirty."

Sylvia added the final rosebuds to my hair and attached the veil. By one-ten no one had returned, so we headed down to the lobby. I was becoming frantic. Where was everyone? The limousine driver wanted to know if there was anything he could do. He offered to take me to the church and then return for everyone else.

"Well, do you think you could go find my mom and the rest of the people? I think they're in the Crystal Room downstairs. They must have lost track of the time."

"Yes, Miss, I certainly will."

I started to pace. It was now one-twenty, and somehow we had to make the thirty- to forty-minute drive in ten minutes! In a quandary I stood quietly by myself, feeling as if I were in some strange movie.

"Shooting a commercial?" a couple asked as the bellboy helped them in with their luggage.

"Oh . . . no . . ." I stammered, nearly in tears once again. "I'm a bride. I mean, I'm a real bride."

Their faces registered shock as they passed through the entrance to the hotel. "What's she doing out here all by herself?" I heard them say.

We were already quite late when the limousine pulled into the parking lot of Saint Matthew's Church in Pacific Palisades. The lovely steeple seemed sheltered amid the autumn branches and cascading vines, serene and gentle. Rupert Allan took my arm and led me down the redwood steps through the wild and rustic garden to an area a few yards from the church, where about thirty members of the press were waiting. I had assumed that Terry would be right behind us, but he was nowhere to be seen.

As the questions began, I tried to concentrate and answer as coherently as I could. But on another level I was thinking bridal thoughts: I needed to speak with the musicians, check the lighting in the church, was my train getting dirty out here in the garden? It's hard enough to be a bride, let alone discuss over a thousand years of church tradition at the same time!

Finally I looked around in desperation. "Has anyone seen the groom?" I asked.

At that moment Terry, dressed in a black tuxedo, came hurrying down the steps toward us. As he moved to me and slipped his arm around my waist, I felt a warm sensation of relief and security, and I melted into his side for support. There was a calm about Terry all throughout our wedding day. Whereas I was a bundle of nervous energy, it seemed as if Terry was surrounded by a cool, peaceful breeze wherever he walked.

"Father Sweeney, we saw you arrive earlier in your Roman collar.

Were you thinking of getting married in your clerics? Why did you change?"

"At one point I was, but unfortunately there are some in the Church who would perceive such an action as a protest. I'm not here to protest or to challenge the current policy. I'm here to express my love for my bride."

"Do you think there will ever be a married priesthood?"

"Absolutely. There was before and there will be again. It was good enough for Jesus; it should be good enough for His church. Whether or not that change will come in our lifetime, I don't know—but it has to change."

"Do you have trouble reconciling what is happening here today?"

"I love God, I love the priesthood, and I love this woman. I love Pamela. They are not incompatible."

"Father, how will you live with the knowledge that once you marry Pamela here today, you will never be able to practice again as a priest? How will you deal with that?"

Terry became suddenly quiet. His lips trembled, and I felt his whole body quiver against mine as the cameras turned. I looked at my fiancé. My heart knew his heart—the sleepless nights and years of contemplation, the heart-wrenching decisions. Fighting back tears, he looked at the reporter and whispered in a voice racked with emotion, "With great pain."

Rupert interrupted. "I think that should be all for now." Emotionally drained, we said a few words of thanks and headed back toward the church. We held on to one another tightly, and the smiles and excitement gradually returned to Terry's face.

"How long were you down there?" he asked incredulously.

"A long time. What happened to you?"

"You won't believe this, Shoopy, but I've never worn tuxedo studs before . . . and . . . well, I couldn't figure out how to get the studs into those little holes!"

After the wedding photos had been taken, I sought to find some stillness in the frenzy of the day. Off in a corner of the dressing room where my mother, my bridesmaids, and I waited for the ceremony to begin, I closed my eyes. There were only a few minutes left. My entire body was shaking so, that I fought to calm myself by taking deep breaths. I tried to shut out the voices, the music. I wanted to think only of my vows, my vows before God. Over and over I repeated them silently to myself as, little by little, my composure returned. A knock came at the door. "We're ready, Mrs. Bergin."

Mom led the way to the back of the church, where Gary Bachlund's operatic voice met us with the haunting love song "Perhaps Love," the same song Terry had played for me in his dorm room so long ago. Ginger pulled the bridal veil down over my face and gave me a final embrace. As I took Bill's arm, I noticed that he, too, was trembling. The violins began, and stepping into the church, I crossed the threshold into a new life.

> . . . The flash of love is a flash of fire
> A flame of Yahweh Himself.

So love sears through all division, all fears, all pain. Love has brought you and me, Pamela, to this moment.

"Who gives this woman to be wed?" Father Kreitler asked.

"Her mother and I," Bill replied.

Pamela took my arm, looked through her tears into my eyes. I led her into the sanctuary.

Father Kreitler welcomed everyone, then asked God's blessing on our marriage. Behind the altar on the wall of the sanctuary was an artist's rendering—an enormous wood carving some twelve feet in diameter. It was a carving of the earth, but an earth created by flames. Had this artist, too, felt the fires of love in his heart? Was he trying to tell us that the final measure of all religion and its greatest sacrifice is love? I held Pamela's hand gently, smiled into her eyes. I felt deeply grateful that our hearts had been touched by those flames and that our families and friends were with us to celebrate this grace.

After the wedding guests were seated, Elizabeth Corrigan read from Romans, chapter eight. I remembered how Bishop Corrigan had first introduced us to his wife: "She is the blessing in my life." Her gentleness and happy spirit resonated in her voice.

"Nothing therefore can come between us and the love of Christ, even if we are troubled or worried, or being per-secuted, or lacking food or clothes, or being threatened or even attacked.

"These are the trials through which we triumph, by the power of Him who loved us. For I am certain of this: neither death nor life, no angel, no prince, nothing that exists, noth-ing still to come, not any power, or height or depth, nor any created thing, can ever come between us and the love of God made visible in Christ Jesus our Lord."

Pamela looked back at me, her eyes glistening with peace and conviction.

As Gregory Peck walked up the steps of the sanctuary, holding his leather-bound King James version of the Bible, I thought of that Easter Sunday four years earlier when he and his wife had walked up to me after Mass: "I'm Gregory Peck, Father. This is my wife, Veronique. Thank you for your homily." I remembered him gladly saying yes to hosting my documentary on the homeless. And when I had resigned from the Jesuits, he'd invited me to his home to express his concern and to ask me if he could help in any way. "If you are going to challenge the Church," he'd said, "do so with dignity."

He opened his Bible to I Corinthians 13:1–13 and began speaking as much from memory as reading:

"Though I speak with the tongue of men and of angels, and have not charity, I am become as sounding brass, or a tinkling cymbal. And though I have the gift of prophecy, and under-stand all mysteries, and all knowledge; and though I have all faith, so that I could remove mountains, and have not charity, I am nothing."

The entire church was silent, riveted to the power of the words and the conviction with which they were spoken. For some in the church this was the first and perhaps only time they would ever hear these spiritual insights of Saint Paul, forged from a life of sacrifice and total love of Christ.

"And though I bestow all my goods to feed the poor, and though I give my body to be burned, and have not charity, it profiteth me nothing."

Hearing this prompted me to ask God to bless our marriage with charity.

"Charity suffereth long, and is kind; charity envieth not; charity vaunteth not itself, is not puffed up . . ."

The words floated through my ears and down into my soul. *How difficult it is, Lord, to love, to really love, without measuring, guarding, counting the cost, expecting return in kind. How easy it is to turn ridiculed love into resentment, abused love into hate. Forgive me, Lord, for giving in to despair, for not seeing rejection from the Society and the hierarchy as part of Your Plan. Forgive me for the times I hurt Pamela—for my blindness to love.*

". . . beareth all things, believeth all things, hopeth all things, endureth all things. Charity never faileth: but whether there be prophecies, they shall fail; whether there be tongues, they shall cease; whether there be knowledge, it shall vanish away. . . ."

I turned to Pamela and looked silently into her eyes.

". . . For now we see through a glass, darkly; but then face to face: now I know in part; but then I shall know even as I am known. And now abideth faith, hope, charity, these three; but the greatest of these is charity."

She looked up at me attentively, her eyes radiant.
The entire congregation stood while Bishop Corrigan read the

Gospel from Matthew 5:1–12. I remembered the first time I had spoken to him on the phone. He had joked about his hearing problem and said I should pick a date when Pamela and I could meet him in person to discuss whether he would witness our marriage. I suggested a date; he said, "Wonderful!" And when we'd arrived three weeks later, a crowd of people had been walking out of his house. It had been his sixtieth wedding anniversary! Bishop Corrigan had shared with us the obstacles he had encountered after he'd decided it was time for the Episcopal church to ordain women. And now this delightful, deeply spiritual man was standing before us:

> ". . . Blessed are the poor in spirit, for theirs is the kingdom of heaven. Blessed are those who mourn, for they shall be comforted. Blessed are the meek, for they shall inherit the earth. Blessed are those who hunger and thirst for righteousness, for they shall be satisfied. . . ."

I was filled with gratitude to God for the blessing being showered on us.

After Bishop Corrigan finished the Gospel, the wedding guests sat down and listened to a homily from Father Gregory Richards on the Sacrament of Marriage being the only Sacrament realized not by the priest, but by the faithful themselves. So powerful is conjugal love, so intimate is its bond, that the power of the Sacrament is conferred not by the priest, but by the bride and the groom. The priest stands only as witness to the new spiritual reality born directly from the love of husband and wife.

Pamela nestled into me more closely as he finished speaking. Father Kreitler turned and faced us, opened up his wedding book again, and began.

I handed my bouquet to Ginger and turned toward my beloved.

> "In the name of God, I, Pamela, take you, Terry, to be my husband, to have and to hold from this day forward, through

tears and sorrow, laughter and joy, in sickness and in health, for richer, for poorer, to love and to cherish as long as we both shall live. This is my solemn vow. And my prayer, both in life and after death, is that in whatever way most pleases God I will love you throughout eternity."

Eternity. It seems I've already loved you for eternity. Taking my hand in his, Terry looked through my bridal veil into my eyes as if he knew what I was thinking.

"Pamela, I give you this ring as a symbol of my vow, and with all that I am, and all that I have, I honor you, in the name of the Father, and of the Son, and of the Holy Spirit."

He slipped the ring on my finger. I looked down at my hand and back into his eyes. Suddenly the words *bound in heaven* rang clear in my heart. *"Honor . . . I will honor you."* How humbling the words were. An image of Jesus washing the feet of his disciples crossed my mind. I was aware of the silence around us, the stillness in the church, the beating of my heart.

When it was time for us to present the bread and the wine, Terry led me through the opening in the Communion rail up to the altar, where we placed the chalice and the basket of hosts. As he then guided me back down from the altar to our waiting families for the Kiss of Peace, it felt wonderful to know that I could begin to rely on my husband's strength even at this very moment. Bill and Mom hugged us warmly. I smiled at Sally's husband, Bill Vaun, who had helped usher and now sat in the back of the church, as we crossed the aisle to Terry's family: to Angie and Owen, Therese, Dan, and all the children. Dudley and Dori sat in the pew behind them on the aisle.

"Peace, Dudley," Terry said as he moved to embrace his brother. I stood alone in the aisle and watched. Few people in the church knew the significance of that embrace. Probably not even Dudley realized how deeply hurt Terry was that his brother had refused to stand with him at the altar as his best man on his wedding day. I felt sad that conflicting principles stood in the way of perhaps a

more important value—that of family. At one of the most important moments in Terry's life, his brother was not beside him. I tried
to hold back the tears as Terry reached out to Dudley, and I prayed
that in the moments of Communion as we knelt before God,
healing would begin to take place for both of them.

> *"Our Father, who art in Heaven,*
> *Hallowed be Thy name. . . ."*

As I knelt at the altar for the very first time next to my husband,
I looked at the crucifix above us. I knew our love would be blessed
by God. The chalice was placed into my hands, and tears stung my
eyes as Marie Hodgson's clear voice rang high through the beams
of the house of God and fluttered down like the carressing wings
of an angel.

> *"Now, behold, He comes*
> *Robed in clouds of Light. . . ."*

Terry and I had not been sure how many people would choose
to receive Communion at our wedding. Our friends came from
various religious backgrounds, and the Catholics among them were
not supposed to accept the Eucharist anywhere but in a Catholic
church. It had been a question debated by many in Terry's family
as to what would be appropriate. From the time he was a little boy,
Michael had been taught by Pat and Rosemarie that a church was
where you went to express your beliefs, but that God was within
your own heart. And although Rosemarie had said that she was
going to receive Communion, she told Michael that he was free to
do whatever made him most comfortable.

Father Kreitler extended his arms to the congregation and said
with a warm smile, "All baptized Christians are, of course, welcome here at the Lord's table."

And one by one, they came to receive the body and blood of
Christ. Terry and I sat off to the side as our friends waited for their
turn to kneel at the Communion rail. We were amazed at how
many people rose from their seats. Whatever personal doubts they
may have had were put away for today.

When the organ began again, I turned to Terry. Perhaps only the two of us and Jim Brown knew the significance of *Suscipe, Domine,* which Terry had asked Gary Bachlund to sing during Communion. It was the song played when Terry had made his Jesuit vows and later during his ordination ceremony—and now, on his wedding day. Though it was sung in Latin, the words meant,

> *"Take, Lord, all my liberty.*
> *Accept my memory, my understanding, my entire will.*
> *All these you have given me,*
> *Use them in whatever way most pleases you.*
> *Grant me only your love and your grace—*
> *With these I am rich enough and desire nothing more."*

Terry turned to me and smiled tentatively. "Do you like it?" he asked.

"It's beautiful. . . . Are you all right?"

"Yes."

As he listened to it now, Terry's face was peaceful.

And still more people came. Terry squeezed my hand and gestured toward the congregation. Michael, dressed in a tuxedo, was making his way to the Communion rail. He looked courageous and very proud as he knelt down; and in that moment, he had made his own personal decision. After having listened to the discussions, Michael had chosen to celebrate our love with us and to show his support of that love by receiving Communion. Looking at Michael in his tuxedo, it seemed as if he were standing in for his father, and suddenly, because of this wonderful thirteen-year-old boy, Pat's love was all around us.

> *"Let the little children come to me,*
> *and do not stop them,*
> *for of such are the kingdom of heaven."*

When the last of our friends had received Communion, Terry and I once again knelt at the altar for a final blessing. At last, he helped me to my feet and very tenderly lifted the veil from my face.

And with that gesture all the waiting, the doubt, the isolation of my life in the shadows disappeared. As my husband's lips tenderly touched mine, elation, relief, amazement all blended together in the word *miracle.*

"And now may I present to you, Reverend and Mrs. Terrance Sweeney."

With the crescendo of the thunderous march of the theme from *Terms of Endearment,* my priest-husband and I walked back down the aisle together.

As we reached the rear of the church, I raised my bouquet high into the air above my head in sheer exaltation. It was a gesture of triumph, of freedom. My husband took me into his arms and held me tightly for a long, private moment as church bells began to chime through the November evening air.

The receiving line was a flurry of introductions, smiles, and congratulatory embraces. Even after champagne had been flowing for over an hour, there were more than a hundred people standing patiently in line waiting to greet us personally. Sensitive to the guests' comfort, Julie and Bill suggested we break off the receiving line and invite the remaining guests to enjoy the hors d'oeuvres and cocktails.

Rosemarie and Sally disappeared with Pamela into the powder room to remove her veil while I mingled with the guests. Three violins and a piano underscored the laughter and happy conversations. Even though many of the people had never met one another before, normal social reserve seemed to have given way to a genuine enthusiasm and conviviality. Perhaps it was the loveliness of the church and the wedding, or the graciousness of Pamela's parents hosting such a magnificent reception, or that so many good people had gathered at the same time in the same place—whatever it was, the spirit of the party was extraordinarily joyful.

Some twenty minutes after Pamela rejoined me, the lights dimmed twice, and the partitions separating the cocktail lounge from the Crystal Room were drawn back. There were sighs of delight as the guests stepped down into the ballroom to the welcoming melody played by Jay Sessum and his orchestra. A magnificent chandelier, centered over the dance floor, cast a warm glow throughout the room. The tables were elegantly decorated with floral centerpieces, crystal, and white linen. Throughout the room Julie had placed lush ficus trees trimmed with small white lights. Their reflection in mirrored pillars created the effect of a twinkling fairyland. Julie's and Bill's loving attention to the details of this reception had created a magical and romantic ambience.

When everyone was seated, the lights throughout the Crystal Room were turned down to a soft glow. "Ladies and gentlemen, in their first dance together as husband and wife, I would like to introduce to you, Terry and Pamela Sweeney." The orchestra started playing "Homecoming" as I escorted Pamela down the long staircase into the ballroom.

She looked at me with the tenderest smile as I took her into my arms and began to dance across the open floor. Enveloped by the ethereal music, I felt her body and her heart so close to mine that I soon became aware of only one body, one heart—and for moments that drifted out of time, I felt flooded with such sweetness and joy that I wondered if, through the infinite energy of love, we had floated right through the veil of life into the everlasting banquet of heaven. This is what heaven is: love, dancing, friends.

Time returned as Pamela's parents, then mine, joined us on the dance floor. Then the entire wedding party.

Through tears, I looked into Pamela's eyes and said,

"I love you, my wife. . . ."

She hugged me warmly and replied,

"I love you, my husband. . . ."

AFTERWORD

The phone rings. As soon as I hear the trembling voice on the other end of the line, I recognize immediately the hesitation, the despair, the cry for help.

Since our marriage Terry and I have been privileged to serve on the board of advisers for Good Tidings, a nonprofit support group for priests and women who are in love. The organization was founded, under tragic circumstances, by Maggie Olsen when a close friend committed suicide after her priest-lover broke off their relationship. It is now run by Cathy and her priest-husband, Joe Grenier, and ministers to over seven hundred women, over three hundred priests, and at present three bishops, who are involved in relationships. These people have nowhere else to turn.

Terry and I have been contacted by a number of these couples, not only in the Archdiocese of Los Angeles, but from around the country and from as far away as Austria. Although the Vatican would have us believe otherwise, priests do fall in love, and they do cry out for help.

Priests and the women they love have sat on our couch in despair and torment. Sometimes together, sometimes independently, they have come to share their struggles. Often priests who would like to marry have serious financial concerns. Since they have lived lives of service without much income, the prospect of marriage forces them to ask how they would support themselves and a wife. The ministry of the priesthood is all they know, and many have no idea how to look for a new profession. For the women, most often, this dilemma is unimportant; just fulfilling their love is enough. Because canon law still mandates celibacy for priests, these priests face a bitter choice. Some choose the priesthood; some choose love. Whatever decision is made, there is a painful sacrifice. Each time I witness their anguished tears, I long for the day that priesthood and love will become a compatible blessing in the eyes of the Church.

Only a few weeks ago Terry's brother, Dudley, remarked that he thought the best example of priesthood might consist of husband and wife, both ministering to the community as priests. His comment not only warmed our hearts, but reflected an awakening that seems to be taking place worldwide.

In June 1988, seven months after our marriage, the First National Conference of Married Roman Catholic Clergy was held in Washington, D.C. Under the auspices of CORPUS (Corps of Reserve Priests United for Service), the conference was attended not only by married Roman Catholic priests and their wives, but also by many priests still functioning within the structure of the Church. Some were involved in relationships, some supported the issue silently, and still others, including at least one canon lawyer, were simply curious. It was a source of great joy to be in the company of so many spiritual, loving people who had shared a similar sacrifice. My husband was asked to give the closing address. Many of those in the audience had chosen love on instinct alone. Terry's arguments questioning the morality of mandatory celibacy released a floodgate of emotion in many of them. Listening to Terry speak, I knew that the future of which all of us dreamed would one day become a reality.

Every day I am filled with gratitude to my husband for his courage, his dignity, his kindness, and his love. The tranquillity, the harmony of heart and spirit we now feel has enriched our marriage, and though the difficulties of the past will never be forgotten, they are greatly diminished. We go forward now in pursuit of our common goal: the right of those called by God to the priesthood to choose for themselves either celibacy or marriage.

As I awake each morning in the warmth of my husband's embrace, his cheerful smile, and the enthusiasm with which he greets each new day of our marriage, I feel I have found my heaven on earth—and I know, now, that love is the greatest blessing in the world.

—PAMELA

Against the backdrop of the Catholic Church's mandatory celibacy tradition, Pamela and I have tried to recount how we met, fell in love, and married. It took an entire book to describe this journey. Any attempt to capture in the few pages of an Afterword all that we have enjoyed and discovered in the five years of our marriage would prove inadequate. Suffice it to say here that love is life's joy, and when two people experience the extraordinary grace of conjugal love, there is nothing on earth more precious. Perhaps this is why Jesus was so strong in his defense of the marriage bond, and why Saint Paul said that those who say "marriage is forbidden" were uttering the "doctrines of demons."

Two months and eleven days after Pamela and I were married, Archbishop Mahony wrote me a letter saying that for as long as I "persist" in my "present marital status," which he characterized as an "irregular canonical union," he was banning me from Communion.

Under this pope it is nearly impossible for a priest to be "granted permission to marry." So, in effect, the Archbishop was ordering me to stop receiving the Eucharist until I had divorced my wife.

Father James Coriden, past president of the Canon Law Society of America, felt the Archbishop's ban had breached the current code of canon law. With Coriden's help I sent a formal appeal to the Vatican Congregation for Clergy asking them to rescind the ban. Rome upheld the Archbishop's censure.

In correspondence totaling over 150 pages, I have forwarded to Pope John Paul II and to other prominent church officials the theological and historical data leading to the conclusion that the mandatory celibacy discipline is unchristian. Reactions to this material have been silence or the imposition of further sanctions, but not a single rebuttal of the conclusion or its supporting evidence.

In 1990 I conducted a follow-up poll to complement my 1985 survey that the Church attempted to suppress. This 1990 study surveyed the U.S. bishops and the Canadian bishops. These results, as well as the conclusions I derived from more than a decade of research into the issues of authority, married clergy, and women priests were published in 1992 in my book *A Church Divided.*

That book, and this, are but two more accounts of the human mind and heart seeking to know the truth and to experience that grace which should be the final measure of all religion, love. These books are an attempt to explain why the canonical foundations for the Church's policy excluding marriage and women from the priesthood are inimical to the spirit of Jesus. This policy has its origins not in the teachings of Jesus, not in the God-given dignity and equality of human beings, not in faith or love, but in power and gender. As this institutional cancer is brought to light, there will be a great struggle within the Church. Furthermore, this conflict will not stop simply with priesthood issues. It will stop only after the entire authority structure of the Roman Catholic Church has been reformed.

When the Church once again recognizes that authority does not come from office, or apostolic succession, or hierarchical consecration, or purportedly infallible definitions; when the Church once again recognizes that it was born not in the power and glory of Constantine but in the shame and humiliation of Jesus' crucifixion, there will once more be hope. For it is only in focusing on the heart of Christ that the true meaning of Christianity is found.

As the Vatican struggles to assert its authority, as it silences dissenting theologians, as it rebuffs all efforts toward collegial and shared authority, as it suspends married priests and women priests from Czechoslovakia who risked their lives under Communist rule, as it scorns married priests the world over as betrayers of their vocation, as it claims absolute power over the priesthood, the sacrament of marriage, and even over the Eucharist, the Vatican will eventually come face-to-face with the two-edged sword of the living God—the sword of love and faith.

As this sword touches the hearts of the faithful and inspires them to follow more closely in the footsteps of their Master—in caring for their families, feeding the hungry, clothing the naked, comforting the afflicted, curing the sick, proclaiming the good news of God's kingdom—the Vatican will then find itself facing a worldwide community who recognizes only that authority which emanates from faith and love. The institutional church will either shed its hierarchical mantle to become once again a servant of God and God's people, or it will collapse with a death cry far more agonizing than that of the Roman empire. And this death, not based on faith and love, will have no resurrection.

Jesus said, "Love one another as I have loved you." His love gave sight to the blind, peace to the brokenhearted, hope to the despairing. And because His love came from God and led others back to God, it could not be buried.

God has placed in my heart love for my beautiful wife, for the priesthood, and for the Lord. Church laws and directives are banning me from Communion, suspending my priesthood, invalidating my marriage, and urging me to abandon my wife.

Strengthened by Pamela's joyful embrace and by the soothing fire of God in my heart, I finally welcome the Church's cross only because the One who has carried it before me has shown with His life that, first and last, all that matters is love.

—TERRY

ABOUT THE AUTHORS

Terrance A. Sweeney holds a Ph.D. in theology from the Graduate Theological Union in Berkeley, and an M.A. in communications from Loyola Marymount University. He has written three other books, most recently *A Church Divided*, as well as several television scripts. He has won five Emmys as a television producer, and served as technical advisor on *The Thorn Birds*.

Pamela Shoop Sweeney is a successful movie and television actress, who has starred with Tom Selleck in "Magnum, P.I." and with Angela Lansbury in "Murder, She Wrote." She has appeared in over 150 television productions, as well as a TV special with Bob Hope, numerous stage plays, and five feature films. She co-starred opposite Jack Palance in *Dead on Arrival*.

Terry and Pamela live in Sherman Oaks, California.